PRAISE FOR
GOSPELBOUND

"In our time, the most committed young evangelical Christians are often the least likely to want to use the word *evangelical* at all. And who can blame them? Evangelicalism has veered recklessly in recent years from tragedy to scandal to farce. The end result is often cynicism. But that's not the final word. This book offers neither spin control nor image maintenance for the evangelical tribe, but genuine hope. Evangelicalism has fallen on hard times; the gospel has not. My hope is that this book helps us wake up to find, as the old hymn says, 'the dungeon flamed with light.'"

—RUSSELL MOORE, president of the Ethics and Religious Liberty Commission of the Southern Baptist Convention

"*Gospelbound* helps us fix our eyes on eternity while practically living Christ-centered lives in this present age. This book could not be more timely."

—RUTH CHOU SIMONS, artist, founder of gracelaced.com, and bestselling author of *Beholding and Becoming* and *GraceLaced*

"The heart of the gospel is the work of God to make all things new. And the heart of *Gospelbound* is to breathe new life into this anxious age. Through stories both global and local, Collin Hansen and Sarah Eekhoff Zylstra give us an informed, up-to-the-minute account of the transformative work Christ can do in our hearts, our churches, and our culture. It's at once a mighty wind and a gentle spring zephyr."

—MINDY BELZ, senior editor of *World* magazine and author of *They Say We Are Infidels*

"Much of what we read about the church today is discouraging—division and dysfunction, apathy and apostasy, moral failures of leaders and malaise among members. Have we simply become too compromised, too comfortable, and too cavalier about the world's ills to make any real difference? *Gospelbound* pushes back against pessimism and defeatism with insightful commentary and inspiring stories. In these pages you'll discover organizations, individuals, and families whose love for Christ is welling up and overflowing onto a world that is desperately in need of saving grace and Christlike kindness and mercy. The beauty is breathtaking."

—NANCY GUTHRIE, author and Bible teacher

"*Gospelbound* is the book we need right now: clear eyed about the challenges we face but joyfully insistent that the life offered to us in Jesus is our refuge and strength. Readers will be encouraged to read about faithful Christians who have discovered this in their own lives and find companions for their own pursuit of faithfulness."

—MICHAEL WEAR, author of *Reclaiming Hope: Lessons Learned in the Obama White House About the Future of Faith in America*

"In a time of intense fear and suspicion, Hansen and Zylstra turn our focus to the 'solid joys and lasting pleasures none but Zion's children know.' This book is not only filled with scriptural medicine but also applies the salve to our terrible insecurities."

—MICHAEL HORTON, J. Gresham Machen Professor of Theology and Apologetics at Westminster Seminary California

"*Gospelbound* is a true account of everyday Christians like us prevailing in hard times. We really are 'more than conquerors' (Romans 8:37). How? By treating the living Christ as real—right where we live. Collin Hansen and Sarah Eekhoff Zylstra paint the picture of that rugged faith, proving Christ's faithfulness today."

—RAY ORTLUND, author of *The Death of Porn: Men of Integrity Building a World of Nobility*

"I was surprised by how hard it was to put down *Gospelbound*. The authors have woven together up-to-the-minute stories of how God is working all around us, presenting us with a much-needed vision of life in Christ. It is both irresistibly appealing and terrifically challenging. I'd like every believer under thirty to read this book."

—JOHN YATES, former pastor of the Falls Church Anglican and author of *How a Man Prays for His Family*

"One of the best antidotes I have found for anxiety is to drink a tall glass of water. This book is a wellspring of assurance in the desert of our current dismay. Collin and Sarah take up the ancient and faithful task of telling forth the wondrous works of God through his servants. They lift our eyes and reorient us to the goodness of God. If you're thirsty for good news, here is an opportunity to drink deeply."

—JEN WILKIN, author and Bible teacher

GOSPELBOUND

GOSPELBOUND

Living with Resolute Hope
in an Anxious Age

COLLIN HANSEN AND
SARAH EEKHOFF ZYLSTRA

MULTNOMAH

Published in the United States by Multnomah, an imprint of Random House, a division of Penguin Random House LLC.

MULTNOMAH® and its mountain colophon are registered trademarks of Penguin Random House LLC.

Portions of this work appeared, sometimes in different form, on The Gospel Coalition (thegospelcoalition.org).

Grateful acknowledgment is made to the following for permission to use the material below:
The Barna Group, Ltd.: Previously published excerpts and data from "Americans Describe Their Views About Life After Death" from Barna, October 21, 2003, copyright © 2003 by the Barna Group, Ltd. Used by permission of the Barna Group, Ltd. All rights reserved.
Lyman Stone: Previously published excerpts from *Promise and Peril: The History of American Religiosity and Its Recent Decline* (Washington, DC: American Enterprise Institute, April 2020), copyright © 2020 by the American Enterprise Institute. Used by permission of Lyman Stone. All rights reserved.

LIBRARY OF CONGRESS CATALOGING-IN-PUBLICATION DATA
Names: Hansen, Collin, author. | Zylstra, Sarah Eekhoff, author.
Title: Gospelbound : living with resolute hope in an anxious age / Collin Hansen & Sarah Eekhoff Zylstra.
Description: First edition. | Colorado Springs : Multnomah, [2021] | Includes bibliographical references.
Identifiers: LCCN 2020039068 | ISBN 9780593193570 (paperback : acid-free paper) | ISBN 9780593193587 (ebook)
Subjects: LCSH: Hope—Religious aspects—Christianity. | Christianity and culture—United States. | United States—Social conditions—21st century.
Classification: LCC BV4638 .H286 2021 | DDC 234/.25—dc23
LC record available at https://lccn.loc.gov/2020039068

Printed in the United States of America on acid-free paper

waterbrookmultnomah.com

2 4 6 8 9 7 5 3 1

First Edition

Title page art: iStock.com/Saemilee

SPECIAL SALES Most Multnomah books are available at special quantity discounts when purchased in bulk by corporations, organizations, and special-interest groups. Custom imprinting or excerpting can also be done to fit special needs. For information, please email specialmarketscms@penguinrandomhouse.com.

Für Elise
—COLLIN

In memory of my father,
Timothy Ray Eekhoff (1953–1994),
who loved both good theology
and a good story
—SARAH

CONTENTS

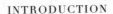

Why You're Anxious and Afraid

America seems to be in the midst of a full-blown panic attack," the *New Republic* observed in 2019.[1] Maybe you've noticed.

The symptoms started in the late 1990s—high school students began having trouble sleeping and thinking, college students were more likely to feel overwhelmed, and adults scored higher on depression studies.[2] Between 1999 and 2017, suicide rates increased 33 percent.[3]

I (Collin) caught a glimpse of this anxiety spread when I asked a longtime friend about his ministry to young adults. We'd been young together ourselves, meeting at the selective, competitive university we both attended.

"What's changed with young people over the last twenty years?" I asked him.

"Remember how hard it was for our classmates?" he asked. He meant the pressure to perform well, the anxiety of landing a prestigious job, the press of grades and graduate school applications. "Well, that's everywhere now."

He didn't mean that the average American is fretting about graduate school but that, over time, the tight vibration of anxiety had intensified and spread. It's no longer just the Ivy Leaguers who are living under immense pressure. Everyone seems to be feeling it.

When polling company Gallup asked Americans in 2018 whether they'd felt stress during much of the day before, 55 percent said yes—up from 44 percent in 2008, when the country was at the bottom of the Great Recession. Forty-five percent said they felt worry a lot, up from 34 percent in 2008.[4]

Then came 2020.

By mid-March, COVID-19 had shut down and stressed out most of the country. People worried about getting sick, about going to work (what if they exposed themselves or their families to the disease?), and about not going to work (how could they pay the bills?). They worried that the nation's health-care system would be overrun, that their local hospitals would run out of ventilators, that doctors wouldn't have enough personal protective equipment. At the same time, they worried about their savings accounts, about local businesses closing, about the economy sliding into recession.

The instability was exhausting. I (Sarah) would gather with friends once a week in a parking lot (so we could sit far enough apart in the fresh air) and compare notes: Whose job is changing? How many times were you able to leave the house this week? Which neighbor is making masks we can buy? How are we going to facilitate our children's e-learning while working from home?

By the end of March, 45 percent of Americans said stress from worrying about the disease was negatively affecting their mental health.[5] In April, a government emergency hotline for emotional distress heard from twenty thousand people—compared with 1,790 in April 2019.[6] An online therapy company said the number of clients jumped 65 percent from February to April.[7]

Then, just as states were beginning to relax their shelter-in-place restrictions, a white police officer in Minneapolis spent around eight minutes kneeling on the neck of African American George Floyd.[8] Floyd's death was caught on camera, and the video was circulated widely online. Anxiety levels, especially among African Americans and Asian Americans, spiked.[9] Protestors marched in nearly every American city, and some marches broke into looting and rioting. Social media exploded with debates over law enforcement and Confederate statues.

And that was before COVID cases spiked again, before many schools opted for e-learning, before the presidential election had even kicked off in earnest.

No wonder we're anxious.

. . . .

The Death of God?

BUT WE'RE NOT just anxious. We're also afraid. Because while God can certainly inspire holy fear (Hebrews 10:31), a world without him is even scarier.

When Friedrich Nietzsche declared the death of God more than a century ago,[10] he glimpsed in part what we can see more clearly today—a declining social need for religion. During the twentieth century, as the countries of Western Europe became more educated and then wealthier, they lost much of their Christian faith. By 2018, Pew Research Center found that, in countries where people go to school longer, they attend church less often. Where lifespans are the longest, worship attendance is least common. And in wealthy countries, people pray less often.[11]

Except in the United States.

"America's unique synthesis of wealth and worship has puzzled international observers and foiled their grandest theories of a global secular takeover," Derek Thompson wrote in the *Atlantic*. "Stubbornly pious Americans threw a wrench in the secularization thesis. Deep into the 20th century, more than nine in 10 Americans said they believed in God and belonged to an organized religion, with the great majority of them calling themselves Christian."[12]

That number held steady through the 1980s. In fact, for years "we believed that . . . the mission field was [only] overseas," author and speaker Tim Keller told church leaders at a conference on gospel-centered urban ministry.[13] Cultural Christianity was so strong that nonbelievers showed up at Billy Graham evangelistic events in church buses. "When he gave you a twenty-minute Bible talk, you already had structures, a DNA, a worldview," apologist Sam Chan told us. For most, conversion was largely a matter of tipping over into believing what you already had been taught.

Back then, belief was "thick," Keller said. "Fifty years ago, virtually everybody had generic religious beliefs. They believed in a personal God, in an afterlife, in guilt and sin." Not only that, but most Americans "also tended to respect [Christianity], or at least feel they ought to show some respect," he said.[14]

In the nineties, though, Christianity began to slip. It's hard to say exactly why—Thompson suggested perhaps the end of the Cold War (which relaxed patriotic feelings and perhaps loyalty to our country's religion), the alignment of evangelicals with the Republican Party (which may have confused the identities of both), or 9/11 (an event whose ideological roots made religion seem dangerous).[15]

In 1987, 88 percent of Americans told Pew they "never doubt the existence of God."[16] But by 2017, only 56 percent believed in "God as described in the Bible."[17] Church attendance fell from 54 percent in 2007 to 45 percent in 2018/2019. Meanwhile, self-identified Christians dropped from 78 percent to 65 percent of the American population.[18]

Those former Christians aren't converting to another religion. They're dropping the faith—or at least an organized version of it—altogether. The percent of "nones," or those who describe their religion as "nothing in particular," rose from 8 percent in 1990 to 26 percent in 2018/2019.[19]

But the number of "evangelical or born again" Christians in America has stayed largely the same—28 percent in 2009 and 25 percent in 2018/2019.[20]

So, what's going on?

Maybe the best way to understand the change is this: The number of committed believers (at least as most heartfelt Christians would define them) has remained steady. But nominal believers (researcher Ed Stetzer labeled them cultural and congregational—or Christmas and Easter—Christians) are slowly dropping their religious identity and, with it, their religious worldview.

"Nominal people tend not to stay nominal," Stetzer wrote in *Christians in the Age of Outrage.* "And why would they? Unless there is cultural pressure and guilt (hello, Irish Catholics on Long Island, where I grew up!), there is no reason to keep following traditions that don't have meaning."[21]

That's why same-sex marriage, illegal until 2015, is now so mainstream that opposing it—or simply refusing to participate in celebrating it—is grounds for a lawsuit. (Without a religious or theological reason to oppose it, why would you?) That's why transgenderism and nonbinary sexuality slid so quickly into cultural acceptance. That's why universities—many of which were founded by Christians—are now refusing to recognize Christian student groups that require leaders to hold to a traditional view of marriage.[22]

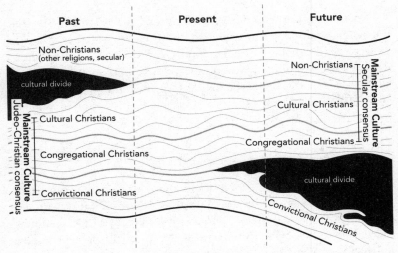

Source: Ed Stetzer, *Christians in the Age of Outrage: How to Bring Our Best When the World Is at Its Worst* (Carol Stream, IL: Tyndale, 2018), 28. Used with permission.

The nominal slide is also one key reason that cultural respect for Christianity is dropping. Confidence levels in religion fell from 66 percent in the mid-1980s to 36 percent in 2019, according to Gallup.[23] Pew reported that only about half of Americans think religion does more good than harm in society (55 percent), strengthens morality in society (53 percent), or brings people together (50 percent).[24]

These changes are real, and a nominal Christian culture's disconnect from God has real consequences, even in the secular world. One of them is widespread anxiety and fear. If God's not in charge, who is? How do we know what's wrong or right—especially when the standards may change again tomorrow? If no one is holding our future, how can we make sure it's happy and secure?

Christians aren't exempt from worrying about the many changes that affect our culture—otherwise Jesus would not have needed to tell us not to be anxious (Matthew 6:25). If anything, Christians may have even *more* reason to feel unbalanced and a little scared. Why?

Not because of our faith—there isn't anything wrong with God or his plan of salvation. We know his love and his grace and his beauty.

And not really because of sin. We already know our world is broken. We know people are blinded and twisted. It's been that way since Eden.

No, the source of our anxiety in America is where those two—our unchanging faith and our changing culture—rub together. Many of us aren't used to being misunderstood, to being opposed, to having to defend what we thought was long-standing common sense. Anxiety and fear follow this perceived loss of security and support.

In addition, we're living in an era of media distortion unmatched in modern memory.

Media Versus Religion

IN 2007, PEW Research Center asked journalists whether they regularly attended religious services. As far as we can tell, it was the last time anybody's asked. Back then, about 8 percent of national news journalists (down from 14 percent in 1999) and 14 percent of local journalists (down from 22 percent in 1999) went every week, compared with about 40 percent of the general public.[25]

The lack of exposure to and understanding of Christianity—and all other faiths—affects media coverage of events. Increasingly, *evangelical* is portrayed as a synonym for *white conservative Republican*, even though a third of Protestants are people of color[26] and even though religious people do a lot more than vote.

Don't misunderstand us: We love the news. (So much so that we both have journalism degrees.) And we believe that you can trust reputable sources to report on what's happening in the world. God pours *buckets* of common grace on us all through secular news outlets that help us follow voting trends, track scientific breakthroughs, and engage safety concerns. You'll see many reports and surveys cited in this book.

Yet nobody's denying that the news industry has endured a rough few years. Newspaper circulation is now at its lowest level since 1940,[27] and the audience for television news is mostly older than fifty.[28] Revenues have plummeted. The number of newsroom employees dropped 25 percent between 2008 and 2018.[29] Even the 2020 boost from Americans tuning in to constant coronavirus coverage didn't help for long.[30]

The main culprit is the rise of news websites and social media—52 percent of Americans now get news from Facebook.[31] But the news industry also suffers from a collapsing reputation, pushed down both by accusations of "fake news" from politicians and by stories that turn out to be false or poorly reported. More than half of people on social media told Pew they expect news there to be "largely inaccurate."[32] Odds are that if you were online during the pandemic, you saw coronavirus and vaccine news that seemed completely fabricated. (It might have been.)

By its nature, the news generally isn't calming or encouraging. One of the first things we learned in journalism school is that conflict makes the headlines. Negative stories—of pandemics or job losses or denominational splits—are also more likely than positive stories to be unusual or timely, which makes them more likely to be reported.

There's an economic reason for this practice. It *works*. Negative magazine covers sell more copies. Negative television stories cause attention to spike. (People's reactions to positive news stories are about the same as when they're looking at a blank gray screen, researchers found.)[33] Even people who *say* they want positive news are more likely to *click* on negative headlines.[34]

The more people read a story, the more advertisers will pay a news outlet to get in front of those eyes, the more revenue that news organization will make, and the more bills it can pay. Most news, after all, is a business. And reporting on conflict helps the bottom line.

I (Collin) have appeared on a number of national news programs, most of which have been hosted by professional and courteous journalists. But in 2020, I caught a behind-the-scenes glimpse of why so many Americans distrust the news. I was invited to appear on a reputable nightly news program and spoke at length the day before the recording with an inquisitive producer. I wasn't told, though, until shortly before the recording that my segment would be adversarial. Or the identity of my supposed adversary. I did know we'd be talking about politics. (In fact, it's been a long time since I've been invited by mainstream media to talk about anything except politics.)

I had never talked with the journalist before the program started. Nor could I see her or the person I was supposed to be debating (that's common for TV news). With slanted questions, the host tried to amplify my disagreements with the other guest. Problem is, I largely agreed with what that guest said! So she tried to ask us the same questions from new angles. Then the other guest started agreeing with me! Clearly, this was not what the producers had expected or desired. Cordial, qualified analysis doesn't go viral on social media and attract viewers.

The inherent weakness of the news—which as an institution informs and helps us—is that it can also scare and divide us. And the less familiar journalists are with Christianity, the harder it is for them to give accurate and nuanced coverage to a faith that to many seems to be archaic and ignorant, sexist and homophobic.

Social Media

THE SITUATION DOESN'T improve when we turn to social media. About one in three American adults told Pew in 2019 that they're online "almost constantly." Eight in ten use the internet at least once a day.[35] The revenue that comes from your clicks is "an incentive for any number of depressing modern media trends, including clickbait headlines, the proliferation of hastily written 'hot takes,' and increasingly homogeneous coverage as everyone chases the same trending news stories, so as not to miss out on the traffic they will bring," wrote editor Michael Luo,[36] who oversees the digital presence of the *New Yorker*.

As a result of this constant flow of information, advertising, memes, and hot takes, "people vastly overestimate what they know, and their unjustifiably strong opinions are reinforced by other people who are similarly ill-informed, creating self-reinforcing communities of misinformation," he wrote. We rarely get the whole story. We're easily influenced—the information we have on a given topic is usually not enough to give a full or nuanced picture, leading us to believe that people who come to different conclusions than we do must be crazy. Or worse yet, the *enemy*.

That's why people who vaccinate can't understand those who won't and why those who vote Republican think Democrats are wrong on everything and why those who support gun control—or abortion or criminal justice reform or private health care—have such a hard time understanding the other point of view. We're bombarding ourselves with just a few facts that leave no room for nuance, tucked into stories meant to scare us into reading more. It's anxiety on a cultural scale, monetizing our angst and pitting us against one another.

What's the result? Look around! Everyone feels like the last soldier of sanity, facing an overwhelming enemy who is irrational, evil, and hell-bent on the destruction of all we hold holy. This is why we can condemn whole swaths of people—so long as they seem distant and faceless. And, in the back of our mind, we know they're doing the same thing to us.

The story changes, though, when we're talking about real people, people we know and love. It's why, when polled, Americans say they like their local public school (55 percent) but not public schools nationwide (25 percent),[37] why they like their local government (67 percent) but not the national one (35 percent).[38] It's why you can love your niece, who votes Democrat, but hate Democrats in general.

It's why you can feel anxious and angry with the country as a whole but still love your neighbors.

That's a clue for where we Christians should turn our attention.

A Different Kind of News

In 2016, the two of us took a gamble. Collin asked me (Sarah) to write news that wasn't being reported anywhere else—stories of Christians caring for the weak, loving their enemies, and suffering with joy. He wanted me to look for places where the Spirit of God was working in a big way and then write it down.

"Obviously, I'm not going to do that," I told Collin. "That's not *real* news. That's more like puffy public relations pieces on Christians."

"It won't be like that," Collin told me. "We won't do puff pieces. We'll tell the uncomfortable parts too. We'll be honest when it seems like God isn't showing up. We'll be truthful about the suffering as well as the joy."

I trust Collin's news judgment, and we love working together, so I figured we could give it a shot. Neither of us was sure anybody would read our stories anyway—we know negative news gets the clicks. And we weren't sure how much activity we'd even find. Was anybody actually living like this? Would we run out of stories in a few months?

It's been four years, and we have heard more stories of Christians living sacrificial, gospel-centered, kingdom-advancing, God-glorifying lives than we can publish. These stories aren't puffy—

they're *hard*. They're gritty and real. But they also won't make you anxious or afraid. They'll inspire you with possibilities, spur you to worship the God who leads and provides and surprises. They'll encourage you to see fresh opportunities as your faith in God grows. We believe this because they've done this for us.

I (Collin) am not naturally inclined to look for the positive. Editors tend to be wired for critical analysis. You don't find many journalists known for their hopefulness. We've seen too much. We know too much about what happens behind the scenes.

But Sarah and I aren't just journalists. We're also Christians. We believe in the gospel—*good news* for sinners and our fallen world longing for renewal. We follow the risen Jesus, who invites us to watch and wait: "Behold, I am making all things new" (Revelation 21:5).

Are negative things happening in our broken world? Every day. But is God working things for good? Are there really people following him so faithfully that they give up their suburban comfort to love low-income neighbors or they obey God's Word instead of following the world's path to sexual fulfillment? Does anyone still take these words of Jesus seriously: "Whoever finds his life will lose it, and whoever loses his life for my sake will find it" (Matthew 10:39)?

Absolutely. We've seen them. We've talked with them. We've learned from them. And we are thrilled to get to share them with you.

GOSPELBOUND

CHAPTER 1

Resolute Hope

*We rejoice in our sufferings, knowing that suffering produces endur-
ance, and endurance produces character, and character produces hope,
and hope does not put us to shame, because God's love has been poured
into our hearts through the Holy Spirit who has been given to us.*
—ROMANS 5:3–5

It's the humidity I (Collin) remember most. After a long day of intern work, I reluctantly left behind the air-conditioned Cannon
House Office Building for my second shift, the one that actually paid.
It was the first summer after the 9/11 attacks, and I had sought work
in Washington, DC, in a burst of patriotic zeal.

I wanted to serve my country. I ended up in the basement of party
headquarters, dialing for dollars.

Four nights a week and all day Saturday, I called up devoted party
members across the country to ask for another donation. I wasn't
very good at it. I'd get on the phone with an elderly business owner
in South Dakota and talk for thirty minutes about the congressional
campaign and education policy. In the end, he'd politely tell me he'd
already donated to his representative in the House.

My colleagues who made the most money never stayed on the line
longer than three minutes. Their strategy was simple and effective:
scare Grandma with a story about how the other party wants to destroy the country, and then ask her to read those sixteen digits on her
credit card. I never discerned any patriotic zeal in my most successful
colleagues. I never observed any particular devotion to the party that
employed them.

On long, sweat-soaked walks home after California had gone to bed, I had a lot of time to think about the hope I invested in politics. I never stopped caring about the issues. But I realized I could never play the game to get ahead.

From those conversations in the basement of party headquarters, I understand when Christians are tempted to trust in politicians to protect the church, our perceived interests, or our loved ones. Politicians have real influence. Government leaders, elected or appointed, decide vital moral and ethical issues, such as whether killing unborn babies should be allowed, whether gender is fluid in the eyes of the law, and whether Christian organizations can set their own hiring standards. They decide whether justice will be done for unarmed victims of police brutality and whether young soldiers will be sent into war on the other side of the world. Elections have consequences. Politics matters.

Understandably, Christians want to win every seeming fight for righteousness. We want to be safe. We want to be in charge. We want election victories and righteous judges and religious freedom and growing churches and friendly neighbors and safe schools and everything else. In other words, we want "on earth as it is in heaven" (Matthew 6:10), and we'd rather not have to wait until Jesus returns.

It's a good instinct—we're meant to be cultivating our world, bringing renewal to whatever corners we occupy. But sometimes Christians chase power the Bible doesn't tell us to expect (1 Corinthians 1:28). And it's not as if Christians in power always wield it for justice. Sadly, it's often quite the opposite—for example, during what some perceive as the golden age of the 1950s, powerful white church members were segregating, threatening, and discriminating against African Americans.

Power isn't going to save us. Even Jesus, the only human who could have wielded it perfectly, "did not count equality with God a thing to be grasped, but emptied himself, by taking the form of a servant" (Philippians 2:6–7). Jesus built his church to withstand—even to be corrected by and thrive in—opposition. The church was born into a regime that would hunt and hurt her, and she spread by running for her life. Over and over, Christianity seeped into cultures after being scattered by persecution. What was supposed to destroy her made her stronger.

If we start with a more realistic expectation—that the default should be marginalization or even suffering for Christ—then the church in America still looks privileged and even protected. The #blessings tagged on social media—rapid career promotions, happy and matching families, and a stream of Amazon Prime boxes—seem more like the prosperity gospel (believing that following Jesus will make life more pleasant or comfortable) than the vision of discipleship we see in the Bible.

From that perspective, sliding out of a privileged position may not be a bad thing for the American church. What if our proximity to power of all kinds is not making us stronger but is *sapping* our potential for genuine Christlike faith and action?

In 2020, just before the World Health Organization declared coronavirus a public health emergency, I (Sarah) flew to a conference of Asian Christians in Kuala Lumpur.

Many of the church leaders I met came from China (minus those quarantined in Wuhan). I don't know when or if I'll ever see them again this side of heaven. But I'll never forget sitting across from them and asking about their stories. In their demeanor I saw calm grace under the relentless pressure of government restrictions.

"Hardship reveals a reality of earthly life—we are bound for another home," said S. E. Wang,[1] who works with house church pastors (his name has been changed to protect his identity). The biggest threat to Chinese Christians isn't having their churches closed or pastors imprisoned, he said.

"We are sojourners on earth, and things like the worship of money and secularism are trying to persuade us that we are permanent residents," he told me. "When the tension eases between your earthly identity and your heavenly identity—that's the biggest threat."

Because if we feel comfortable here, in a world we know is broken and sinful, what does that say about us?

"Persecution helps with that," Wang said. "Even cancer tells you that earth is not your home. Hardship reveals reality—that we are bound for another home, another life."

God doesn't want us to settle in here. And as we see over and over in the Old Testament, discipline is the way God gets the attention of his people, reclaims their love for him, and purifies them from sinful practices that would wreck them.

"Discipline is God's love," Wang said. "He disciplines those he loves. He's training and refining his church and will bring her up in full maturity. We don't see discipline as negative. It shows God's grace and favor."

Wang didn't make that up—he got it straight from Scripture. "It is for discipline that you have to endure," the author of Hebrews wrote. "God is treating you as sons. For what son is there whom his father does not discipline?" (12:7).

What does this say, then, about the American church? In all our concern about persecution, have we neglected the goodness of our heavenly Father's discipline?[2]

Maybe we don't need to worry so much about losing privilege and power we were never meant to have. Because we have received "a kingdom that cannot be shaken" (verse 28), there is always hope.

Living with Resolute Hope

THE KEY TO living with resolute hope is to think big and small—at the same time. Thinking big means trusting God: "The Lord will rescue me from every evil deed and bring me safely into his heavenly kingdom" (2 Timothy 4:18). Remembering the Lord's vast power, perfect plan, and deep love for us helps us relax into his care. When we think big, our hope rests on promises that have never failed and power strong enough to cast stars into the sky and Satan down from heaven (Isaiah 40:26; Luke 10:18).

Thinking small means looking across the street rather than scrolling social media on our phones. It means digging into the simple, ordinary rhythms of life—befriending the coffee shop barista, helping the neighbor with his car, or volunteering at church. By looking for ways we can make a difference, we see evidence of God working through us. That, in turn, makes us more hopeful.

For example, during the COVID shutdown, my (Sarah's) church offered Zoom Bible studies as a way to connect while we were socially distanced. The simple act of regularly meeting with other believers to hear their love of God and his church lifted my spirits. I could see God at work in their lives, and that gave me hope when not much of our news—of shutdowns, racial injustice, and overwhelmed hospitals—could.

Maybe you sometimes feel anxious about the rising number of "nones." But think small: The unbelieving girl next door? You've known her a long time, and you love her.

The angry shouts of LGBTQ activists may worry you. But your same-sex-attracted colleague? You see how God has gifted him for work, even if you disagree with his lifestyle.

Planned Parenthood's rhetoric might make you feel ill. But the friend who is unexpectedly pregnant? You want to encourage and support her—you wish her only the best.

Even if your enemy lives next door, if you're a Christian, Jesus said you must love and pray for him or her (Matthew 5:44). Not only does that behavior benefit your neighbor—and you—but it also thwarts the work of our ultimate foe, Satan, whose lies bring pain to all who believe them.

We know that many feel their hope is being shaken—maybe that's you. And that's where we want to help. We want to give you perspective from Christians throughout history and around the world so that, in the power of the gospel, we do not lose heart.

In the pages of the Bible, in the stories of the early church, and in the lives of everyday Christians, we see a different story. We see a tremendous amount of hope—but not a giddy, ridiculous, naive hope, like some fantasy that you'll inherit millions from some heretofore-unknown uncle.

Instead, the two of us see Christians with a realistic, honest, solid hope. Across time and space, Christians hope that God will help them—and he always does. They hope that he will use them—and he does. They hope that someday all things will be made right—and they certainly will.

Their hope isn't soft or silly. It's real and robust because it hopes in something true. It's rooted not in their ability but in God's character. This hope grows with time as God's faithfulness proves itself over and over. We're calling it "resolute hope" because it doesn't sway in the winds of politics or wobble under the pressure of delayed (or even unrealized) results. It doesn't crack when the election doesn't go the right way or the test shows cancer or the temptation persists.

This hope is anchored in the past and aimed at the future. It plays the long game—a hope that can see the score at the end and works while it waits for the buzzer.

Gospelbound

FOR NOW, WE all live in a fallen world. Christians know that even as we work to show God's light and love to this world, the job won't be complete until Jesus returns. We know that in this world we'll lose many battles against evil. We know that Jesus warned that the world will hate us (Matthew 5:11; John 15:18).

But for many of us in historically Christian America, these warnings have been hypothetical for so long that we don't know what actual opposition looks like or how to minister from the margins.

It's an important skill to recover, because as culture slowly secularizes—or at least looks outside Christianity for purpose and meaning—American Christians have a brand-new opportunity.

We must not waste it. Christians shouldn't be embarrassed about our old-fashioned beliefs, hiding them or apologizing for them. A defensive posture hardly commends our faith to the world. It's no way to reach out to those who need Jesus.

We also shouldn't be antagonistic, lying our way into political power or forcing backroom deals. Nothing good comes from attacking people on social media or fixating on the small number of issues where we might disagree with another Christian. All-out offensive is not only exhausting but also off-putting. It's no way to draw others to Jesus.

So what should we do? Learn from those who are living with faithfulness from a strong foundation, despite the challenges that roar around them.

The two of us have seen Christians care for the weak by keeping a mission hospital open during the Ebola crisis. We've seen Christians live with integrity by choosing celibacy even though they feel same-sex attractions. We've seen Christians suffer with joy through physical paralysis, love their enemies through church splits, and show hospitality by sitting with strangers at church.

We've seen a marketing manager pull hundreds of women from the sex industry, a family befriend the meth dealer across the street (and lead him to Christ), and a healthy black church in Iowa merge with a growing white church so they could be a picture of God's multiethnic kingdom. We've seen a classical education movement that puts Christ in the center of the curriculum, men and women who give up vacations to make meals after natural disasters, and churches that sacrifice their best leaders and their budgets to plant new churches.

And that's just in the United States. Globally, we've seen thousands of children rescued from sex trafficking in the Philippines, Chinese house churches choosing God over government, and a network of gospel-centered churches growing on—of all places—the Arabian Peninsula.

We've been calling these Christians *gospelbound* because they're tied to the gospel of Jesus Christ that turned the ancient world upside down. They're bound by love to tackle today's challenges with hope that the gospel will prevail. And they're bound for glory someday because Jesus is coming again.

As we collected these stories of hope, seven themes kept coming to the fore. Over and over, we saw these gospelbound Christians *embrace the future, live with honor, suffer with joy, care for the weak, set another seat at the table, love their enemies, and give away their freedom.* We saw how these practices matched biblical teaching and historic Christian examples. We saw how relevant, countercultural, and timeless they are. And we began to ask, *How can we all live this way?*

These hopeful, gospelbound Christians show us the way to firm faith in an anxious age. They teach us how to live in the world with love, without falling in love with the world. They lay out a clear and compelling distinction between the way of Jesus and the way of our culture.

As our country loses the light of the gospel, stories like these just glow brighter.

So read on, and learn with us what it looks like to live with resolute hope in shaky times.

Then let's go and do likewise.

CHAPTER 2

Gospelbound Christians Embrace the Future

If we have been united with him in a death like his, we shall certainly be united with him in a resurrection like his.

—ROMANS 6:5

I (Collin) am not a Southern Baptist. You don't meet many Southern Baptists while growing up in South Dakota. We Methodists had to fight the Lutherans and Catholics for a seat at the post-church dinner table. As a child I'm not sure that I even knew the Southern Baptist Convention (SBC) is the largest Protestant denomination in the United States. I remember only that I thought they hated Disney or something.

Since moving to the South, I've learned a lot about my Baptist neighbors. If you know a Southern Baptist (or if you are one), you've probably noticed they're big on congregational meetings, soul winning, and altar calls. In 2016, the denomination formally encouraged pastors to share the gospel with unbelievers every week, Bible study teachers to ask whether anyone would like to repent and believe, and congregations to intentionally increase the number of those baptized each year.[1]

You could say Southern Baptists are embracing the future: their eyes are firmly fixed on heaven. More than anything else, they ask God to save people from an eternity in hell—they want to see people headed for the joy of being with Jesus in heaven. In fact, it might seem like that's all they're interested in. Are they perhaps too heavenly minded to be of any earthly good?

On the other hand, perhaps you know of people or organizations that are so busy feeding or housing or educating people that evangelism is nearly forgotten—that's the Methodism of my youth. You've probably heard someone use this quote: "Preach the gospel at all times. When necessary, use words." (It's often attributed to Saint Francis of Assisi, who not only didn't say it but also preached with words in up to five villages a day.[2]) Are they working so hard to meet physical needs that spiritual needs are being neglected?

For decades, Christians have been wrestling with what deserves more time and effort—preparing souls for heaven or caring for the poor.[3] And since we have finite time and energy, we need to make wise choices.

But we don't need to pick between loving God and loving neighbor. In fact, we don't even need to balance them. The more we love God and the more we eagerly embrace the future he's promised us, the more clearly we'll recognize the time we live in. And the better we'll be able to love our neighbors. Just consider what popular media probably never told you about the Southern Baptists.

Gospelbound Christians Work While They Wait

IN 1967, A Texas hurricane named Beulah spun off 115 tornadoes and killed almost sixty people. When it was over, a group of Baptist men were aghast at the wreckage.

"In a nutshell, some guys said, 'We have to do something. People are hurting and in need,'" said David Melber, who used to head up the SBC's disaster-relief efforts. The group of men gathered some ingredients and portable camp stoves and headed to southern Texas.

They kept at it, showing up after hurricanes and tornadoes and floods to offer meals to those in need. Four years later, after receiving a $25,000 mission offering, they bought a used eighteen-wheeler and converted it into a feeding unit. The next year, they used it to dish up 2,500 meals after a flash flood in central Texas.

Other state conventions followed their example—four more started their own disaster-relief efforts by 1976; another nine joined by 1988. Volunteers showed up after hundreds of local tornadoes and floods, an earthquake in Nicaragua in 1972 (their first international response), and a hurricane in Honduras in 1974.

"Back then, people would throw a chain saw in the back of a pickup truck and take off for the coast—totally untrained, not knowing what to do but willing to help someone," former disaster-relief director Cliff Satterwhite told Baptist Press in 2009. "Today, we wouldn't think of a chainsaw team going out without hardhats, chaps and goggles. No one wore that stuff back then. We were flying by the seat of our pants during [Hurricane] Hugo. A lot of [the] work was unofficial."[4]

Relief organizations measure time by disasters: If you ask SBC's North American Mission Board (NAMB) for a history of their organization, they'll give you a bullet list of bombings, hurricanes, floods, and earthquakes. Growth in finances and volunteers rises not slowly and steadily but in surges after regional or national tragedies.

For example, Hugo catapulted South Carolina's state response team into existence. Over the next twenty years, the state went from zero to 6,800 volunteers. At the same time, they gained 129 "units," which is what NAMB calls the trailers or trucks outfitted for a specific purpose—in addition to kitchens, some of them house rows of showers, washing machines, childcare areas, or cubicles with satellite phones and electricity for communication.

Nationally, volunteer numbers also shot up after Hugo, then again three years later after Hurricane Andrew.[5] Southern Baptists came "by the hundreds and multiplied hundreds every weekend," said Cecil Seagle, director of the Brotherhood Commission for the Florida Baptist Convention, in 1993.

By 1997, the SBC had more than 13,700 volunteers. By 2000, it had nearly 21,000. By 2004, it was up to about 31,000. Then Hurricane Katrina pounded into the Gulf Coast and blew previous volunteer efforts—even 9/11—out of the water.

Over seven months, 21,000 volunteers served 14.6 million meals in New Orleans (up from 2 million in 2001 and 3.5 million earlier in 2005) and spent 1.5 million hours caring for 7,800 children, mudding out 17,000 buildings, and doing 27,800 loads of laundry. They purified 21,600 gallons of water and sent more than 3,000 ham radio messages.

The enormous effort raised the Southern Baptist profile even higher,[6] marking them as a sought-after partner and a model for others. (Jim Burton, NAMB's then-director of volunteer mobilization, was asked to write a project-management textbook chapter on Southern Baptist disaster planning and logistics.)

Partnerships with the Red Cross, the Salvation Army, and the Federal Emergency Management Agency (FEMA) were also growing. The four saw one another again and again after floods, fires, and storms. Each time they met, the organizations refined their roles a little more. The Red Cross or FEMA buys the food, the Southern Baptists prepare it, and the Red Cross serves it from shelters or delivers it to neighborhoods. (If you've seen a Baptist potluck, you'll know why they left the food preparation to the Baptists.)

And when FEMA assesses a neighborhood for damage, it hands the list of addresses and needs over to the SBC and the Red Cross, which split it up. The Red Cross primarily provides emergency medical care, sets up temporary shelters, hands out meals, and occasionally offers financial help. The Southern Baptists cook the meals, help with cleanup and repairs, provide water and showers, and offer trained childcare.

"We could not fulfill our mission without the Southern Baptists," Red Cross president Gail McGovern told Southern Baptists in a 2014 promotional video. "And more importantly, the people that we're serving couldn't get through this without you."[7]

Five decades after the camp stoves in Texas, the Southern Baptists have sixty-five thousand trained volunteers. The SBC's disaster response is so massive it financially trails only the Red Cross and the Salvation Army—and has more trained disaster-relief volunteers than either one.

When Sarah told me (Collin) this statistic, I almost didn't believe her. How could I have not known the size and scope of these Baptist relief efforts? It also made me wonder what else normal Christians are doing every day to help strangers in need—the work we're not told about—and how I can join in.

What's the Time?

THOSE SIXTY-FIVE THOUSAND SBC volunteers aren't cooking meals in trailers because it's a fun thing to do on spring break. They aren't tearing out carpet because they're being paid. They don't remove soggy Sheetrock to get on TV. So why are they doing it?

Because they have a right view of time.

People generally view time in one of two ways. First, many lean toward nostalgia. They see the world getting worse and worse and long for someone or something to restore order. They imagine a past golden era that we must recover—perhaps the time of hearty and pious pioneers or of calm and capable 1950s families. I (Collin) am especially inclined in this direction. I love to get caught up in the drama of history and imagine what I would do in a different time and place. I can't help but judge our current day as lacking interest by comparison. Maybe that's why I identify with Owen Wilson's character in the Woody Allen film *Midnight in Paris*.

But as Wilson's character learns, nostalgia is a liar. There is no golden era. If you had the chance to go back, you wouldn't—and not only because you couldn't survive without antibiotics and Wi-Fi. People in the 1880s or 1950s didn't live in utopia. Their culture was as sinful and unpleasant as ours, just in different ways. In addition, your golden era might not be someone else's golden era. What's good for you and people like you might have been bad for someone else. Nostalgia fails in love for neighbor.

Given that we can't go back anyway and the past is a mirage, nostalgia is unlivable. It's beside the point. It can breed only discontent, making you anxious and afraid that you'll never recover the good old days. And it makes you furious with those who aren't aiming in the same direction you are.

The second view of time is progressivism. It believes everything is getting better and better. History doesn't have much to teach us except how enlightened we are by comparison. Eventually, when every vestige of the confining past has been conquered, we will enjoy full freedom and enlightenment. I (Sarah) sometimes lean too far in this direction. I'm naturally optimistic and a little bit perfectionistic, so I'm constantly working to make things better. If I don't keep checking the posture of my heart before God, I can get both anxious and exhausted.

Because, like nostalgia, progressivism is a mirage—you never actually arrive. There is no utopia except the new heavens and the new earth. And attempts to force one don't end well—consider the chaotic bloodbath of the French Revolution, the Stalinist starvation of Ukraine, the deadly deterioration of Venezuela.

Anyway, you can't live in the future. Comparing the present with an imaginary future paradise just fuels dissatisfaction. It makes you anxious, afraid that the future might not arrive in your lifetime. It makes you fear and loathe the people you think inhibit its arrival.

We need a better view of time. And we can find one in ancient Rome.

The Early Christian View of Time

IT MIGHT BE the most surprising development in world history—how an obscure, crucified Galilean prophet conquered the world's greatest empire without lifting a sword. So how did it happen? In large part, because of how early Christians thought about time.

Ancient Rome wasn't antireligion; in fact, the opposite was true. Jesus was crucified in a culture flooded with gods and goddesses. The Roman deities wore togas and lived on Mount Olympus and needed a lot of attention from the mortals.

The humans eagerly complied. They worked hard to appease big names like Jupiter and Minerva and Apollo, who they believed would hand out favors if they were flattered enough. But the Romans didn't stop there. By one reckoning, there were thirty thousand Roman gods, including Vulcan, the fire god; Fornax, the corn-baking god; and Sterculus, the manure heap god. Romans gave gifts in January to Tellus, the planting god; held a parade in May for Mars, the earth god; and cooked a feast in December for the soil gods.[8] All year long they sacrificed at the many temples, built household shrines, and retold the stories of their gods' deeds.

In this culture, where emperors themselves were nearly deities and the office of high priest was a political position, there was no such thing as separation of church and state. The gods were needed for military victories and economic success and to legitimize leaders. Being a good citizen, then, meant being highly religious.

Many nations conquered by Rome were also polytheistic, and they added the Roman gods to their list of deities. Rome often returned the favor, figuring the more gods, the better.

The Jews, however, were noticeably different. They worshipped only one God, kept rituals like circumcision and the Sabbath, and held their own feast days. At first (before the Jewish rebellion in

AD 66), the Romans didn't mind too much. The Jews seemed like a peculiar ethnic group quietly following their ancestral traditions. They weren't bothering anybody, and for the most part, Rome didn't bother them.

Christians, though, were even more different than the Jews. They were not confined to one ethnic group, but spread to all races and classes of people. They were not following their forebearers in worship of an ancient deity (something the Romans could respect in the Jews) but pledged allegiance to a Savior many of them had met on the shores of Galilee or the streets of Jerusalem. And they didn't just ignore the Roman gods (like the Jews did); Christians condemned them.

They also had a different view of time, which affected everything they did. Christians are confident of a better future. We're both realistic (we know we can never achieve perfection in our fallen world) and ever hopeful (we know our work has eternal significance). Christians know a time will come when we no longer need to broker peace between two quarreling friends, pick up trash, or teach a child to read. And every time we do these good deeds, we see the world a little more like it was supposed to be and like it will be when Jesus returns.

This hope sustained Christians for the first one hundred years after Jesus was crucified, and the church grew modestly. By AD 150, their numbers were up to forty thousand, according to one estimate. Just fifty years later, though, there were 218,000 Christians. And by AD 250, the number of Christians had skyrocketed to 1.17 million.[9]

If you were a Roman, you could pity a small and strange religious sect. You could even abuse them for sport. But as the number of Christians grew, they began to feel like a legitimate threat. Many Romans worried that the gods would frown on this rebellious group. And sure enough, in the 200s, barbarians began to invade along Roman borders, peasants tried to revolt, and the leadership destabilized so much that the government went through twenty-six emperors in fifty years. It was easy to conclude that the gods were punishing the whole Roman Empire because the Christians wouldn't bow to them.

It didn't help that it was easy to misunderstand Christianity. You know what it's like sometimes to explain Christian jargon to someone who can't remember the last time he went to church. The Eucharist sounded like cannibalism—drink my blood and eat my flesh? Talk of "loving our brothers and sisters" sounded like incest. And anyway, the powerful and prideful Romans were not naturally inclined to follow a God who humiliated himself by becoming human and getting himself killed trying to save a bunch of people. Many regarded Christianity, according to author Steven Smith, as "contemptible nonsense."[10] Persecution began in earnest. We're not talking a bit of social disapproval. We're talking gruesome death.

It shouldn't have been too hard for the Romans to stamp out this odd little sect—while their numbers had grown, they were still only around 1 percent of the population of the Roman Empire.[11] But even when their leaders were beheaded, crucified, fed to lions, and burned alive, their numbers kept growing. In fact, the passionate faith of the fallen inflamed the faith of those left behind.

"Let there come upon me fire and cross, struggles with wild beasts, cutting and tearing asunder, rackings of bones, mangling of limbs, crushing of my whole body, and cruel tortures of the devil, if so I may attain to Jesus Christ!" wrote Justin Martyr, condemned to be beheaded for refusing to renounce his faith.[12]

This forward-looking faith—anticipating a joyful existence with the risen Jesus after death—was mind boggling. Roman religion was all about obtaining blessings in this life; there was no clear idea of what came next. Some believed that life just stopped. "I was not, I have been, I am not, I do not want" was such a popular funeral inscription that it was eventually just abbreviated.[13] Others believed that people descended to a dark underworld, either to be punished or to live a ho-hum existence in the Asphodel Meadows. Heaven was reserved for the gods and divine kings; normal people didn't go there.

The idea that Christ went to prepare a place for believers, that they could be with him in paradise, was a far brighter hope. Not only did it remove the fear of death, but this future also gave present life a deeper, heavier meaning while lightening burdens of pain and sorrow. Imagine the difference it would make in our evangelism if we grasped this news as truly good, now and forever. You're not burdening your friend when you tell her about Jesus. You're sharing a resolute hope that will help her find meaning and joy no matter what troubles may come.

Consider the case of Perpetua, a legendary figure in the early church.[14] I (Collin) love to introduce my church members to her when I teach an annual class on living our faith in public. Even though few of us will face her impossible choices, we can still be inspired by her courage. Born around AD 182, Perpetua was raised in the upper classes of Carthage, an early stronghold of Christianity, which made it a target of persecution. The mother of a small child, Perpetua was arrested in 203 as she prepared to be baptized.

Perpetua's father did not approve of her faith in Jesus Christ. Many of us today can relate to this experience of family disapproval, increasingly so even in the West. Her father begged her to recant so the Roman authorities would spare her life. He bemoaned how she made him look bad. He spoke of the fate of her son if he lost his mother. And still Perpetua would not forsake the future she could not see for the family she could.

Perpetua was taken into an arena to be mauled by wild animals. She was attacked by a wild heifer before a sword ended her life.

Some might think she was foolish. (If Jesus isn't coming back, then she was.) Or maybe you can see why the great theologian Augustine considered her a hero. For Christians, to live is Christ, and to die is gain (Philippians 1:21). Gospelbound Christians like Perpetua embrace a future they cannot see.

"Though you have not seen him, you love him," Peter said of Jesus in 1 Peter 1:8–9. "Though you do not now see him, you believe in him and rejoice with joy that is inexpressible and filled with glory, obtaining the outcome of your faith, the salvation of your souls."

With such a great future in front of us, what should we do while we're waiting? Blend in with the world as best we can to minimize any conflict? Hold our breath and hope nobody notices us until it's all over? Begin every conversation with "Do you know the Lord?"

Christians from Perpetua to the Southern Baptists live out something called "inaugurated eschatology," which basically means that while we wait for heaven, we're working toward it. Since Christ has come, we already have the promised Spirit, the law of God written on our new hearts, and the power to obey God and do his will. Where we live and work and move in the world, we're able to—with God's help—fix some of what is broken and right some of what is wrong. Through us, some of heaven is breaking through on earth.

We know that we do not do this perfectly. Even with our best intentions and efforts, we mess up all the time. We're slow to see needs, incompetent in our repairs, bumbling in our relationships. We're still sinful people living in a sinful world that has not yet been fully redeemed. This can be frustrating. I (Collin) struggle to make peace with this fallen world. I want to arrive, to see all my plans come to fruition, to watch all my dreams come true. But that's not life in this world.

We live between sin and redemption, between Jesus's resurrection and his coming again, between this world and the perfect one to come.

The apostle Peter helps us straddle those two worlds. "The day of the Lord will come like a thief," he wrote in 2 Peter 3:10, "and then the heavens will pass away with a roar, and the heavenly bodies will be burned up and dissolved, and the earth and the works that are done on it will be exposed."

But waiting for "the day of the Lord" doesn't panic or paralyze us. "Since all these things are thus to be dissolved, what sort of people ought you to be in lives of holiness and godliness," Peter wrote. "Therefore, beloved, since you are waiting for these, be diligent to be found by him without spot or blemish, and at peace" (verses 11, 14).

We are to be holy, godly, diligent, at peace. We do good on earth because we set our minds on heaven. We work while we wait.

Here's how C. S. Lewis put it in his book *Mere Christianity:*

> A continual looking forward to the eternal world is not (as some modern people think) a form of escapism or wishful thinking, but one of the things a Christian is meant to do. It does not mean that we are to leave the present world as it is. . . . It is since Christians have largely ceased to think of the other world that they have become so ineffective in this. Aim at Heaven and you will get earth "thrown in": aim at earth and you will get neither.[15]

Gospelbound Christians embrace the future by working diligently in the present. But we don't want to work on just anything. Our time is short. How do we know, then, how to spend our time, however long it may be?

Gospelbound Christians prioritize their tasks the way God does.

Gospelbound Christians
Prioritize the Way God Does

For a small stretch of time during graduate school, I (Sarah) lived in Washington, DC. Except for the fact that I was living apart from my husband—who was in school in Chicago—I loved it. The city is beautiful and busy, and when you're working there, you feel the weight of the important decisions being made.

If you're ambitious, DC is the perfect place to live. That's what twenty-eight-year-old John Folmar was doing, hoping to make it big. After graduating from Duke Law School, he got a job as a legislative counsel for an influential senator.

"I was where I wanted to be," he wrote in *The Underestimated Gospel*. "And yet when I got there, I was empty and unsatisfied."[16]

While out for a run one day, he spotted Capitol Hill Baptist Church and figured he could "make some connections or meet influential people" there. He began attending, started meeting pastor Mark Dever for a morning Bible study, and realized "that I was a moral failure, that I couldn't turn over a new leaf but needed a new life."[17]

Capitol Hill Baptist introduced John to Jesus and to Keri Harrison, who also worked on the Hill. She was the chief counsel of the House Judiciary Subcommittee on the Constitution and would eventually write the Partial-Birth Abortion Ban.

As John and Keri dated, fell in love, and got married, John started feeling the tug to ministry. He ignored it, assuming Dever made everyone feel that way.

"My whole life was geared toward political office," he told us. "And it was difficult to give that up."

But the call to ministry was strong, and John wound up in seminary, then worked as an assistant pastor at Capitol Hill Baptist. Both John and Keri were interested enough in missions that when the call came for a pastor of an international church in Dubai, they said yes almost before Dever finished asking whether they'd want to go.

In just a few years, the Folmars had traded high-profile legal careers for the sand and Sharia law of the Arabian Peninsula.

They weren't the first to follow that path. Forty-five years earlier, doctors Pat and Marian Kennedy arrived in the United Arab Emirates, before the country even formally existed. At the invitation of two local sheikhs, they set up in a mud-brick guesthouse and delivered their first baby before they'd even unpacked.

In a place where obstetric care was so crude that a third of mothers and half of children died in childbirth, the Kennedys delivered sixty-seven babies during their first full year in UAE. Four years later, they delivered 770.[18] With more than two hundred patients arriving each morning and no replacement doctors, the Kennedys worked for years without taking leave. Their thirteen-year-old son wasn't playing baseball with his friends; he was helping with gallbladder and hernia operations.[19]

Nothing was easy. There were no roads—just barren desert crossed with donkey and camel paths. There was no running water and no electricity, which made basic cleaning and medicine storage difficult. The Kennedys mixed water, sugar, and salt to make their own intravenous fluids. With no support staff, the doctors also cleaned and maintained the rooms. With few supplies, they treated everything from broken bones to tuberculosis to eye diseases.

Then heavy rain destroyed their mud-brick facility. They moved to another building, this one made of palm branches and corrugated aluminum. Six months later, a cookfire burned it down.

The Kennedys kept at it. Their selfless service won so much goodwill that the hospital—now a world-class facility—is still allowed to place Arabic-language Bibles in the rooms and offer staff prayers with patients. I (Collin) learned their story while teaching Scripture to Christians who worked in their hospital. Many regard the Arabian Peninsula as closed to the gospel. But that's not what you see when you visit. When Christians show they're willing to move to the other side of the world and sacrifice wealth and fame, it's natural for skeptical unbelievers to ask why. And that's especially the case when those Christians love them, both body and soul.

Relative religious tolerance continued even after oil was discovered off the shore of Dubai in 1966. The tiny port town exploded into a bustling global destination, and the surrounding emirates swiftly formed into an organized country.[20] Today UAE's population is ten million. Of those, less than 12 percent are Emirati citizens—

the rest are hired foreigners.[21] That's important because although the UAE constitution declares all citizens Muslim, other people are largely free to choose their own religion.

"In day-to-day life, it's easy to share the gospel with someone who has never heard it before," Keri said. For example, the tailor making her son a suit is a Muslim from Albania. "All I had to say was 'Do you know what an evangelical Christian believes?' and I could share the gospel with him," she said.

Week after week, John preaches the Bible at United Christian Church of Dubai (UCCD). The church began to grow, from five hundred to six hundred to more than eight hundred. Keri started a women's inductive Bible study that now draws more than one hundred women.

The Folmars were "a drink of water in a dry and weary land," said one former elder. UCCD has planted three churches and continues to train pastors from neighboring countries.

"There is incredible hunger and spiritual poverty in the countries next to us and across the water from us," UCCD elder Etienne Nel said. "We trust the Lord and pray that the Spirit would be at work, convicting people and giving glory to his name. . . . We want to be an effective church—a city on a hill."

Prioritizing the Things of God

BOTH THE FOLMARS and the Kennedys believed so wholeheartedly in a longer arc, in a future they cannot see, that they gave up comfortable homes and lucrative careers and easy friendships in order to move to UAE.

If this world is all there is, these life choices seem extreme. Everybody loves a self-sacrificing hero; fewer are willing to actually become one—because if the hero doesn't get the girl in the end, he's just a fool. The bigger the risk, the less willing we are to take it—unless the payoff is extreme. Mission work is always a long shot; therefore, missionary math adds up only if you multiply by eternity.

This is the future Christians eagerly await—a renewed life in brand-new physical bodies (Philippians 3:21) on a brand-new physical earth (Isaiah 65:17) with feasting (Luke 13:29) and singing (Revelation 5:9–10). If you're looking forward to living safely, building houses, and planting gardens (Ezekiel 28:26) in close relationship (1 Thessalonians 4:17) with an exciting God who loves you, then spending your short, hard years here doing his work is exactly the right priority.

For the Kennedys, that meant bringing medical care to the desert. For the Folmars, it meant taking the gospel to those who hadn't heard it. For the Southern Baptists, it means talking about Jesus while cooking meals for those who have lost everything. For the two of us, it means writing stories that reveal God at work, which shows us and our readers his faithful love, which helps us all love and obey him. For you, it may mean working with integrity, loving your extended family, or sharing Jesus with a coworker.

Gospelbound Christians are working hard, prioritizing the things of God. They're also giving away their time, their sleep, their lives. They aren't giving away their margins or their extras. They're giving away their best. Mark Dever didn't send just anyone to Dubai. He sent a couple with exceptional potential. Because that's how the kingdom of God advances around the world. And because you can afford to do that when you're living not only for the moment or yourself but also for a future beyond the horizon of tomorrow.

Gospelbound Christians Give Away the Best

AT THE SUMMIT Church in North Carolina, the children's facility is shaped like an airplane hangar.

The classrooms are marked like a terminal, with signs such as "Gate K1," "Gate 24," and "Summit Airlines" marking the way. Maps of the world hang prominently. And the sign over the exit says, "You are sent."

It's the refrain of the ten-thousand-attendee church—played on repeat.

When babies are born, parents are commissioned to raise them "as arrows to be launched out into the world," said Todd Unzicker, who was the pastor of sending at the Summit. By the time children finish middle school, the Summit wants them to have experienced a domestic, short-term mission trip with their family. By early high school, they're encouraged to do a trip somewhere in the Americas; by senior year, around twenty-five of them—out of 250—will have committed to spending three weeks living with the Summit's overseas missionaries.

The Summit asks every college student to give one summer to a mission trip—not to take a beach vacation or barhop across Europe but to serve others in the name of Jesus. Then the Summit asks for two years of mission work or church-planting participation after graduation. The Summit asks baby boomers for something similar, encouraging them to give the first two years of their retirement not to golf or grandkids but to being part of a church plant.

When new believers are baptized, they're asked whether they believe Jesus saved them from sin and whether they're willing to "do whatever he has called them to do and go wherever he has called them to go." When communion is served, it's sometimes presided over by missionaries on video, breaking bread in Africa or India or the Middle East. Every month, short-term and long-term missionaries and church planters are publicly commissioned; when they return, they're given a standing ovation. What you celebrate, others will emulate.

J. D. Greear, the pastor at Summit, connects every one of his sermons to missions or church planting in some way. Instead of "You are dismissed" or "Go in peace," the Summit pastors end each service with the words "Summit, you are sent."

"Preaching that, week in and week out over ten years, has had a big impact on the culture of the church," said Mike McDaniel, who was the pastor of church planting and leadership development at Summit. In 2018, the Summit celebrated sending out its one thousandth person in fifteen years. The church has given money and members to more than forty church plants in the United States and more than two hundred overseas. For the first time in 2017, the average combined attendance of the plants (10,171) bested that of the Summit itself (9,973).

If you aren't a Christian—or even if you are—it may seem to you that the Summit has designed a recipe for disaster. Why would you train leaders just to send them away? Why would you raise funds only to hand them over to another church? Why would you put so much energy into a program that siphons people—with their money and good ideas and ability to volunteer—away from your congregation?

But the Summit's strategy makes sense if you believe that Jesus rose from the dead and now reigns from the right hand of the Father.

"If Christ has not been raised, then our preaching is in vain and your faith is in vain," Paul wrote to the Corinthians. "If Christ has not been raised, your faith is futile and you are still in your sins. Then those also who have fallen asleep in Christ have perished. If in Christ we have hope in this life only, we are of all people most to be pitied" (1 Corinthians 15:14, 17–19).

Christians do a lot of things that don't make sense: risk their lives to care for the weak, uphold unpopular views on sexuality, give away their money, and send away their best friends to live among unbelieving neighbors. If Christ is still in the tomb, that behavior is sad and ridiculous. We're wasting not just our own time and energy but also everyone else's. If Jesus isn't raised and it doesn't make any difference in eternity whether we believe in anything he did or said, then Christianity is not benign. It's cancerous. And Southern Baptists like Greear should be ashamed of their evangelistic zeal. You don't admire a friend who waits on a future that will never arrive. You pity him.

But if it is true—if Jesus did rise from the dead—that changes everything. So why don't more self-professed Christians act that way?

Why Americans Aren't Worried About the Afterlife

We've seen that ancient Romans didn't worry much about heaven or hell. But modern Americans—while they'll tell you they believe in heaven—aren't overly concerned about the afterlife either.

From 2007 to 2014, Pew Research Center found that American belief in God dropped from 71 percent to 63 percent.[22] At the same time, belief in the existence of heaven barely budged (74 percent to 72 percent).[23] So what gives? Why would you believe in the afterlife if you don't believe in God? Probably because the idea of an eternal paradise is so attractive, especially when you're standing at a graveside or facing your own declining health. Murmuring "He's in a better place" or "Now she's smiling down on us" is more comforting than "We'll never see him again" or "Now she doesn't exist."

But vague religious clichés are junk food. Maybe they feel good in the moment, but they don't contribute to a healthy life. When you separate heaven from the reason martyrs like Perpetua were willing to die to get there—namely, to be with God—it's nothing more than hazy projection or vain longing.

As Barna Group reported in 2003, while 46 percent of people believed that heaven is "a state of eternal existence in God's presence," sizable minorities said it is "an actual place of rest and reward where souls go after death" (30 percent) or "symbolic" (14 percent).[24] They're likely picturing a heaven like the one portrayed by the popular show *The Good Place*—a godless paradise where you get everything you want.

Most people think that's where they're going (two-thirds of those Barna surveyed),[25] though not everyone thinks believing in Jesus is the only way to do that. LifeWay Research found that 45 percent of Americans believe "there are many ways to heaven." About four in ten said heaven is open to people who have never heard of Jesus, and three in ten said there will be a chance for people to follow God after they die.[26] The shift from the days of the early Christian martyrs is drastic: imagine telling them you want to go to heaven but not to be with Jesus.

Even those who believe in hell aren't worried about going there. Just one-half of 1 percent told Barna they thought they were going to hell after death, a place most described as "a state of eternal separation from God's presence" (39 percent) or "an actual place of torment and suffering where people's souls go after death" (32 percent).[27]

To many Americans today, hell—if it exists—sounds like a place populated only by Adolf Hitler and Osama bin Laden. Heaven, on the other hand, looks boring. In *The Good Place* finale, three of the main characters end up choosing to leave heaven and become energy dust—essentially committing suicide—because they ran out of things to do.

No wonder reaction to the afterlife is often ho-hum.

"Would it be nice not to die?" one person wrote to the *Atlantic* blogger Andrew Sullivan when he asked what atheists thought would happen to them after they die. "Maybe, certainly sounds interesting (although I could see myself wishing fervently for death to put me out of my boredom when I turned a million, and considering it an inhuman and sadistic torment to deny that to me . . .). How do I feel about [death]? Meh."

Another replied, "I think that when I die I'll cease to exist, and in some ways I'm happy about that. . . . I don't want to live forever."

And another said, "Life after I am dead will be just like life before I was born. I don't regret not being here sooner than I was, and I had no sensation of existence before my birth. So it will be after my death."[28]

No wonder many Americans have turned away from Christianity. They think they're facing either paradise or oblivion—neither inspiring nor terrifying. No wonder religion is seen as so peripheral to life. Eternity with Jesus, saved from judgment by his blood on the cross, is our whole thing.

And no wonder gospelbound Christians stand out when they prioritize what God does, choosing to give away their best. No wonder they radiate joy that can come only by experiencing—and anticipating—new life with Jesus. No wonder they'll risk anything to introduce the world to the risen Christ. Because whether we want to admit it or not, time is running out.

The Gospelbound View of Time

OUR VIEW OF time makes an enormous difference in the way we live today.

We don't need to long for the past, even for the Garden of Eden. We know we can't return there. And while we look forward to the future, when life with Jesus will be perfect, we know we can't expect perfection from our lives on earth. Man-made utopia is the stuff of nightmares.

So we choose neither nostalgia nor progressivism.

In the same way, we reject the false dichotomy of loving God *or* loving neighbor, of evangelism *or* mercy ministry. Yes, time is limited, but that's one reason God gave us one another. While one Christian may start a workplace Bible study for nonbelievers, another may volunteer at a pregnancy center. Doing one doesn't mean there's no room for the other.

We choose both.

We can do that because love isn't a limited resource. It comes from God. And the more we give it away, by adopting a child or moving to the Middle East or mentoring a new believer, the more he gives us. He sets before us the tasks *and* gives us the financial, physical, and emotional means to complete them.

Gospelbound Christians can work with joy, knowing the things we do for God—and with his Spirit's strength—have eternal value. We are not overly discouraged by how dark and broken our world is, how utterly unstable and vulnerable we are. In our jobs, the two of us see that darkness and brokenness clearly. But then we look beyond them, to a new creation where we get to laugh and work and worship and explore with God and with others we love.

That, in turn, helps us be more patient with problems, more hopeful about people, and more willing to jump in to help. Since the work we do here matters for eternity, it's worth our time to be productive, to work with excellence, to invest in relationships.

And our good service—done with peaceful hearts that trust in God's character, with gentleness and care for others, and with the best of our ability—can attract those around us to this same hope. The choices of gospelbound Christians—made with eyes fixed on eternity, feet ready for God's leading, and hands open to his providence—look beautifully different to those around us. We live in such a way that others "may hear of [us] that [we] are standing firm in one spirit, with one mind striving side by side for the faith of the gospel, and not frightened in anything by [our] opponents" (Philippians 1:27–28).

We're not afraid of this world. We're waiting for another one, "for new heavens and a new earth in which righteousness dwells" (2 Peter 3:13).

Take a deep breath and exhale. If you believe in the risen Jesus, this is your future. His promise will not fail. Jesus came once, and righteousness dwelled among us. When he died on the cross, he exchanged our sin for his perfect goodness. When he returns, righteousness will never leave. We'll be freed from sin and freed from sinning!

Since we already know this promise is true, we can endure the frustrations of this "not yet" time, of the brokenness all around us. Because his promise cannot fail, you can keep picking up fallen branches and wiping up mud. You can keep delivering babies in the desert or preaching the gospel to church members who can barely understand you. You can send away a chunk of your budget and your best leaders to a new church plant on the other side of town—even the other side of the world.

You can work with excellence, with dedication to the tasks God has set in front of you, and with a cheerful willingness to give him—and his image bearers around you—your best.

The two of us want you to think much more of heaven. Stick your head in the clouds. Remember that our lives here—plagued with fighting, material poverty, and actual plagues—are not what God intended for us. Remember that he has something better planned for our future and that there is nothing in heaven and earth that can keep him from fulfilling his promises.

And while your head is in the sky, plant your feet on the earth. While you wait in hope for Christ to return, get to work. There's so much to do: Visit the lonely; feed the hungry; care for the sick. Nurture a child; tell someone about Jesus; cultivate a garden. Encourage a friend; wash some dishes; plant a church.

We embrace the future, and because of that, we work by faith.

CHAPTER 3

Gospelbound Christians
Live with Honor

Repay no one evil for evil, but give thought to do what is honorable in the sight of all.

—ROMANS 12:17

Ten years ago, Becket Cook was a perfect example of success in America.[1] He'd thrown off the Catholic shackles of his youth, come out of the closet as gay, and moved to Hollywood. He had a natural eye for production design, kept meeting the right people, and climbed the entertainment industry's ladder up and up and *up*.

Eventually he was working with stars such as Meryl Streep and Katy Perry. He flew around the world to design photo shoots for magazines like *Vogue* and *Harper's Bazaar*. He acted with Nick Offerman in a movie that premiered at the Sundance Film Festival, went to a party at Prince's house, and swam in Drew Barrymore's pool.

By all the world's measures, Cook had arrived. He was free from religious expectations and financial worries. He'd chased his dreams and found himself, and he was living his best life.

He'd won.

But there was a problem. Contrary to expectations, winning didn't make him deliriously and endlessly happy.

"Despite many wonderful and exciting experiences, I still felt like something was missing," Cook wrote in his memoir. "I had no explanation for it. I couldn't have dreamed of asking for more, yet everything somehow felt hazy. Though I didn't articulate them, the questions kept coming. *Who am I? What am I doing here? What's the meaning of life?"*[2]

He went to therapy for years, trying to get to know himself but feeling like he was going in circles. He attended plays in New York and London, looking for a story line that would communicate some larger truth, but ended up with more questions. He loved the spiritual experience that often came with observing art, but it was fleeting and never quite enough.

And then one day, while at a fashion party in Paris, he felt an overwhelming, intense sense of emptiness.

"There I was, in the middle of Paris at an ultrachic fashion party, feeling dead inside," he wrote. "I thought, *If this stuff isn't doing it for me anymore, what on earth will? I've done everything, met everyone, been everywhere. What am I going to do for the next fifty or sixty years of my life?"*[3]

Looking for Meaning in Yourself

It's not just Cook asking these questions. It's an entire generation raised to believe that they can be anything they want if they just search inside themselves and try hard enough. So, what happens when you get everything you want and it's still not enough? What if your problem is success?

Cook did everything right, according to the modern American dream. He found freedom from the stifling expectations of authority. Two or three generations ago, Cook's life choices would've been unthinkable. Back then, many children grew up to follow their parents' professions, live in their parents' towns, vote for their parents' political party, attend their parents' churches. Family and home and behavior expectations lay across generations like a weighted blanket.

Sometimes that blanket was comforting. There were common expectations of behavior: If you couldn't afford it, you didn't buy it. If you promised to do something, you did it. If an older person asked you to do something, you obeyed. You knew who you were and where you belonged—you were born where you were supposed to be, into a family and maybe even a profession you were supposed to have. You didn't worry about it.

I (Collin) have traced my direct family history as far back as I can, and I can't find anyone through my father's generation who did anything but farm or work with farmers. Sometimes I feel like I failed by not following in their footsteps. I know how to toss hay bales and to feed cattle from birth. But I'm not sure anyone who's seen me drive (or worse, try to fix) a tractor would think I made the wrong choice by becoming a writer.

Sometimes the weight of generational expectations felt suffocating to our ancestors. Sometimes it meant embarrassments no one forgot, abuse you couldn't escape, or talents you couldn't develop. In its worst forms, it meant racial segregation and limited opportunities for women.

The children born in the years after World War II famously threw off the shackles of the past. "If there were a hippie code, it would include these flexible guidelines," *Time* magazine wrote in 1967. "Do your own thing, wherever you have to do it and whenever you want. Drop out. Leave society as you have known it. Leave it utterly. Blow the mind of every straight person you can reach. Turn them on, if not to drugs, then to beauty, love, honesty, fun."[4]

Rebelling against convention sounds fun, and while there's been some tugging back and forth, America has gradually loosened more and more of its social restrictions. *Honor* and *duty*, two words that popped up often in older literature, are rarely heard these days. The lifestyle they described—doing what's right even when you don't want to, curtailing your freedom for someone else—is also harder to justify. Many social stigmas have disappeared. It's okay to have sex anywhere, with anyone. It's okay to leave your spouse, to ghost your friends, to never check your voice mail. Your only obligation is to be yourself, to follow your heart, to find yourself by looking inside yourself. If you don't feel like doing something, then that's a sign you shouldn't try.

Even though Americans keep telling one another these mantras, there isn't much evidence that they actually work. British singer-songwriters IDER released "You've Got Your Whole Life Ahead of You Baby" in 2018:

> I'm trying to enjoy myself, love myself
> Who the f— is myself?[5]

"Who is myself," indeed? Having to come up with your own meaning and purpose in life—when the options are limitless and you have no idea which way is right for you—is daunting and exhausting.

And once you get there—to more Instagram followers than you'd ever dreamed of, to the job with the corner office, to the good-looking spouse, to the ultrachic party in Paris—then what? What do you shoot for next? More of the same?

Why don't so-called freedom and success bring peace and stability? Because it's a lot of pressure to pretend you're God and in control of your life. You didn't create the world; you didn't choose to be born; you don't know what's going to happen next. Attempting to make decisions without considering why he created you and what he's done for you and what he asks of you is an exercise in futility. It's like going in circles or trying to solve a problem without enough information.

Added to this is the pressure of social media. It turns out we're not free to do or say what we want. Now we're just one bad move from our fifteen minutes of infamy. So you have to find yourself inside yourself, but you have to make sure that self is socially acceptable before you show your face online.

No wonder we're exhausted and anxious.

Finding Meaning Outside Yourself

THE SOLUTION FOUND by gospelbound Christians might surprise you. It is to live with honor.

Honor probably isn't a word you've heard lately. It means "to hold in high respect" and "to keep an agreement" as well as "adherence to what is right or to a conventional standard of conduct."[6] It's doing the right thing when it's not easy, when it doesn't feel good, when you don't want to. It's choosing to act—or not act—for others instead of for yourself. It's choosing to wear a mask to protect others even if it feels uncomfortable, choosing to keep an appointment when a more fun option came up in the meantime, choosing to do what your boss asked even if your colleagues don't.

Honorable behavior can be difficult. But honor is also durable. It lasts longer than an afternoon Twitter storm. It doesn't tank with the markets or change with new fashions.

You know it when you see it. It's the man who stops to help the stranded motorist on Jericho Road. It's the woman at the water cooler who's always ready to lend a sympathetic ear yet never succumbs to office gossip. It's when you're so sure of whom God made you to be, you don't need to worry so much about what everyone else thinks of you. You're wearing your own oxygen mask; now you can help others put on theirs.

We were made for honor by a God who defines it.

From the first breath he gave to Adam, God has shown himself to be honorable, a God who remembers his promises, who keeps his word. He gave Adam and Eve everything they needed and more, including a relationship with him. When they sinned, he provided both discipline and a path to redemption. For centuries, he honored Israel by choosing her, providing for her, disciplining her, loving her. Every time she broke her promises, he kept his.

We see God's honor illustrated most graphically in the story of Hosea. God ordered the prophet to get married to symbolize the relationship between God and his people, Israel. The woman, Gomer, already had a reputation for being promiscuous with her sexual favors. Hosea went in eyes wide open, knowing she would cheat on him.

And she did. After giving birth to three of Hosea's children, she left him to shack up with another man. Hosea was now well within his rights to divorce her. She had dishonored him and their marriage in a painful and public way.

But God told Hosea to chase Gomer down. To add insult to injury, Hosea had to pay six ounces of silver and about nine bushels of barley to get back what was his in the first place. No wonder he told her, "You must dwell as mine for many days. You shall not play the whore, or belong to another man; so will I also be to you" (Hosea 3:3).

Hosea's heartbreaking marriage is like God's relationship with his people—first Israel, now all believers in Jesus Christ. God knew from the beginning that we would not honor our end of the "I'll be your God, and you'll be my people" deal. So he proved himself honorable enough for both sides of the covenant, paying with the life of his own Son for our redemption from sin.

He doesn't stop behaving with honor, even when we inevitably prove faithless. He chases us with his love, justifying and sanctifying us while we sleep with sin. Instead of pushing us away, he gives us the

Holy Spirit, honoring us with his presence, with full access to him every time we pray.

Honor reflects the One who gives it.

Every time the sun rises, every time the tide turns, every time the leaves change and drop, creation testifies to the faithfulness of its Maker. Every time two plus two makes four, every time gravity pulls our feet to the ground, every time friction produces heat, God's integrity is proved. He always does the right thing. You can depend on him, no matter how you feel, because he doesn't change.

You may not feel like you can count on much. But gospelbound Christians rest, knowing that God cannot act dishonorably toward us.

How to Live with Honor

ASSURED BY THIS honor and empowered by the Holy Spirit, gospelbound Christians extend the same honor to others.

"Outdo one another in showing honor," Paul wrote in Romans 12:10. He was writing to people who were used to bowing before authority and admiring athletic champions. They knew how to speak with deference to those with power and money. They even knew how to submit themselves to religious leaders.

But that's not what Paul was talking about.

Honor one another, he told the church in Rome. Don't think of yourselves more highly than you ought. Recognize that everyone has different gifts. Don't be haughty. Love one another. Rejoice with one another. Live in harmony with one another. Be thoughtful about how to live with honor (verses 3–17).

How much safer would you feel in a community marked by these values?

Drawing on God's character, Paul was explaining a selfless, others-focused honor. It doesn't just defer to kings. It values slaves. It doesn't just apply to friends. It's for our foes too. It comes to us from God, so we share it with others. This sense of honor once shaped the way many understood good and evil: we do the right thing, even if it's not convenient, even if it doesn't feel good, even if no one ever notices.

It's the opposite of keeping your options open and constantly checking in with yourself to see whether things are still working for you.

It's looking not for comfort but for need. It's praying through a decision and then sticking with it—even if you later wish you were at the movies instead of the food pantry or with someone besides your spouse or in a life different from your own. Living without honor looks inward; living with it looks outward.

If you're lucky, someone has modeled honor for you. That person for me (Collin) was Grandpa Daniel, who lived less than a mile from me while I grew up. He didn't do anything the annals of history will record. He farmed as his father had before him. He raised four children, including my mother. He was married to my grandma more than fifty years. Rarely do I see a politician or movie star I would want my son to emulate. But I'll tell him all about Grandpa Daniel.

Despite such honorable examples, we all know that the "you do you," "find yourself" language is attractive. Who doesn't want to follow their heart or be themselves? But a few serious problems arise when we switch from outward-facing honor to inward-looking "authenticity."

First, it assumes the human heart is good and a reliable guide. But as you can see in Becket Cook's story (and maybe in your own experience), following your heart without reference to a standard of honorable conduct is liable to make you miserable.

Second, it assumes the highest good in this world is that you achieve your own happiness. But Cook learned what generations before him knew intuitively: happiness comes not through self-fulfillment but rather through commitment to others and doing what is right according to a code of honor (in this case, biblical ethics).

Third, it assumes anybody trying to tell you what to do (including your parents, the church, or God) is interrupting or derailing your journey to finding what makes you happy. You are the only one wise enough and good enough to know what's best for you. And sure, it can be helpful to learn from your own mistakes, as Cook did. But not everything we learn from previous generations is wrong. Wouldn't you want to know from honorable examples what a life well lived looks like?

Here's the thing. It turns out that, by trading in one set of demands, we're buying another. Real freedom is not lack of boundaries, mainly because that's impossible. We're always hemmed in by something, whether it be time or money or energy or social approval or the Bible. We're humans, not gods. We operate inside constraints.

Rather, real freedom is recognizing the *correct* boundaries. Becket Cook's questions—*Who am I? What am I doing here? What's the meaning of life?*—aren't just for philosophy majors. Everyone answers them, either consciously or not. And your answer determines how you choose your boundaries.

For example, I (Sarah) answer like this: I am a child of God, a sinner saved by grace. I was born to know God, which makes me love him, which makes me worship and serve him with joy. I am living inside the greatest story ever told, that of God's never-ending pursuit of his people.

I don't think I'll ever end up at an ultrachic party of celebrities in France. But if I did—or if Cook relived those days—the experience would be completely different. Because our meaning is built not on where we are or whom we know or how much we've achieved but on *which direction we're facing.*

Facing In: A Story of Sexual "Fulfillment"

IN THESE POLARIZED times, you see a lot of recrimination over the other side's dishonorable acts. One side decries the other for dishonorable sexual acts. The other complains about dishonorable business dealings. In some ways you can see how both sides of our so-called culture war trade others-focused honor for self-focused fulfillment. Both sides face in when they should face out.

On the left, sexual fulfillment is considered a fundamental human right. Sleep with as many people as you want, watch as much pornography as you want, and start as young as you want. Choose your gender, the gender of the person you sleep with, or whether you'd rather skip gender altogether. Demand emotional support of anyone's right to engage in almost any sexual behavior without judgment from anyone else.

Judgment is key. Freedom alone isn't enough. In the privacy of your own home, you can do anything you like, so long as it doesn't harm anyone else or involve anyone underage. But the parades and protests haven't stopped. Demands have shifted to transgender public bathrooms,[7] enforced nondiscrimination hiring laws[8] (even for religious institutions),[9] and the admittance of biological males who identify as women into female sporting competitions.[10]

"When pursuing your desire for same-gender sex and romance would publicly mark you as a hero—brave and strong—denying it makes you a villain," our friend Rachel Gilson wrote in *Born Again This Way*.[11]

In her freshman year of college, Gilson was the hero. She was in love with her girlfriend, studying in a selective humanities program at Yale University, and drinking unlimited amounts of alcohol. "It seemed too good to be true," she wrote in her testimony for *Christianity Today*.[12] But before long, she found out her girlfriend was cheating on her "with an undereducated, semi-homeless guy out in Tahoe."

"On Christmas morning, as I read *Don Quixote* on her futon (while she had sex with her boyfriend in the other room), I wondered what my life had become," Gilson wrote.[13] She hadn't lost her social standing—she was still at Yale, still hoping to marry a woman someday—but that life wasn't delivering any peace or happiness.

Back at school, she heard a lecture on French philosopher René Descartes and began wondering whether God is real. She asked Google and, through her reading online, found a Jesus she really liked. The trouble was, she wasn't sure he'd like her.

Gilson asked two Christian girls she knew (who were dating each other), and they explained how the Bible doesn't really oppose homosexuality. But when Gilson looked up the verses they referred her to, she wasn't convinced the girls were right. Frustrated with the Bible, she gave up until she spotted C. S. Lewis's *Mere Christianity* on her friend's bookshelf. She stole it.

"I read and read," she wrote. "One day, as I read between classes in the library, I set it down, mid-chapter, as it dawned on me: There *was* a God—my heart and my head could no longer deny it."[14]

Gilson didn't suddenly become attracted to men that day. Even now, sixteen years later, with a husband and a daughter, she still experiences same-sex attraction. But she knows that "obedience will never lead us away from God's blessing—it will always lead us toward it."[15] This is the promise he makes to us, on his honor.

God's words "flow out of his deep love toward us," she told me (Collin) on the *Gospelbound* podcast. "If we divorce ethics from his character, then we're already off track. . . . Always consider what he's saying from the source of his character—because some of what he had said seemed arbitrary and cruel to me, but the reality was God's character isn't arbitrary or cruel. And so I was forced to recognize that I probably wasn't understanding the words well."

A perfectly loving and good God "is not going to tell me things that are going to contribute to my insanity or contribute to my degradation," she said.

God's approval of us—obtained for us through Jesus's death on the cross for our sins—gives a far deeper peace and joy than society's approval ever could. Best of all, he doesn't take it away when we mess up or when we don't change quickly enough to be trendy.

Not only that, but his standards of honorable behavior are for our benefit. He's not limiting sex to marriage of a man and a woman because he doesn't like us. He calls us to honorable behavior because he loves us.

For gospelbound Christians, living with honor means living for God, whether or not society approves. Because when we stray from God's plans, the weak and vulnerable suffer most.

Facing In: Sexual Unfulfillment

IN THE GARDEN of Eden, God created sex as a way for a married man and woman to be intimate and to produce children. While the narrative of Scripture has plenty of examples of his people's failure to live up to his original intention for sexuality, he's always been clear about his standards: "A man shall leave his father and his mother and hold fast to his wife, and they shall become one flesh" (Genesis 2:24) and "Each man should have his own wife and each woman her own husband" (1 Corinthians 7:2). He's also clear about the way he sees sexuality outside those boundary markers—they are "dishonorable passions" and "shameless acts" (Romans 1:26–27).

Jesus didn't give us a new sexual ethic—in fact, he strengthened the old one. "Everyone who looks at a woman with lustful intent has already committed adultery with her in his heart," he said in the Sermon on the Mount. "If your right eye causes you to sin, tear it out and throw it away. For it is better that you lose one of your members than that your whole body be thrown into hell" (Matthew 5:28–29).

It's not as if Jesus and Paul lived in a culture devoted to modesty.

In the wider Roman Empire, freeborn men weren't expected to contain their sex lives to their wives or even to the female gender. Prostitutes served openly in the temples of the gods; pornography was displayed on the walls of homes and public places. For men, having sex with a young man didn't make you weird or even gay; in some circles, it made you normal.

But that sexual liberty didn't mean the Romans were blissfully happy. Roman sexuality was about dominance, which meant freeborn Roman men imposed themselves on weaker men, women, and children. Pedophilia was common. Women were easily exchanged among men. Slaves were consistently raped. The only people enjoying themselves were free Roman men.

In this context, the Christian sexual ethic—which limited intercourse to two faithful marriage partners—was revolutionary. Even *honorable*.

"Our early Christian ancestors did not confess biblical chastity in a safe culture that naturally agreed with them," Matthew Rueger wrote in *Sexual Morality in a Christless World*. "The sexual morality they taught and practiced stood out as unnatural to the Roman world. . . . Christian sexual ethics that limited intercourse to the marriage of a man and a woman were not merely different from Roman ethics; they were utterly against Roman ideals of virtue and love."[16]

Sound familiar? Though America's sexual ethic still clings to a few rules—everyone involved should be a consenting adult—our culture has been busy redefining virtue and love to mean chasing anything that makes you feel good. And those who would stand in your way—even with a question or a word of caution—need to be cut down for making you feel guilty or bad about yourself.

Then as now, the marginalized biblical sexual ethic looks weird, even restrictive. But as Rachel Gilson and Becket Cook can tell you, here's the trouble with chasing what feels good: you can't catch it. And then what?

I (Collin) help lead a large and youthful church. We have a lot of opportunities to talk about sex and marriage. It's not uncommon for me to be leading a small group with at least five newly married or engaged couples. But even among committed Christians, I find a lot of confusion about these topics, in part because churches get so distracted by the hot topics that they miss the basics. They worry so much about the headlines or what's happening "out there" that they don't give attention to what's happening "in here."

It's rare for us to deal with dramatic cases like Cook and Gilson. More commonly I sit across from a tearful wife and mother who can't understand why her husband won't stop playing video games so he can get a job and care for his child. Or with a young wife who regrets breaking her marriage vows. Or with a single man who's lost confidence after several women have rejected him.

If we're looking for an era when everyone in the church acted honorably regarding sex, we won't find it. Every generation has fallen short in one way or another. And in every generation, without any standard of honorable conduct, the vulnerable suffer most. Today they're neglected and told it's freedom. They're rejected and told it's authenticity. Tears of loneliness will be the price of liberation.

Already we can see that the promise of satisfaction from the ongoing sexual revolution has largely fallen flat. Like in Rome, sexual liberty has not led to great joy in America. Just check the stats.

Since the 1980s, the rates of marriage and church attendance have declined.[17] You'd think that, without those two restrictors of sexual behavior, young people would be happily engaging in all kinds of nonstop sex. Instead, the opposite has happened. Young people are having less sex—and are less happy—than the married, churchgoing generation before them.

"The United States is in the middle of a 'sex recession,'" the *Atlantic* observed. "Nowhere has this sex recession proved more consequential than among young adults, *especially* young men."[18] In 2018, the number of American adults who said they hadn't had sex in the past year rose to an all-time high of 23 percent. The demographic having the least sex is, predictably, those older than sixty. But those having the second-least amount of sex are eighteen to twenty-nine.[19] Today's young people are having significantly less sex than their parents are.

The expectation is that movie-like sex would happen spontaneously, after a few drinks with an attractive partner picked on a dating app. But the relaxed nature of the hookup culture, which is supposed to make casual sex easier, ends up muting it altogether. Turns out, people like to have sex with people they like. (Whoever would have thought?) Sharing intimacy casually with a near stranger doesn't feel safe or enjoyable—or (we'd add) *honorable*. Of the twenty thousand college students surveyed by the Online College Social Life Survey from 2005 to 2011, the median number of hookups over four years was only five—and a majority of students said they wished they had more chances to get into a long-term relationship.[20]

Additionally, it will likely not surprise you that sex primarily learned by watching porn and practiced only sporadically through hookups is not good sex.[21] "If you are a young woman," one sex researcher told an *Atlantic* reporter, "and you're having sex and somebody tries to choke you, I just don't know if you'd want to go back for more right away."[22] Only a third of men—and just 11 percent of women—achieve orgasm with a new partner. (By contrast, 84 percent of men and 67 percent of women in a relationship said they reached orgasm in their last sexual encounter.)

It's no wonder, then, that rates of masturbation—easily facilitated by porn and allowing people to skip the mess of relationships—are skyrocketing. From 1992 to 2014, the number of American women who reported masturbating in any given week tripled (to 26 percent), and the number of men doubled (to 54 percent).[23] This uptick in reporting and downtick in actual relationships doesn't bode well for long-term satisfaction.

In practice, modern sexual freedom doesn't actually look like beautiful men and women finding passion with multiple partners. It looks like regular people swiping on Tinder, trying to find someone who will share an awkward conversation before shedding his or her clothes for some uncomfortable coupling—or opting to stay home with a laptop and a vibrator.

Does this sound like joy to you? In 2018, the "happiness level" for young people fell to a record low.[24] The reasons? Researchers W. Bradford Wilcox and Lyman Stone found a few:

- They aren't married. (Married young people are 75 percent more likely to report that they are very happy.)
- They aren't going to church. (Young people who go to church more than once a month are 40 percent more likely to say they are very happy than nonreligious peers.)
- And they aren't having sex. (Weekly sex makes young people 35 percent more likely to report that they are very happy than those who aren't having sex.)[25]

So, how do all these trends connect? Historically, young people often found their spouses in church,[26] where they find support for marriages. And married people have more sex.[27] And regular sex with a person you love makes you happier.

"Thus, while most of the decline in happiness is about declining sex, that's not the end of the story," Wilcox and Stone wrote. "Declining sex is at least partly about family and religious changes that make it harder for people to achieve stable, coupled life at a young age."[28]

There is a better way—the way of honor.

Facing Out: Living with Sexual Honor

IF SEEKING YOUR own fulfillment (either sexual or otherwise) leads directly—and ironically—to lower satisfaction, what should you do instead? How do you get to that elusive joyful fulfillment?

Again we can find a clue in marriage stats.

Married couples who attend church together don't necessarily have better sex than those who don't. Neither do couples where one spouse is religious and the other is not.

But seriously religious couples do.

"When religious married couples view their marital union as a divinely appointed relationship, various aspects of that relationship, including sexual intimacy, may take on spiritual characteristics," researchers wrote. "This may create a sexual sanctification mindset wherein sexual intimacy itself takes on divine importance and may help couples feel more satisfied with their sexual relationship."[29] (Praying and reading religious texts together are another boost to sexual satisfaction.)

These researchers speculate that's because religious people are more likely to work on their relationships, especially if they think God wants them to. And spiritual intimacy probably naturally leads to more emotional and physical intimacy.

But there's even more to it.

"If I, as a Christian, am particular about how I use my body, you might think it's because I have a low view of physical intimacy—because I think it is disgusting or demeaning in some way," Sam Allberry wrote in *Why Does God Care Who I Sleep With?* "Actually it's because I think of bodies—mine, yours and everyone's—like convertibles, not like beat-up trucks. I'm particular about physical intimacy not because I value it *so little*, but because I value it *so much*."[30]

So, here's the twist: On the one hand, gospelbound Christians value sex more than our culture does—so much that we don't just give it away. For single Christians, like Allberry, that means refraining altogether.

On the other hand, gospelbound Christians value sex less than our culture does. We reject the increasingly common view that unless you're having sex the way you want it, you're living an unfulfilled life. A virgin or sexually inactive gospelbound Christian is living just as much of a fulfilling, exciting, interesting, and meaningful life as a married, sexually active gospelbound Christian is.

"To the unmarried and the widows I say that it is good for them to remain single, as I am," Paul wrote in 1 Corinthians 7:8. Those aren't the words of a bitter single man. They come from a gospel-centered, Spirit-filled leader whose letters show him to be productive, joyful, and honorable.

And the beautiful thing is that because honor comes from God, it doesn't depend on our circumstances. So you can live with sexual honor if you've never had sex. After all, that's the case with Jesus himself. Because honor isn't about how relationships define you. It's about how living for God frees you to love everyone, not as objects for your self-fulfillment but as subjects of God's beautiful design.

Our sex lives shouldn't be about us. They should be about glorifying God—by abstaining from sexual immorality, by choosing abstinence if you're single, and by working to please your spouse if you are married. Living in obedience to God is where you will find real fulfillment and meaning.

Becket Cook did.

The Rest of the Story

THE GOD WHO always acts with honor kept pursuing Becket Cook. Six months after his moment of intense despair in Paris, Cook went out for coffee with a friend. While there, he spotted a table of young people with Bibles. He struck up a conversation and ended up invited to their church.

"I asked what their church believed about homosexuality, and they explained that they believed it is a sin," Cook told The Gospel Coalition in an interview. "I appreciated their honesty and that they didn't beat around the bush. But the reason I was able to accept their answer was because I had that moment in Paris. Five years earlier I would have been like, *You guys are insane. You're in the dark ages.* But instead I was like, *Maybe I could be wrong. Maybe this actually is a sin.* So I was open to it in the moment."[31]

That Sunday, he showed up at their church. Two hours later, he left a completely different person.

"I grew up in Catholic schools, and I honestly thought religion was just being a good person, doing good things," Cook said. "I don't think the priests in my high school once explained what the gospel was. Not once. So when [the pastor] was preaching all these things that were the exact opposite of what I thought religion was, I was like, *Whoa.* It all really resonated, and it prompted me to go forward at the end of the service to receive prayer. It was shocking and unexpected to me, a Road to Damascus moment. It was so powerful, so all-consuming. I was all-in."[32]

He really was. Cook spent the next few months meeting the pastor for coffee to talk about Jesus, reading his Bible, and listening to sermons by Tim Keller and John Stott. He enrolled at Talbot School of Theology. Eventually he wrote his testimony in *A Change of Affection: A Gay Man's Incredible Story of Redemption.*

He also quit dating.

"I had such a clean break from it, and it was entirely God's grace upon me to see that it was necessary," Cook said. "Your life is a vapor. You're here for two seconds. What do you want your life to be at the end, when you're on your deathbed? Do you want it to be, 'Oh, I got to satisfy all those urges and got the things I wanted'? Or do you want to be told, 'Well done, good and faithful servant. You spent your life on mission for the kingdom of God'?"[33]

Cook's not the only one stepping out of that path: artist and speaker Jackie Hill Perry, author Rebecca McLaughlin, Rachel Gilson, and Sam Allberry are among many Christians who are attracted to the same sex but are choosing to either remain celibate or enter a heterosexual marriage.

Choosing to be single is "declaring to a world obsessed with sexual and romantic intimacy that these things are not ultimate, and that in

Christ we possess what is," Allberry wrote. "Celibacy isn't a waste of our sexuality; it's a wonderful way of fulfilling it. It's allowing our sexual feelings to point us to the reality of the gospel. We will never ultimately make sense of what our sexuality *is* unless we know what it is *for*—to point us to God's love for us in Christ."[34]

Cook compared it to trading a single meal for a birthright.

"The gain is like Paul said: 'I count everything as loss because of the surpassing worth of knowing Christ Jesus my Lord,'" he said. "The gain is this relationship with God through Christ. Eternal life. It's this impenetrable joy because of not only knowing Christ, but knowing the meaning of life—where I came from, what I'm doing, where I'm going. It gives me such peace."[35]

God may change his sexual desires someday, Cook knows. He said, "We'll see. But for now, I'm happy to just be single and celibate for the rest of my life. I'm happy to deny myself and take up my cross and follow Jesus."[36]

To live with honor.

Any Relationship

LIVING WITH HONOR by obeying God requires not a low view of self but a high view of self *and* others. It's not about chaining ourselves to archaic rules but about seeing how selfless commitments draw out the best in humanity. It's not about chasing our own happiness but about following God and discovering far deeper and more exciting joys than we could ever conceive.

Those principles apply to sex but also to every other area of human relationships. One example is money. Just as some on the left have traded honor for sexual freedom, some on the right have done the same thing with economic freedom.

It's not that free trade is bad. In fact, free markets have arguably done more than anything else to lift the world out of poverty.

"When people exchange goods and services honestly and freely together, both parties increase their flourishing, specializing their work and becoming more efficient at it," wrote Justin Lonas of the Chalmers Center. "For example, a woodcutter trades firewood to a blacksmith for a new axe, and both are now better equipped to do their work, reducing wasted time and resources."[37]

Trade dignifies both parties in a way that charity can't, Lonas said. "God made us to depend on each other, to flourish alongside each other, just like all the other ecosystems he has made."[38]

Occasionally a country will attempt to smooth out the ups and downs of trade by putting everything under government control. But time and again—think Russia and China and Venezuela—restrictions meant to lift the poor end up impoverishing everyone. Communism or socialism depends on omniscient government employees acting with perfect wisdom and foresight and selflessness—it's doomed before it even starts.

But free markets can run into their own problems. The trouble comes when trading partners, like sex partners, swap honorable behavior for the unrestricted pursuit of pleasure or wealth. Like with sex, people stop acting with honor when their view of wealth is too high ("Money will solve all my problems and make me happy") and, at the same time, too low ("It doesn't really matter if I get my money ethically or what I spend it on").

And like with sex, too much freedom doesn't lead to happiness. It's by facing outward, by restraining yourself to honorable behavior, that you'll find joy and meaning.

Let us tell you a few stories to illustrate.

Facing In: Economic "Fulfillment"

THE HOUSING BOOM in the early 2000s seemed like a golden goose. No matter what, property values kept rising. But you know what happened—blinded by what seemed like easy money, lenders stopped being careful with mortgages, handing them out to people with poor credit histories.

They could do that, in part, because investment banking (which makes more money but is riskier) was permitted at regular banks (where you have your checking and savings accounts). Having those two things under one roof means that your deposits can then be used to fund risky investments. This setup was part of the reason for the four thousand bank failures after the stock market crash of 1929. So in 1933, the government said those two operations had to happen at separate institutions.

But by the 1980s, banks were complaining that they couldn't earn enough on their low-risk options to compete with foreign financial firms. They asked for more freedom, and in 1999, they got it.

That wasn't the only excess of freedom. Derivative regulations, leverage rules for five Wall Street banks, and antipredatory state laws were all loosened or ignored. Each of those things happened not by accident but as a result of heavy, expensive, persistent lobbying by the financial industry.

Even that would have been okay if all the bankers and investors had behaved with honor—if they'd made responsible loans, told the truth, and taken the time to understand what they were selling and purchasing. But you don't usually ask for more freedom to play with money if you're planning to operate by strict standards. In fact, one study found that the more aggressively a bank lobbied before 2008, the worse its loans performed during the financial crisis.[39]

Chasing wealth as an ultimate good is so dangerous that Paul warned specifically about it: "The love of money is a root of all kinds of evils. It is through this craving that some have wandered away from the faith and pierced themselves with many pangs" (1 Timothy 6:10).

People who worship money will trade long-term health for short-term gain, and they'll hand out promotions and large bonuses to anyone who does the same. They'll ignore red flags to churn out a record number of high-risk mortgages. They'll hide those mortgages by bundling them and passing them off as secure debt. And they'll ignore anyone who tries to blow the whistle.

But though your net worth may skyrocket at first, trading honorable behavior for more and more freedom to chase your own happiness doesn't ever end well.

In 2008, a growing number of at-risk people couldn't make their mortgage payments, and the foreclosure rate began climbing. Banks and investment companies holding bad debt scrambled to get rid of it, but nobody wanted to disclose having it, and nobody wanted to unwittingly buy someone else's. IndyMac Bank, Lehman Brothers, and Washington Mutual failed. The stock market tanked, and Americans lost $8 trillion in value. Home prices plummeted, and unemployment climbed to 10 percent. The crisis—America's worst economic disaster since the Great Depression—was large enough to depress markets globally and to earn the name the Great Recession.

It would be simplistic to say that relaxed laws alone caused the recession. But it isn't wrong to say that a headlong rush past honorable behavior—and the rules that enforced that behavior—did.

So, if unlimited freedom isn't the right way, what is? How can we behave honorably in the marketplace?

Facing Out:
A Story of Economic Honor

SMACK IN THE middle of the housing bust, former NFL tight end and real estate investor Casey Crawford called his close friend, church planter Stephen Phelan.

"I think God is telling me to start a mortgage company," he said. "Will you fast and pray with me about that?"

"I don't even know if I need to pray about this," Phelan told him, worried about his timing. "I just know it's a bad idea."

But Crawford found a partner, Toby Harris, and they reread the love-God-and-neighbor principles in Matthew 22. "The activities that brought down our economy—clearly, we failed to love our neighbors as ourselves," Crawford told us. "We wanted to change the way people thought about lending in the United States."

They're doing it. Movement Mortgage honors customers by pre-approving them before they start shopping so they know what they can spend, by turning around most loan applications in seven business days, and by working with minority communities to raise home ownership levels. Under this model, in twelve years, Movement grew to more than four thousand employees who close about $30 billion in loans annually, making it the sixth largest retail mortgage lender in the country.

"We do our best to operate in the secular marketplace in a way that will glorify God, treating people with love and using proceeds to love people who have been marginalized," communications director Adam O'Daniel said. So far, more than $65 million in profit has been paid out in dividends to Movement Foundation—Crawford made the nonprofit a majority owner of the company—which has used the money to fund charter schools, affordable housing, and health care in low-income communities.

When companies such as Movement live with honor, they don't

look like those around them. That doesn't just mean they have Bible verses on the walls (though Movement does). It means there is something noticeably different about the way they operate. It means their actions line up with biblical values such as telling the truth, serving those who can't reciprocate, and stopping to rest regularly.

This type of distinctly honorable living crops up over and over again in the faith-and-work movement we've watched growing over the past few decades. As pastors and authors and speakers try to make stronger connections between the gospel and everyday spreadsheets and emails and meetings, honor—choosing to do what's right no matter what it costs you—is part of the foundation.

The fruit from this movement is remarkable. I (Sarah) have sat in rooms with hundreds of entrepreneurs seeking to reimagine their business models in light of the gospel. They're starting car washes (that offer ownership to employees) and hotels (that refuse to sell porn) and coffee shops (that aim to be community gathering places).

Instead of diluting the gospel, this expansive view of God's sovereignty over everything—even sales calls and service contracts—has caused me to worship him more fully in everyday life. I've learned there is no boardroom, no front desk, no budget plan that is neutral before God. We can glorify God and love our neighbors through generous pay to employees, quality products and customer service, and transparent bookkeeping.

But if that's true, then so is the opposite.

Facing In or Out: No Neutral Business

Living with honor doesn't always lead to the financial success of Movement Mortgage. Sometimes it means losing your job after blowing the whistle, losing a deal after being honest, or losing a client after taking responsibility for a mistake. It can be hard to know the right thing to do and then hard to do it.

It can also be tempting to fudge a little on the numbers or to tell a small lie or to let someone else's lie pass without comment—especially when it seems like it wouldn't really hurt anything. People don't expect you to live with integrity all the time, do they? Everybody takes shortcuts, right?

In the early 1990s, Bernie Madoff wanted to give his investors good returns. But the country was in a recession, and he couldn't do it. So he made it up, taking capital from one investor to pay high returns on someone else's investment.

"All of a sudden, these banks which wouldn't give you the time of day, they're willing to give you a billion dollars," he told *New York* magazine. "It wasn't like I needed the money. It was just that I thought it was a temporary thing, and all of a sudden, everybody is throwing billions of dollars at you. Saying, 'Listen, if you can do this stuff for us, we'll be your clients forever.' "[40]

The scheme worked—and kept working for years. By 2008, Madoff was worth $823 million. He owned four homes, four boats, and half a charter jet.[41] He'd been with his wife since she was thirteen, and both of their sons worked closely with him in what they thought was a legitimate business. If you'd met him, you would've thought he had it all. By the world's standards, he was absolutely winning.

But by the end of the year, Madoff confessed to his sons that the nearly $65 billion he was supposed to be managing for his clients didn't actually exist. He'd finally run out of fabricated returns.

Madoff is number two on *Forbes*'s list of the ten biggest frauds in recent US history. The first is Enron, which collapsed in 2001 after Kenneth Lay and Jeffrey Skilling used fraudulent accounting to hide the company's debts. Also included are WorldCom (which pretended to survive the dot-com bubble burst by recording expenses as investments) and Tyco (where the CEO and CFO stole more than $150 million from the company).[42]

Leaving the path of honor to chase wealth may net you some nice things. But eventually, lying and stealing leave a legacy of empty bank accounts, ruined lives, and lawsuits. Madoff's life is a parable of someone who has neglected to live with honor—someone who lives for the here and now, who worries only about himself.

"It was a nightmare for me," Madoff said. "When I say nightmare, imagine carrying this secret. Look, imagine going home every night not being able to tell your wife, living with this ax over your head, not telling your sons, my brother, seeing them every day in the business and not being able to confide in them."[43]

Today Madoff is in jail. One of his sons committed suicide; the other won't speak to him. Neither will his wife. "Not a day goes by that I don't suffer," he told the reporter. "Trust me, I'm not okay. And never will be."[44]

Contrast that with an investor with honor, who holds to such a high standard he won't even put his clients' money into a company that produces cigarettes or donates to Planned Parenthood or mistreats its employees.

Facing Out: Eventide

WHEN FINNY KURUVILLA was in medical school, he was living on a stipend of between $10,000 and $20,000 a year. It wasn't much, but he was single, living in student housing, and eating ramen. So he ended up with some money left over.

He asked his mom what he should do with it. His mom, a teller at Bank of America, told him to invest it.

Good idea, he thought. But it turned out to be easier said than done.

"If you look at a mutual fund fact sheet, you can see the top ten companies they're holding," Kuruvilla told us. "I'm a pretty strong Christian—some would say too radical. I looked at the top holdings and didn't want to invest in tobacco or gambling or pornography."

The problem was, "virtually every mutual fund in America has one or all of those elements in them," he said.

Kuruvilla is a smart guy—he was getting his MD from Harvard Medical School at the same time he was getting his PhD from Harvard University, and he followed them up with a master's in electrical engineering and computer science from Massachusetts Institute of Technology. So he decided to try investing on his own, in companies that offered excellent—meaning both virtuous and high-quality—products or services.

He'd been doing that for about ten years—and doing well—when his fellow church member Robin John asked for prayer about his future. John was working for the Bank of New York Mellon but wondering whether God had something else for him. Together, Kuruvilla and John thought they could maybe start a Christian mutual fund.

And then one Sunday, as they were discussing their plans, a visitor overheard them. "Okay, I know what a mutual fund is," Tim Weinhold told them. "And I know what it means to be a Christian. Put those together for me."

Well, you should avoid companies that invest in pornography or gambling or abortions, they told him.

"It's more than that," Weinhold replied. "You have to ask yourself, *What is God's intent for business?*"

It was a light-bulb moment, one that led the brand-new Eventide Asset Management to invest in companies that created "compelling value for the global common good"[45]—in other words, companies that prospered by providing quality goods and services, stewarding creation, and treating employees, customers, and stockholders with integrity. Eventide's investments included a pharmaceutical company working to cure intestinal diseases, a paper company with sustainable practices, and a company supporting open-source software.

The team researched extensively and chose carefully. During Eventide's first five years, it earned an average of almost 15 percent per year, nearly double the overall market return of 8 percent.[46] (Please note that past performance does not guarantee future results.)

Where Madoff's market-beating numbers were fake, Eventide's were coming from solid companies that followed ethical business practices. In 2013, the *New York Times* ranked Eventide as "the best performing mutual fund with over $50 Million in assets" over five years.[47] Financial research firm Morningstar put Eventide in the top 1 percent of US mid-cap growth mutual funds.[48] And the *Wall Street Journal*, which lists the top ten performers every quarter, had included Eventide twelve times already.[49]

Eventide is part of a rising trend of socially responsible investing but with specifically Christian principles.

"I'd say 95 percent or more of people in church today have no idea what investing is or how to think about their faith as it applies to investment decisions," Eventide managing partner Jason Myhre said. His dream is that "when Christians turn to think about investments, they understand it clearly and know how to apply their faith to this decision-making process."

"We can strategically allocate our dollars toward culture-making that is moving the world closer to God's original intent," Myhre told us. "That's the exciting dimension—we're expanding the beauty and provision of the garden across the world for human benefit and God's glory."

Living *from* Honor

THE IRONY IS beautiful and awful. Those who push away from God's standards of honorable living in search of freedom end up tangled tighter and tighter in behavior and consequences that cut off joy and life. And those who seek to align themselves more and more with honorable living as described in the Bible end up with the joy and freedom of knowing they did the right thing.

Be careful, though: It's impossible for human beings, born sinful into a sinful world, to perfectly align their hearts and minds with the goodness laid out by God. We cannot live honorably just by trying hard.

Gospelbound Christians know this. We also know that Jesus already lived a perfectly honorable life for us. Because we are united with Christ in his death and resurrection, Jesus's perfection belongs to us.

So we live with honor by resting in the honor already given to us. We live *from* a place of honor. We're already honorable, thanks to Jesus. We receive it—and, in turn, live it out and give it to others—through the power and wisdom of the Spirit.

And that means our honor is God's. When Becket Cook opts for celibacy, God receives the glory because only God's power and grace enable him to make that choice. When Rachel Gilson chooses her husband, when Movement Mortgage gives a family an honest assessment of how much house they can afford, when Eventide invests in a company that is producing excellent products while caring well for its employees, God is glorified. Because without his power and grace, we cannot please God (Romans 8:8).

Living with honor isn't always easy—that's kind of the point. But living *without* honor isn't easy either. And in the end, God's ways are always right. They lead to a clean conscience, a peaceful soul, and a joyful heart. That's why, if someone were to offer you all the fame and fortune in the world, you wouldn't trade it for living with honor before God.

CHAPTER 4

Gospelbound Christians Suffer with Joy

I consider that the sufferings of this present time are not worth comparing with the glory that is to be revealed to us.

—Romans 8:18

When I (Sarah) was in Kuala Lumpur in 2020, I watched thousands of Asian Christians—who live under constant government scrutiny—worship God with joy. Many had taken a risk just to come to the conference, and despite such pressure, none of them looked like they were about to give up their faith. They listened to speakers, bought Christian books, and talked calmly about what they had endured.

That's not to say they were emotionless. Clearly, it was scary for them to be threatened or arrested or to see the same done to their friends and families. There were disagreements over what lines to draw. (Is it okay for a pastor to send his sermon to the police if they request it? What if they ask you to put a Communist flag in the sanctuary? What if they ask for a list of parishioners?)

These Christians weren't unaware of the danger or unfazed by the pain. But they chose to follow Jesus in it. They *trusted* him to get them through. And when he did—and he always did—they were filled with love for him.

That was abundantly clear in Maggie's story (her name has been changed to protect her identity).[1] She's small but feisty, the wife of a house church pastor in a country where his profession is illegal. When some church leaders they know were arrested, a group of Christians—including Maggie and her husband—went to see whether they could take care of the church members.

After visiting the wife of an elder who was arrested, Maggie's husband and his fellow pastor left the house. Maggie paused to use the bathroom.

"When I went out, I saw a police car stopped there, and my husband and that brother in Christ were taken into the police car," she told me. "I thought the policeman must know I was also with them."

She started moving toward the situation, then watched in surprise as the police officer ignored her and shut the car door. She ran quickly back into the house, that night shifting to another elder's home.

Left on her own, Maggie didn't retreat to safety. Instead, she spent the week visiting and encouraging wives whose husbands were arrested. She's since stayed in contact, supporting them through regular online communication and counseling.

This wasn't Maggie's first brush with persecution—and almost certainly won't be her last. In May 2019, government officials rushed into her own church multiple times.

"My husband says that even if the government threatens to take the church away from us, we still should not compromise anything in the faith," she said. They both know that could happen—two of their close relatives have been jailed for their faith, one for six years and another for sixteen. But that isn't as discouraging as it sounds: Maggie has heard many stories from both about how God is with them in prison.

"The Lord, through prayer, has made it possible for us to joyfully suffer," she said of her experience. "He has also guarded our hearts throughout the entire time."

Her voice was so full of emotion, of love for God, that it made my eyes well up.

"God promises to be with us in suffering," she said. "He does not abandon us. . . . If the holy Father, who created heaven and earth, and the holy Son, who saved us from sin, and the Holy Spirit, who is in us and continues to [counsel us]—if the three in one are with us, what more will we need?"

I heard Maggie's story referenced often while I was in Malaysia—her experience was so unexpected and her response to forge on was so bold that it's easy to see God at work in it.

"There are severe persecutions, but there are also blessings, growth, and good testimonies," one house church pastor told me.[2] He encourages his congregation with stories of God's providence but also grounds them in Scripture on suffering—adjusting their expectations, preparing them. Later I talked with a thirty-eight-year-old project manager who attends his church in Shanghai.

If faced with jail, "I'm not scared at all. It's only temporary," she said. Her voice was calm and firm.

"But what about your husband?" I asked.

"My God will look after my family," she told me, both earnest and smiling. "So what should I worry about? If I have Christ, I have nothing to lose."[3]

Waning Religious Privilege

DOES THIS ATTITUDE sound admirable to you? Or just strange? American Christians, at least in the white majority, have rarely been treated this way for their faith in Jesus. If anything, our country has historically been biased *toward* Protestant Christianity. Our national language includes phrases like "In God we trust" and "One nation under God" and "God bless America." We have lived in remarkable religious privilege.

But as our country drifts away from cultural Christianity, we can sense that atmosphere changing. "Churches in the Western part of the world are experiencing more opposition than we have in a thousand years," Tim Keller said in 2020.[4]

Rather than in state-sponsored arrests, you're more likely in the West to see this shift in our cultural or ethical dilemmas. Religious freedom attorney Luke Goodrich sees it in disagreements over gay rights, abortion rights, and nondiscrimination laws that prevent organizations from hiring only those who agree with their religious beliefs.[5] We've seen Christian individuals sued for not baking a cake for a same-sex wedding, Christian student groups that have lost their official status and freedom to meet on university campuses because they wouldn't let their leaders engage in homosexual behaviors, and Christian nonprofits and colleges pressured to cover abortifacients in their employee health insurance plans. In most of these situations, Christians are faced with no good option. By following their consciences, they've ended up in the middle of controversy, litigation, or other social fallout.

Nobody wants to go to court, face fines, or close down his or her store or school or adoption agency. Nobody chooses persecution. And to people unaccustomed to opposition, it can be even more disorienting and anxiety producing.

Compared with their Chinese counterparts, American Christians are especially unprepared to suffer with joy, partially because we've been society's favorite for so long. But also because so many have bought into a lie about what the Bible says about suffering.

No Magic Genie

"Growing up in the Hinn family empire was like belonging to some hybrid of the royal family and the mafia," televangelist Benny Hinn's nephew Costi Hinn wrote in *Christianity Today*. "Our lifestyle was lavish, our loyalty was enforced, and our version of the gospel was big business." Jesus was "more of a magic genie than the King of Kings," Hinn wrote. "Rubbing him the right way—by giving money and having enough faith—would unlock your spiritual inheritance."[6]

Not a spiritual inheritance as you might think of it—the future joys of heaven or even the fruit of the Spirit here on earth. The Hinns taught that God's goal is to give you a fat bank account, nice cars, and a vacation home on the beach. He's making you a deal—you send prayers and money to the preacher, and he'll land you that promotion or cure that disease.

The falsehood of the prosperity gospel—also called the health-and-wealth gospel—began in America in the late 1800s and developed throughout the 1900s.

Consider this Joel Osteen sermon that's been watched more than 3.8 million times.[7] (One viewer was Oprah Winfrey, who said it changed her life.)[8]

"I want to talk to you today about the power of 'I am,'" Osteen began. "What follows these two simple words will determine what kind of life you live. 'I am blessed. I am strong. I am healthy.' Or 'I am slow. I am unattractive. I am a terrible mother.' The 'I am's that are coming out of your mouth will bring either success or failure."

Changing your self-talk will enable God to bless you, he said. He offered Abraham's wife, Sarah, as an example.

"She was eighty years old—never had a baby," Osteen said. "She felt like she had let Abraham down. Her self-esteem is so low. I can imagine some of her 'I am's. 'I am a failure. I am inferior. I am not good enough. I am unattractive.' Now she's got this promise that as an older woman she's going to have a baby. God knew that it would never come to pass unless he could convince Sarah to change her 'I am's. It was so imperative that she have this new mindset, God actually changed her name from Sarai to Sarah."

Invite good things into your life, he said, and "I believe and declare you will overcome every obstacle, defeat every enemy, and you will become everything that God's created you to be."

The prosperity gospel says exactly what many Americans want to hear, explained Russell Woodbridge, a professor at the Ukrainian Baptist Theological Seminary. "Americans tend to have a lofty view of human nature and potential. The prosperity gospel says you are good and have the ability to bend circumstances to your will. Simply change your thinking and your words, believe, and then God—your personal cosmic bellhop—will give you a push on the road to success."[9]

This idea spread like crazy in the United States and then the world, in part because it seems to work. If you have a good attitude and work hard, you probably will keep your job, gain a promotion, and earn more money.

But what if you don't?

What happens to the prosperity gospel in the first economic downturn, the first fever and cough, the first miscarriage? Either God isn't all powerful, or you didn't believe enough. So prosperity pupils get wound tighter and tighter into working more and praying more and believing more and giving more. And when it doesn't work—or even if it seems to for a time—there is no rest, because something bad is always either happening to us or about to befall us.

I (Collin) will never forget the years my wife and I pleaded to God for a child. It's an all-or-nothing request: either your wife gets pregnant or she doesn't. You can't pretend that God answered, just in a slightly different way, like you asked for a new house and got a new boat instead.

I found unusual comfort in this suffering. I realized that God had never promised me a child. So it wasn't right of me to be upset at him for something he didn't owe me. I found that real joy—the kind of joy that doesn't depend on our circumstances—comes from God himself. And what he promises is far greater than I would ever naturally think to ask for myself.

> God, being rich in mercy, because of the great love with which he loved us, even when we were dead in our trespasses, made us alive together with Christ—by grace you have been saved—and raised us up with him and seated us with him in the heavenly places in Christ Jesus, so that in the coming ages he might show the immeasurable riches of his grace in kindness toward us in Christ Jesus. (Ephesians 2:4–7)

I see this kind of resolute hope and joy in gospelbound Christians. Not only do they accept suffering from God's hand—they even find joy amid their pain. How can we follow their lead and find that joy ourselves?

Pro tip: It's often easier to handle hardship if you know it's coming. If you know your company is bringing in less money, you can anticipate layoffs and perhaps even begin looking for other employment. If your car starts making weird noises, you can take it to the mechanic before you're stuck on the side of the highway. If COVID-19 swept through another country first, you could see that you'd need to stock the hospitals with personal protective equipment and start working on a vaccine.

In order to find joy in our suffering, we need to expect it. Gospelbound Christians suffer with joy because they trust God's Word, draw inspiration from history, and follow the example of other Christians around the world.

Preparing for Suffering: Lessons from the Bible

THE BIBLE TELLS us how the world is supposed to be, how it is right now, and how it will be in the future. Here we read the ultimate cause of our tragic condition: the fall into sin (Genesis 3; Romans 8:22).

We weren't made for a place where parents bury their children, where terrorists strap on bombs, where a virus can wreak havoc on billions of lives. We weren't supposed to be in a place where divorce splits families, where doctors cut babies out of their mothers, where dictators rob their countries blind.

Gospelbound Christians feel the sharp pinch of being in the wrong spot. They work hard to make the world more just, and they pray that God's will would be done "on earth as it is in heaven" (Matthew 6:10). Yet they know that until Jesus returns, even their best efforts are sometimes akin to painting a dirt wall or covering a concrete bed with a thin blanket. They're temporary at best, futile at worst.

We don't want to stay here.

We *won't* stay here.

We are pilgrims.

Jesus promised that he would go ahead to prepare a place for us (John 14:2), a place where moth and rust do not destroy and thieves do not break in and steal (Matthew 6:20). The Bible also tells us that, in the new heaven and new earth, God will dwell with us—that he will wipe away our tears, that there will be no mourning or crying or pain. We will be his people, and he will be our God (Revelation 21:3–4).

That's where we belong. And in reminding us of that home, our sufferings turn our affections toward what is good and lasting.

"We rejoice in our sufferings," Paul wrote in Romans 5:3. He said much the same thing several chapters later: "Rejoice in hope, be patient in tribulation, be constant in prayer" (12:12). He said it again to the Philippians: "Rejoice in the Lord always; again I will say, rejoice" (Philippians 4:4). And to the Thessalonians: "Rejoice always, pray without ceasing, give thanks in all circumstances" (1 Thessalonians 5:16–18). And to the Colossians: "I rejoice in my sufferings for your sake" (Colossians 1:24).

Why? Toward what end? Paul explained: "We rejoice in our sufferings, knowing that suffering produces endurance, and endurance produces character, and character produces hope, and hope does not put us to shame" (Romans 5:3–5).

It's not like Paul enjoyed beatings and imprisonments and shipwrecks. Still, he rejoiced in how God used them to produce endurance, character, and ultimately hope. Likewise, we hate the broken leg or racial discrimination or mental illness. But if we let those experiences drive us to depend on God and lean on his grace, then we rejoice as we look forward to eternity with him.

For most of history, the Bible's expectations about suffering would have seemed like common sense. Now, however, many Americans struggle to relate to the biblical norm. Most of us have reliable heat in our homes and food in our stores and entertainment in our Netflix accounts, even during a global pandemic. We expect that doctors can heal us. Cheap fuel takes us anywhere we want to go. We can buy nearly everything via Amazon. If something is uncomfortable or inconvenient—say, going out for groceries or physically depositing a check at a bank—someone invents an app to solve the problem.

We also expect our Christian beliefs to be, if not adhered to, at least respected. Because until recently, they were.

We give thanks to God for these good gifts. The only trouble is, they tempt us to expect that a pain-free life is normal. But if even the perfectly loving, perfectly holy Jesus suffered, then so will we. Instead of escaping pain, Jesus endured the cross on the orders of the religious and political authorities. How much more will the world hate us as we stumble after our sinless Savior!

"If the world hates you, know that it has hated me before it hated you," Jesus told his disciples in John 15. "If you were of the world, the world would love you as its own; but because you are not of the world, but I chose you out of the world, therefore the world hates you" (verses 18–19).

And then, a verse later, "If they persecuted me, they will also persecute you."

Light and dark, good and evil don't peacefully coexist. "Whoever is not with me is against me, and whoever does not gather with me scatters," Jesus explained when tossing a demon out of a man (Luke 11:23). Even though you can't always see it, a spiritual battle is raging all around you. If we are identified with the light, then darkness will always align against us.

In other words, Christian suffering reminds us—again and again and, in case you forgot, again—that we live an "already, not yet" life. We're already saved but not yet made perfect. We carry in us both the pain of this sinful physical existence and the Holy Spirit. We're caught between two worlds.

Many American Christians have grown too comfortable with this world. But we don't have to look back too far to see how different life has been for others. Their joyful suffering warns us not to settle for a full fridge and a cold heart.

Preparing for Suffering: Lessons from the Past

John Perkins grew up in a sharecropping family on a southern plantation, with an absentee father and a mother who died of malnutrition when he was seven months old. He remembers the sting of a white boy's BB gun (and the frustration of knowing he couldn't fight back), going around to the main house's back door, and watching old black men step off the sidewalk to let white women pass by.

His antipathy toward white men flared hotter when his older brother, Clyde, safely home from World War II, was shot and killed by a town marshal. His crime? Blocking the marshal's club from hitting him a second time. The behavior that warranted the first strike? Talking too loudly.

Perkins was furious; to keep him safe, his family sent him west to California. There his son Spencer began attending a Bible class at a local church. Eventually he took Perkins along.

"In that Sunday school, I finally met Jesus," Perkins wrote in *One Blood: Parting Words to the Church on Race*. "Almost immediately God began to do something radical in my heart. He began to challenge my prejudices and my hatred toward others. I had learned to hate the white people in Mississippi. . . . And if I had not met Jesus I would have died carrying that heavy burden of hate to my grave. But He began to strip it away, layer by layer."[10]

He went back to Mississippi, thinking "the gospel could burn through those racial barriers," he told Charles Marsh in a 2009 interview. "Then I faced the harsh reality."[11] In 1962, two people were killed and hundreds injured in riots over James Meredith's admission to the University of Mississippi.[12] The next year, three black students sparked a riot by sitting at the "Whites Only" counter at Woolworth's in Jackson.[13] A year later, three Freedom Summer workers were famously killed and their bodies hidden by Ku Klux Klansmen.[14]

In the early 1960s, Perkins founded the Voice of Calvary, the umbrella ministry under which he tucked a day-care center, an adult-education center, a thrift store, a health center, and more.

Early in 1970, Perkins headed to the Rankin County Jail in Brandon, Mississippi, to post bail for some of his arrested civil rights demonstrators. Before he could even get into the building, highway patrol officers met him with their fists. Perkins survived the night, but five months later, the stress prompted a heart attack and then ulcers. He spent long hours recuperating in a hospital. "I had a lot of time to think," he told Billy Graham Center interviewer Paul Erickson.[15]

"I thought with real sadness of the gospel I believed in with all my heart," he wrote of that time in his 1976 autobiography, *Let Justice Roll Down.* "I believed that gospel was powerful enough to shatter even the hatred of [my hometown of] Mendenhall. But I had not seen it. Especially in the churches."[16]

After thinking for a while, though, he could see flickers of hope. Perkins's doctor was white. One of his attorneys was white. White people supported his ministry with their money and their time. Two white people had even been arrested and beaten alongside him. "God used the black and white nurses and doctors at that hospital to wash my wounds," he wrote in *One Blood.* "For me they were symbolic of the people who had beaten me. What they did healed more than just my broken body. It healed my heart. . . . Oh, how beautiful it would be if we could wash one another's wounds from the evil of racism in the church!"[17]

Perkins spent the next fifty years fighting back—he led demonstrations and filed lawsuits on behalf of blacks on issues of equal pay, hiring practices, treatment of inmates, and voting rights. At the same time, he championed forgiveness and reconciliation.[18]

"John modeled that kind of forgiveness and willingness to deal with white evangelicals in a very wonderful way," theologian and social activist Ron Sider told me (Sarah). "He has played an enormous role in helping white evangelicals make a little bit of progress on racism."

Over the past thirty years, the Southern Baptist Convention has apologized to African Americans for racism,[19] repudiated the Confederate battle flag,[20] and condemned alt-right white supremacy.[21] The Presbyterian Church in America voted to repent of its history of barring blacks from membership, defending white supremacists, and teaching that the Bible sanctioned segregation.[22] Perkins loves denominational apologies ("I love it. I'd love it if they'd do it again."), but the resolutions don't mean that those denominations are now empty of racism. George Floyd's murder and the explosion of protests reveal just how far our nation must still travel down that road.

"There have been a number of local therapeutic reconciliation moments where we feel good in the moment—it's cathartic, we weep, we hug each other, we go golfing together," said pastor C. J. Rhodes (whose work on reconciliation in the church "only makes sense in the larger scope of the work that people like Dr. Perkins have done. I'm a successor of that."). But that reconciliation alone can be shallow, he said. It can lead to the "moderate gradualist perspective"—in other words, white pastors saying of racial injustice, "Hey, let it work itself out."

"Many times white people assume that time alone will eradicate these problems," Ethics & Religious Liberty Commission president and Perkins's friend Russell Moore told me (Sarah). "But time won't do that. . . . In many ways, we're facing some of the exact same problems the church was faced with in the 1960s, and with some of the exact same manifestations of the same arguments."

"I'm just now seeing clearly that the black church can't fix this," Perkins wrote in *One Blood*. "And the white church can't fix this. It must be the reconciled Church, black and white Christians together imaging Christ to the world."[23]

Perkins has lived long and hard enough "to have seen every manifestation of hate," Moore said. "He isn't surprised by it. He isn't intimidated by it. Nor does he allow it to embitter him. Whenever I—in frustration—bring up the continuing racism we have to deal with, John Perkins's reaction is almost always 'Yes, and . . . '—and then he returns to the power of the gospel."

Perkins's suffering is tragic. But it has not been in vain. In only a couple of generations, the patient, joyful suffering of Perkins and many other black Christians changed laws and stigmatized overt racism as unacceptable to most Americans. Perkins looks forward to the day when Jesus will return and all things will be made right. And that brings him joy even amid today's setbacks.

By refusing to hate his enemies, Perkins has overcome evil with good (Romans 12:21). By suffering with joy, he shines light that overcomes the darkness (John 1:5). He follows in a long line of faithful examples in church history. This is the legacy of all who are united by faith in Jesus Christ. God invites us to follow their example as he supplies the faith to endure anything with joy.

Consider the strength and fearlessness of early-church leaders such as Polycarp, an eighty-six-year-old martyr burned alive for his faith—who told the Romans not to bother fastening him to the stake, since he wouldn't run away. Consider the clear thinking and boldness of Protestant Reformers such as Martin Luther, who rejected the Roman Catholic practice of selling forgiveness and access to heaven. Or consider the steady love of early evangelical heroes such as Sarah Edwards, who inspired her husband, Jonathan, and her eleven children with her patience and faithfulness in daily life.

During Perkins's lifetime, black and white Christians may have worshipped the same God, but sometimes it seemed like they lived in different worlds. But now, as Christianity shifts out of the mainstream, even white Christians need to brace for suffering. Perkins and other gospelbound Christians like him show how to suffer with joy to the glory of God without succumbing to despair or revenge.

On the other side of the world, Chinese Christians are teaching the same lesson.

Preparing for Suffering:
Lessons from Christians Around the World

LONG BEFORE COVID-19 popped up in Wuhan, Chinese Christians were thinking about how God wanted them to handle suffering.

During the Cultural Revolution (1966–76), Christians held small worship services behind closed curtains with smuggled Scriptures, whispered singing, and staggered departures. They got baptized at night in nearby rivers. They hid their Bibles under their mattresses. If they got caught, they went to jail.[24] Those generations "didn't have a systematic theology written on paper," said one pastor from northern China. "They could not form a system. But they knew, like me, that God controls everything. They read Romans 8:28, that God works everything together for the good of those who love him. They knew God was in control."

During the 1990s and 2000s, Chinese limits on trade gradually lifted. Goods and services began crossing borders, and so did people. The internet, although restricted, was connected. House churches began to meet a little more openly. They could buy Bibles from government-approved church bookstores and listen to sermons online. A few were able to send pastors to seminary overseas.

But suffering had become such a hallmark of Chinese Christianity that older believers became concerned. How would the next generation know they were Christians unless they were persecuted?[25] They worried that the untested faith of their children would be weaker, China Partnership president S. E. Wang said. *Should we pray for persecution to come?* they wondered.

They didn't have to pray—they just had to wait. It was on its way.

But first, in seminaries and books and internet articles, some Chinese pastors were encountering theologians who had also been thinking about suffering. "We must recognize that as Christ's whole life was nothing but a sort of perpetual cross, so the Christian life in its entirety, not just certain parts, is to be a continual cross," Westminster Theological Seminary professor Richard Gaffin wrote in 1979.[26] His teaching—some of which has been translated into Chinese—has been influential for a number of leading Chinese theologians, including Wang. (Gaffin was born in Beijing while his parents were missionaries in China. Kicked out by Communists in 1949, the family moved to Taiwan and continued to work.)

Sharing in "the fellowship of his sufferings," Gaffin explained, means that "existence in creation under the curse on sin and in the mortal body is not simply borne, be it stoically or in whatever other sinfully self-centered, rebellious way, but borne for Christ and lived in his service."[27]

Here's what's going on: If you have received grace from Christ, if you are washed in his blood, if you are raised to new life with him, then you are *united* with him. His life is your life. So when you serve others, you do so on Jesus's behalf. When you speak the truth in love, when you comfort the lonely, when you nurse the sick, you represent Christ to the world. He is the head; we are members of the body (1 Corinthians 12:27; Colossians 1:18). The work you do is so beautiful and refreshing and holy that Jesus called it being a light or being salt (Matthew 5:13–14).

Being in Christ sustains gospelbound Christians in China when the world conspires against them. Since 2013, Chinese president Xi Jinping has tightened party control over every facet of life. In 2017, the government reiterated that house churches are illegal and that no religious activity—including hosting a home Bible study, donating money to a religious organization, and studying theology at school—could happen without their approval.[28] Xi's government punishes Christians for attending church by docking "social credit" scores—which increasingly determine how likely you are to be able to purchase airline or train tickets, get your rent application approved, or land a job.

Nearly all Chinese house churches have been questioned by the police. Some have been kicked out of their worship space—sometimes out of multiple worship spaces. A few pastors have spent time in jail.

"I don't want to be persecuted," said the pastor from the north. When the police hauled him down to the station, "I was very much scared. My heart beat quickly." They wanted him to publicly recant a statement he'd signed, along with 458 other house church pastors, denouncing the government regulations.[29]

He said no. Instead, he talked about the gospel, answering their questions about eternity and the resurrection.

They told him that religion is ridiculous. That it was dangerous for him to stick his neck out and sign the document. That he should stay out of trouble or things would get worse for him.

"Theology helps at such moments," the pastor said. "God is in control."

He reminds his church members that faith must be tested. And they know it—their services have been raided, their elders hauled to the police station for questioning, their meeting place closed.

"Spiritual disobedience and bodily suffering are both ways we testify to another eternal world and to another glorious King," pastor Wang Yi wrote in 2018,[30] about a year before he would be sentenced to nine years in prison for "inciting to subvert state power" and "illegal business operations."[31] "The cross means being willing to suffer when one does not have to suffer."[32]

Here's what he meant: Before his sentencing, Wang was hauled into the police station multiple times. When that happened, he'd immediately tell the police what his bottom line was—that he would not deny Jesus or forsake his church. He was opening himself up to beatings that way. And he knew it.

"I am putting my physical safety at risk in exchange for the safety of my soul," he told his friend.

That friend, who may someday face the same situation, thinks about it this way: "I pray to God, 'I'm willing to be a chained pastor for you.' And the minute I make that prayer, I am free."

Because once we accept and face the worst, we see—God is there with us.

None of the Chinese pastors I (Sarah) talked to—pastors who had their churches shut down, who didn't know where they were going to meet the next Sunday—felt like they were being persecuted. Pressured, some said. But it wasn't anything that they couldn't, with the Spirit's help, face with joy.

One woman, who spent a month in jail, said, "When I was released from jail, I thought, *That wasn't too bad.*" She'd been able to pray intensely, especially for her fellow inmates. And when she was released, two of them came to her church. "I was full of joy," she said.[33]

A few years ago, a Chinese house church pastor was offered employment in America. He turned it down. While it seemed like the safer option, he knew it wasn't.

"My wife and I were just wanting to protect ourselves" by staying in God's will, he said. "God is in control and leading us to the ultimate glory."

He said that seeing the persecuted Chinese church as heroic is too romantic of a notion. And that what's happening in China isn't unusual if God made us in his image, if he made us to know him, and if suffering strengthens our fellowship with him. "We view it as suffering leads to glory, and this is why we're so empowered—even attracted—to the cross in this world. That's why it's not irrational."[34]

It may be too romantic, but it's a story line we recognize instinctively. In fact, it's the plotline of nearly every action movie. The embattled, underdog hero is in an impossible situation. There's no way he can win against the enemies he faces. But the audience sticks with him because we know what will happen. Against all odds, he will inevitably rise to triumph. And the suffering he endures just makes his victory sweeter.

That's the story line the Chinese pastor sees. Jesus is the ultimate hero, and we belong to him. We point to him; we act for him; we suffer with and for him. We live in the dark middle of the story, when things look bleak and the going is hard. But we already know the end. Jesus has already won on the cross.

Suffering That Sparks into Joy

IN TALKING TO John Perkins, to Chinese Christians, and to others who are suffering—Christians who face violence in Nigeria, who have been imprisoned in Iran, who spent nights watching their Minneapolis neighborhood go up in flames—I (Sarah) have seen evidence of faith built on a Rock.

I've listened to people who are clinging to Jesus in all sorts of troubles, and I've been amazed with them at how he has not let them go. They can often see his discipline or his redirection of them. And they've all told me about his faithfulness.

God calls gospelbound Christians to that kind of trust. In fact, trusting in God—and acting in faith and love—may be the key to protecting our constitutional freedom to worship. (I mean, the key certainly can't be fearing and loathing our enemies.)

In our country's early days, the Quakers—even though many did not consider them to be orthodox Christians—gave us an example. Starting in the colonial era, they faced harsh persecution from Puritans for their preaching and for their refusal to serve in militias and to swear oaths. This infuriated colonists who felt they needed every able body to fight against Native Americans and the British. Some Quakers had their tongues bored through with hot irons, their ears cut off, or their lives ended with a hangman's noose. But they joyfully and peacefully stuck to their convictions.

"Over time, the colonies realized, *Look, we're not getting anywhere by punishing these Quakers*," religious freedom attorney Luke Goodrich told us. "Over time, by steadfastly suffering and doing it joyfully, the Quakers really won some important religious freedom protections."

That's the key for Christians today, he said. "Religious freedom comes not just from good laws. Sometimes religious freedom comes from good people who are willing to suffer for their religious beliefs.

And I think that's really going to be how we maintain religious freedom in the years to come, is our faithfulness to our convictions, our willingness to suffer joyfully."

It's just like Paul instructs us in Romans 12:14: "Bless those who persecute you; bless and do not curse them."

God also uses suffering to change us—for the better, if we'll trust him.

"Paul says that everyone who lives a godly life will be persecuted, so persecution is inevitable," Tim Keller told the pastors at the Kuala Lumpur conference. "Persecution will make you a far better Christian than you would have been or a far worse Christian than you would have been. But it will not leave you as you were."[35]

They've seen it happen. They know pastors who have closed down churches out of fear; in fact, the entire Three-Self Patriotic Movement pledges loyalty to the state in exchange for security.

By contrast, when one young persecuted church was asked how opposition had changed their leaders, they reported improved sermons and more stable faith. Another pastor credited imprisonment with transforming his Christianity from theoretical knowledge to deep, real-life belief.

The suffering that refines us also reveals God's glory. "My power is made perfect in weakness," Jesus told Paul (2 Corinthians 12:9). When we crumble before "insults, hardships, persecutions, and calamities" (verse 10), God holds us up.

We need to be careful, though, because pain doesn't automatically produce righteousness. I (Collin) can recall many times when my own sin brought about suffering, for myself and others, without any evident redemptive purpose. Keller said suffering can also make Christians feel prideful, superior to other people who haven't suffered like they have. Instead of producing joy, he said, self-pity can turn into self-righteousness—or make you feel like you deserve to sin a little.[36]

But the key is not to let suffering provoke us to fear and loathing, no matter how gratifying those responses may feel in the heat of the moment. Jesus invites us to suffer with joy, with faith and love.

Jesus loved us so much that he came right down next to us and then took our place on the cross. "That's the only thing that will get rid of our fears," Keller said. "What was the one thing [Jesus] didn't have in heaven? He didn't have you. He didn't have me. And we were worth it to him, in his infinite love, to come to earth and to be crucified, to stay, to endure."[37]

Jesus came so that we could be united with him. He offers us his perfect righteousness, his strength, his peace. He offers us his love and his joy and his promise that we can be with him forever.

The worst this world can do to us is hasten the day of our faith becoming sight.

"This light momentary affliction is preparing for us an eternal weight of glory beyond all comparison, as we look not to the things that are seen but to the things that are unseen. For the things that are seen are transient, but the things that are unseen are eternal" (2 Corinthians 4:17–18).

Instead of watching the news in anger and fear, wouldn't you rather enjoy the peace of knowing that Jesus will never leave or forsake us in our suffering?

"Suffering usually drives us further from God or closer to God," Keller said. "Sometimes sufferers say, 'I'm angry at God that he let this happen.' But sometimes sufferers say, 'I am so weak. I need God more than ever.'"[38]

If that happens, your suffering can "[drive] you, like a hammer drives a nail, into the love of Jesus Christ," Keller said.[39]

It's not the suffering that brings us joy. It's the hope of things to come. And this is not an uncertain hope. It's based on God's rock-solid faithfulness and his unbreakable promises.

It's a hope so bright and so certain it sparks into joy.

CHAPTER 5

Gospelbound Christians Care for the Weak

We who are strong have an obligation to bear with the failings of the weak, and not to please ourselves.

—ROMANS 15:1

In 2016, International Justice Mission (IJM) was thrilled with their progress in slowing child sex trafficking on the streets in the Philippines.

Over thirteen years, they'd helped rescue more than 1,450 victims and put more than 175 traffickers behind bars. They'd lowered the number of minors being trafficked in three major metro areas by an average of almost 80 percent.

"In all instances, we see a reduction in the prevalence of child trafficking compared to five to six years ago," one Manila government employee told IJM in 2016. "The reduction is very steep, the prevalence in commercial sex establishment was reduced so [much] that we could barely see children in trafficking."[1]

The organization achieved its success by focusing on training local law enforcement to catch and prosecute perpetrators. But just before IJM could check "stop almost all child sex trafficking in the Philippines" off its list, they noticed a new problem.

It started as a smattering of cases in 2011. Philippine law enforcement began to get referrals from Western governments, alerting them to photos or videos of sexually abused Filipino children found on confiscated computers.

"The numbers started going up," Brianna Gehring, IJM's Asia

Pacific chief of staff, told us. "In about 2014 or 2015, we realized it was a major issue." In 2015, more than two thousand IP addresses a month were being reported for suspected use in online child sexual exploitation.

The online version of sexual exploitation was worse in several ways. First, the children were younger—where the average age of commercial sex trafficking victims was sixteen or seventeen, 84 percent of cybersex trafficking victims are younger than eighteen, and 54 percent are younger than twelve.[2] (The youngest child IJM helped rescue from online sexual exploitation was three months old.)

There were also more boys involved in online abuse (about 14 percent), said Maggie Cutrell, the director of media and communications for IJM North America. "In our prior commercial sex trafficking project, we rarely encountered male victims."

And more often than not, the rescues involved families—the victims either were siblings (about 40 percent) or were related in another way, such as cousins (13 percent).

All those trends made sense when IJM looked at the change in perpetrators. Instead of area pimps or bar owners, more than 62 percent of offenders in IJM-supported online sexual abuse cases were relatives or close family friends. Over a third were *parents*.

Eager to lift themselves out of poverty and often believing abuse done by family isn't really abuse, mothers and fathers and aunts and neighbors started selling explicit photos and videos of their children to customers online.

For IJM staff who thought they were nearly home free, this new and darker form of slavery was heartbreaking. "IJM believes that we can see the end of slavery in our lifetime, which seems overwhelming to think about right now," Cutrell told me (Sarah).

When I realized that the perpetrators were moms and dads, I felt like I was going to throw up. These people were poor, but they weren't starving. They had internet access and devices on which to film their children. How could a parent abuse a child to get spending money?

I called Collin, wondering how on earth we were going to tell a story of God at work in this situation. What should have been a joyful story of rescue—all those kids no longer sold for sex on the streets—had turned so much worse.

Perhaps you've felt like I did. Perhaps you've walked with someone out of addiction, only to see him wade back in. Perhaps you've counseled and cared for a pregnant woman, only to learn she chose an abortion. Perhaps you've spent hours helping a homeless person land a job, only to hear he didn't show up the first day. I (Collin) once served on a church committee that helped ex-convicts transition back into freedom. We had seen God work in remarkable ways through this ministry. And then we noticed that someone had stolen the televisions in our church foyer. It felt like two steps forward and three steps back when we recognized the culprit.

Or perhaps you've seen some movement, some victory of goodness over darkness—a life changed, a neighborhood cleaned up, a relationship turned around—only to glance around and see a hundred more problems popping up.

You might wonder whether what you're doing makes any sense at all. We know we'll always have the poor with us (Matthew 26:11), so it follows that caring for the weak is an endless task. How can we keep going when it doesn't seem like we're getting anywhere?

Caring for the Poor, but Not for Their Sake

GOD HAS ALWAYS been clear how he feels about the weak.

"You shall not mistreat any widow or fatherless child," he commanded back in Exodus 22:22.

"When you reap the harvest of your land, you shall not reap your field right up to its edge, neither shall you gather the gleanings after your harvest," he told the Israelites through Moses in Leviticus 19:9–10. "And you shall not strip your vineyard bare, neither shall you gather the fallen grapes of your vineyard. You shall leave them for the poor and for the sojourner: I am the LORD your God."

"He executes justice for the fatherless and the widow, and loves the sojourner, giving him food and clothing," Moses said of God in Deuteronomy 10:18.

In the ancient world, where sharing could mean starving, Israel's concern for the poor was unusual. But God never let up.

"Rescue the weak and the needy," Psalm 82:4 says.

"Learn to do good; seek justice, correct oppression; bring justice to the fatherless, plead the widow's cause," Isaiah 1:17 instructs.

"Religion that is pure and undefiled before God the Father is this:

to visit orphans and widows in their affliction, and to keep oneself unstained from the world," James 1:27 explains.

The Bible's instructions are clear and consistent, and so is God's example. Over and over, we see his love for the weak. He dramatically rescued both Rahab (a foreign prostitute) and Ruth (a widowed foreigner), then fit them into Jesus's family line. He loved David, the youngest and smallest son of Jesse. He picked barren Hannah, teenage Mary, uneducated Peter.

Our God still loves the poor, the small, the shaky; after all, he loves us. He sent Jesus to die so that you and I—weak sinners, thousands of years from being born—could be saved.

When we follow God's commands to care for the poor, it's not because we're trying to save their souls. We know only God can draw them to himself. And we can't always save them from poverty either. Although we can serve a meal or even work to fix a broken justice system, we can't change someone's habits or cure her mental illness or free her from the memory of abuse. While we can sometimes be encouraged—when a perpetrator is caught, when a homeless person moves into permanent housing, when a child we're tutoring learns to read—we cannot depend on those wins for our motivation. After all, we might never get them. Or like IJM, we might find something far worse.

Instead, Christian care for the weak is rooted in our Father's character, modeled on his love for us, and done in obedience to his commands. God's example and commands are firm no matter whether the unemployed gets a job, the gang member flushes his drugs, or the child embraces her adoptive mother.

"When I read 1 Peter, his expectations for the people being won to Christ do not appear to include cultural transformation," author and speaker John Piper told me (Sarah). "The expectation is: Keep on declaring the excellencies of the One who called you, and keep on doing good deeds. Some people will be moved to faith, and others will go on maligning."

Piper lives in Minneapolis, just three miles north of where George Floyd was killed. Most think of it as a poorer inner-city neighborhood. Piper and members of his congregation have been living there for forty years, and while hundreds of lives have been changed, the neighborhood's challenges are ongoing and difficult. The lack of transformation can be discouraging.

But Peter used phrases like "you have been grieved by various trials" (1 Peter 1:6), "when they speak against you as evildoers" (2:12), "endures sorrows while suffering unjustly" (2:19), and "do not be surprised at the fiery trial" (4:12). In other words, the Bible doesn't promise that if you care for the weak, people will trade drugs and violence for hymn sings and stable family structures.

"But they might see your deeds and give glory to God," Piper said. "Your job is to be there, love people, declare the truth, and give a reason for the hope in you. My job is faithfulness. God's is fruitfulness. We want fruit. But staying in the city does not depend on it."

Because leaning into the need—letting someone slap you on both cheeks, giving your cloak as well as your tunic, walking two miles instead of one—isn't only about the person you're helping, Piper said. "It's about you—whether you trust Jesus, love him, bank on him, enough to be taken advantage of. That's what I have to preach to myself over and over again."[3]

That solid, freely given care was so integral to Christianity—and so different from the rest of the world—that the first Christians gained attention for their uncommon generosity to strangers, their adoption of abandoned infants, and their staying in a city wracked by famine, war, and plague to care for the sick and bury the dead.[4]

"It is disgraceful that, when no Jew ever has to beg, and the impious Galilaeans [Christians] support not only their own poor but ours as well, all men see that our people lack aid from us," Roman emperor Julian the Apostate scolded his high priest in Galatia. Figuring that's what made Christianity so popular, he told the priest to do the same things and then tell the people it "was our practice of old."[5]

But it wasn't. Caring for the weak—especially those not in your family or tribe—has always been a particularly Christian value.

We know this from history. In Confucian-influenced China, a person's dignity came from how important his family was, and his social welfare depended largely on those relationships.[6] German führer Adolf Hitler thought Christianity was a ridiculous impediment to natural selection by the survival of the fittest.[7]

In the nineteenth century, philosopher Friedrich Nietzsche despaired over all Christians did to comfort sufferers, encourage the oppressed, and preserve the sick. They were sustaining a population full of weak and poor people, he said, instead of letting nature weed them out. As a result, he believed, the humans in Europe were not evolving as they could have.[8]

Planned Parenthood founder Margaret Sanger felt the same way. "The most urgent problem today is how to limit and discourage the overfertility of the mentally and physically defective," she wrote in 1921.[9] A decade later, she recommended "a stern and rigid policy of sterilization, and segregation to that grade of population whose progeny is already tainted or whose inheritance is such that objectionable traits may be transmitted to offspring."[10]

Nietzsche and Sanger sound eminently sensible—that is, if there is no God. If humans are an accident of nature, there's no reason to keep the weak ones. A global pandemic that wipes out the older crowd should be not fought but embraced. Wouldn't their deaths leave more resources for everybody else?

But in truth, it would be hard to find anyone—even those who work at Planned Parenthood—who would publicly still agree with Sanger. (The abortion giant, which has removed Sanger's name from a Manhattan clinic,[11] now explains her motivation as "the revolutionary idea that women should control their own bodies."[12]) And there have been no popular campaigns to sacrifice the elderly to COVID-19 to lighten the Social Security load or cut the country's health-care costs.

In fact, you can probably think of non-Christian friends or organizations that provide substantial care for the weak—perhaps raising money for cancer research or digging wells in Africa or showing up to help with repairs after hurricanes or tornadoes.

If history shows that caring for the weak is a particularly Christian value, then why do so many of those who don't believe in God still do it? And why do the two of us think that caring for the weak stands out among gospelbound Christians?

Let's turn to one of the most thought-provoking books published in recent years.

Why Serving the Poor Is Popular

EVEN AS A boy, historian Tom Holland was gripped by Roman tales of valor and intrigue. As an adult, he earned his reputation largely by writing about the Roman Empire. And that's how I (Collin) first encountered his work, as I studied the Roman Republic. Holland wrote about Rome as an atheist, so you can imagine my surprise when in late 2019 he released the book *Dominion: How the Christian Revolution Remade the World*.[13] I knew I needed to pick up the book and call him.

As we conversed via video across the Atlantic Ocean, he struck me as a parable of a possible Christian future for the West. Unless we can reconnect with the uniquely Christian values that build what we love about our culture, we're likely to lose them. You won't properly value justice unless you're clear on God's law and his wrath, satisfied by Jesus. You won't value caring for the weak unless you understand yourself to be weak in sin and needing a Savior. You can't have the benefits of Christianity without Christ. A vague notion of Western culture, hazy with Christianity, can't sustain itself for long.

"There is a kind of a cloud of very, very fine dust particles that people in the West are constantly breathing in and being affected by and being influenced by even though they may not realize it," Holland told me (Collin). "And these dust particles come from what I see as being the greatest cultural transformation in the history of humanity, which is the coming of Christianity."

This faith spread so successfully that today 31 percent of the world's population identifies as Christian.[14] Along the way, Christian values—such as human rights, religious freedom, and the idea of consent—were embraced by governments, particularly in the West. Then, as governments colonized and traded and explored, those values spread across the world.

After a while, those ideas were so widely recognized and had been around for so long that many people forgot their origin and what the world looked like before Jesus. By 1948, the United Nations could make a universal declaration of human rights affirming the dignity and freedom of each person on earth but make no mention of *why* that was true—because each person is a valuable image bearer of God.[15]

In so many ways, this is wonderful. That people made by God—even if they don't believe in him—would recognize right motivations and healthy behavior is a gift from our Creator and Sustainer. That countries steeped in animism or atheism would affirm religious freedom and fair court systems in their constitutions—even if they don't put those ideas into practice—is worth celebrating.

This common grace, this ability to recognize good, helps Christians find common cause with non-Christians. You don't need to be a Christian to fight against the Nazis, to march for civil rights, to sew masks and practice social distancing during the COVID-19 outbreak.

So far, the world isn't losing its morality—far from it. Many fight for justice and feed the hungry and protect the marginalized with enthusiasm and passion. We praise God for that. When billionaires like Bill Gates give away their fortunes to fight diseases and help the world's poorest people, we recognize God's provision, even if Gates does not recognize God.

But when you unplug something from its source, it isn't long before things get wonky. Peaceful protesters can stop demanding justice and commit their own injustices by looting stores. Marginalized groups that gain power can stop protecting the downtrodden and begin to oppress them. Politicians who oppose spending by the other side can be happy to be the ones overspending.

In the same way, people who remove Christianity from their care for others start to run into problems. You've probably experienced this frustration yourself. What motivates you to care when you don't see results? When the going gets tough? When the television cameras turn off?

Even when you serve for Christ's sake, you'll be discouraged from time to time. You'll be tempted to question why you're bothering. But in those moments, the Spirit calls you back. You persevere because Jesus came to serve you and to give his life as a ransom for many (Mark 10:45). When you hit a roadblock, you might change methods—from serving meals to offering a cooking class or from working with underresourced schools to working with underresourced hospitals—but your motivation stays the same. Christians *want* to obey God. As long as that's true, they'll keep faithfully seeking ways to serve others.

Christians aren't immune from frustration or burnout. But if they allow those feelings to drive them toward Christ, it can result in a deeper, richer faith, softer hearts toward others, and testimonies of how God always shows up.

Christians can follow a better way. And it can lead us into a resolute hope.

Caring for the Weak Even When
Suffering Never Goes Away

FACED WITH A new and darker evil of parents selling their children, IJM rolled up its sleeves and got to work. In 2013, the three largest church councils in the Philippines launched an anti-human-trafficking movement at an IJM event. Two hundred churches committed to praying for IJM's work, and dozens of their members have donated resources such as furniture or clothing, volunteered to work in shelters, and taught classes on parenting or job skills for survivors reintegrating into society.

One church helped set up an assessment shelter that offers special care and intervention for survivors during the first three months after rescue. A Nazarene church built a shelter that meets a new need—keeping sibling groups together. (Government shelters for children are male or female only. Children are placed there if social services decides it would be unsafe to return them to their homes.)

"IJM is working with the Philippine government and other NGOs to increase the capacity of foster care as a viable option for rescued survivors who are unable to return home," Cutrell said. If the child does go home, "IJM works with the social welfare department to educate non-offending parents and relatives on how to best care for survivors of cybersex trafficking and keep children safe from further exploitation."

Foster care and adoption are new needs, since the average cybersex survivor is just twelve years old. IJM church mobilization manager Gigi Tupas is working with churches to encourage their families to step into that role. "I feel like crying, because I can see how the Lord is working even before we ask for something," she said. "In the early years, we'd be the ones approaching churches. Now it goes both ways—often they approach us." Since 2011, IJM has helped arrest about 140 online child sex traffickers and rescue more than 380 victims.

"There's no question that when you look at the scale of evil and violence, particularly in the developing world, it can leave one hopeless and exhausted," IJM founder Gary Haugen told us. " 'How can I possibly create a divine pivot point in the massive sea of pain and injustice that exists?' But then we're reminded that we serve a God who doesn't ask us to do the miracle. He simply asks us to give him what we already have in our hand."

When we do, "he multiplies our five loaves and two fish to meet the needs of the thousands," Haugen said. "I take refuge, release, and rest in the promise of Christ, who says, 'My yoke is easy and my burden is light.'"

Gospelbound Christians know that, no matter how long they work, no matter how effective their programs, no matter how well designed their policies, they cannot eradicate sin or its effects. The demand for evil will persist until Jesus comes back. While we can make progress on eliminating hunger or poverty or abuse, we cannot save the world from it.

When our natural desire for results is frustrated—as it always is in this broken world—it can cause people to lose their tempers or their motivation. Two out of five social workers in North Carolina, for example, are experiencing burnout—emotional exhaustion, lack of interest in work, and detachment.[16] It's hard to keep working for change when it seems like every problem you solve reveals a dozen more.

If you didn't have the Spirit of God guiding and encouraging you, it would be tough to keep going when the going gets tough.

Caring for the Weak When the Going Gets Tough

I (COLLIN) FIRST heard about Rachelle Starr from my friends in Louisville. She had a story so unusual, so inspiring, that I knew I needed to meet this woman whose work reminded me so much of Jesus's. I've always been fascinated by how Jesus drew together what we're prone to pull apart. How could someone perfectly holy have been perfectly loving toward sinners like prostitutes and drunks? How could someone perfectly pure have spent so much time around people his society had pushed to the margins?

Starr gave me a glimpse of that type of gospel living—not an example that every Christian today should emulate but one that we can all admire as we find our own ways to follow Jesus by caring for the weak.

The first time she walked into a strip club, Starr made sure she wore a turtleneck and no makeup. She also took three girls from her church.

"I didn't want to look assuming," she told me (Sarah). Then we laughed together, unable to picture anything less assuming, except maybe snow pants. Less than two minutes in, the bartender asked Starr and her friends, "What on earth are you girls in here for?"

Starr was big eyed; the daughter of a pastor, she hadn't even been allowed to watch movies with strip clubs in them. The dark room, the neon lights, the loud music, and the dancing girls were all new to her. It was a lot to take in. But she knew exactly what she had to say.

"Jesus has sent me here to do something kind and loving for the women in this club," she told the bartender. Starr can still recite those exact words; she felt like they were straight from God. "Can I bring a meal in?"

"No," answered the bartender. ("Her face was priceless," Starr remembered.) "That's the craziest thing I've ever heard. Absolutely not."

"Can I talk to the manager or the owner?" Starr persisted.

"No," the bartender said. "He's busy."

So Starr and her friends sat at the bar, drinking Sprite and Coke and chatting with the bartender and her customers. "About thirty minutes later, I felt the presence of God move me to go over to a man," Starr said. She introduced herself, shook his hand, and told him, "Jesus sent me here to do something kind and loving for the women in this club."

The man was the owner of the club. His mouth dropped open. "You're what?" She repeated herself. He told her that, in his thirty years of management, he'd seen Christians protesting outside, but he had never knowingly had one in the club.

"Well, here I am," she said.

The next week, Starr walked back into the club, this time with homemade fried chicken, green beans, and macaroni and cheese. "Where are you from?" the women asked as she handed them plates free of charge.

"I'm not from a restaurant," Starr said. "I'm here because Jesus loves you." That was enough to turn some off altogether; several wouldn't eat because they thought the food was poisoned.

But Starr kept going back. "It took us six months to build any sort of trust," she said. "Now I understand why trust is so hard for them. It's hard to believe in God when everybody on earth has failed you."

Buoyed by her success, Starr approached another club. Then another. She began sending teams of two or three Christian friends to each club with a meal every Thursday night. They'd stay for a few hours, serving either in the dressing room ("It's a good way to build relationships, because they're doing their hair and makeup and don't have to pretend to be somebody else") or on the floor ("It's a great witness to everyone who walks in the club").

Within a few weeks, some of the women began asking for help. One was addicted to heroin. Another was homeless and living in her car. Another really wanted to go back to school.

Starr couldn't refer them to anyone else—"I could count on one hand the number of organizations [across the country] doing similar work." So she started investing in one person at a time. The first was an eighteen-year-old who wanted to go to culinary school. Starr, who at one point made wedding cakes as a side job, was immediately empathetic.

"The only thing she had in [her apartment] was a princess sleeping bag," Starr said. "She used her dance duffel bag as her pillow." Starr pulled together donations of household items and was touched by how it changed the young woman's life. "That was the beginning of finding resources and partnerships and programs so that we could truly meet the needs of some of these people."

The next few years were trial and error. Starr tried just offering Bible study classes once or twice a week but soon recognized that the women "needed everyday touches." She built up a huge mentoring program only to realize that not all mentors are equipped to deal with the sometimes-dishonest coping skills women develop to survive trauma. She dipped into social enterprises, having the women make body scrub and lotions to sell online, but they didn't generate enough income to sustain themselves. For a while she offered housing, but she didn't have the staff and training to deal with the substance abuse and mental illness problems that cropped up.

Finally she hit on an idea that worked—a bakery. She would pay the women not only to make cupcakes and cookies but also to take classes in how to balance a household budget, how to recover from addiction, how to parent children, and how to study the Bible.

Today Starr's Scarlet Hope provides meals to twenty-two of Louisville's twenty-three clubs—though this work can be spotty. As management shifts, access can change. "I have never kicked out someone who I wanted here more," one owner told Starr. But her work was taking away his employees, and "I have to put food in my kid's mouth."[17]

His concern was real: Scarlet Hope has helped six hundred women transition into new careers, and hundreds have accepted Christ. More than three hundred volunteers and twenty-one staff now minister to between three hundred and four hundred sex workers, and Starr has started a conference to help others do the same in other cities.

But Starr said that pulling women out of the industry is a slow, one-step-forward-and-two-steps-back process. Even though Scarlet Hope has helped hundreds of women leave the industry, they don't always stay gone. And for every woman who does, "five more walk in the door," Starr said. She's even seen it on a larger scale. When one of the club owners came to Jesus through the influence of Scarlet Hope, she shut down her club. But she sold it to another club owner, and it reopened nine months later.

Also discouraging is the darkness. The women suffer from the emotional and mental scars of childhood abuse, from mental disorders, from the aftermath of abortion decisions. When Starr took a three-month sabbatical, five of the women she had been working with died of drug overdoses.

"That's why we hold these programs so loosely," she said. "It's the gospel that's going to save them, not a program. We never know if we're going to see them again, so we're all about Jesus Christ."

It's hard to keep steady volunteers in the dark places. "You can be working so hard with a woman, and then it's disheartening if she drops off the face of the earth or is put in prison," Emily Williams, Scarlet Hope's assistant network director, said.

The average time a volunteer stays with Scarlet Hope is two years, though some have been with Starr since the beginning. She holds quarterly retreats and trainings to keep them refreshed and connected. "Unity is incredibly important for this type of thing, because you don't want to be disunified in the darkness," she said. From those who stick with it, Starr and Williams have seen beautiful fruit.

"Life is a vapor and then it's gone," Williams said. "[Starr] is choosing to use what little time she has to show Christ to these women. And she's giving other women the opportunity to do the same thing. . . . She is not only touching dancers' lives but has transformed hundreds of Christians' lives."

One of those lives is Starr's. "I myself have changed more by meeting broken people and knowing their desperate need than in twenty-plus years in a church," she said. "For me, this was so uncomfortable and so awkward, and I had no idea what I was doing. I had to 100 percent rely on the Spirit. . . . There hasn't been anything else in my life that has pushed me to know Jesus at an intimate level like this."

I (Sarah) tell Starr's story a lot. It's encouraging to share how effective she's been but also how simply she started. On that first day Starr walked into the strip club, she didn't have plans to start a bakery. She didn't have a curriculum for the workers who wanted to learn a different life. She didn't have a list of volunteers. She just did the one thing she felt God leading her to do. She asked whether she could take dinner to one club one time. And then she stayed open to God's leading.

Even working together, humans cannot solve all the myriad problems that trap people—cycles of poverty and violence, systems of injustice, mental health issues, corruption, poor choices, and inadequate education. Indeed, even the helpers are weak. Bodies break and age; emotions flare and crack; spirits waver and sink. Patience runs thin; strength gives out.

But God isn't asking us to fix every problem. He didn't ask Starr to swoop in and save all the sex workers in Louisville. He just asks her to love him and obey him one day at a time. Until he returns and finally brings his perfect kingdom in its full glory.

As they enjoy the care of Jesus, gospelbound Christians, through his Spirit's energy and wisdom, can keep picking up the burden of caring for the weak. Even when things don't change as quickly or as much as we want them to. And even when caring puts us in danger.

Caring for the Weak in Dangerous Places

MEDICAL MISSIONARY RICK Sacra has been evacuated from ELWA Hospital in Liberia three times. After every time, he turns back up. I (Sarah) spoke with him after the third evacuation. Guess where he was when I talked to him on the phone? Back at the hospital in Liberia.

Sacra's first two evacuations were during civil wars and political unrest—when the fighting veered too close to the hospital, Sacra's mission organization pulled everyone out.

The third time, he was in the United States taking a breather. But he could see the Ebola epidemic ripping across West Africa. It spreads through contact with bodily fluids such as blood and vomit; soon hospitals became the most dangerous places. Health-care workers who weren't infected quit in fear and frustration.[18] One by one, hospitals shut down.

Sacra's colleague Kent Brantly was working at ELWA when he and nurse aide Nancy Writebol came down with the disease. Days later, another nurse was diagnosed and ELWA closed to decontaminate. The Centers for Disease Control and Prevention warned people off all "nonessential travel" to West Africa.

But Sacra was already booking his ticket, worried that, with all the hospitals closed, a million and a half people in Monrovia, Liberia's capital city, would be at risk of dying from routine afflictions like appendicitis or strangulated hernias. Moms who needed a simple C-section would lose their babies and their lives.

He'd be fine, he and his wife, Debbie, reasoned. After all, he'd be working with the general population, not the Ebola patients.

He landed hours before Writebol left, and got to work helping re-open the hospital. Scared of contamination, many staff stayed home. One night the entire hospital staff consisted of Sacra and one pharmacy tech.

Sacra had been in Liberia for four weeks—and, along with two other doctors, oversaw one of the only open obstetric units in Monrovia—when his temperature began to rise. He isolated himself right away. When the tests came back positive for Ebola, he called Debbie.

"She was amazing during that time," he told me. "She never once said, 'What were you thinking?' Never once. She was really incredible."

But other people did. Fellow missionary and longtime friend Dave Decker remembers watching the news about Sacra on a fitness center television. His workout buddy said, "That is the stupidest thing. I can't believe he went there."

He was not alone—comments sections and social media were full of people saying the same thing.[19] But neither the criticism nor the praise ruffled Sacra. He was flown in an isolation unit to Omaha and, at the end of the first week, was able to talk to Decker a little.

"He filled my ear—and I sat there taking notes—about all he saw in Liberia and what he felt needed to be done," Decker said. "Here is this guy who just about died from one of the scariest diseases we can imagine, and his full attention is on a crisis in Liberia."

On September 25, Rick left the hospital. Ten days later, he developed a fever and a cough and had to return. His left eye fogged up. His muscles felt like sawdust. At first, he could do only three minutes on a stationary bike.

By Thanksgiving, he started to feel itchy for Liberia.

By January, he was back in Monrovia.

Perseverance in Dangerous Places

IF YOU AREN'T a gospelbound Christian, Sacra's story might sound both amazing and nonsensical. Even if you admire doctors and nurses who put their lives on the line for others, Sacra's level of commitment and sacrifice can be hard to wrap your mind around.

When I asked Sacra why he keeps going back, he laughed and told me he's stubborn. But it's more than that.

"A crazy thing happens [to missionaries] where you no longer feel like you're in a foreign land with anonymous people," Decker told me. "It becomes home. They're our people, our family."

In many ways, it's a family unit even stronger than the one that shares your last name. These are spiritual siblings united by their mission to save lives, both physically and spiritually.

"The Sacras' commitment represents the best of the missionary enterprise—to be committed to one people, a place, an institution, with radical love and sacrifice," said medical missionary Jon Fielder, whose organization, African Mission Healthcare, awarded Sacra the Gerson L'Chaim Prize for Outstanding Christian Medical Missionary Service. "When I hear stories like these, I am always reminded of the first chapter of Ruth, when Ruth tells Naomi, 'Where you go I will go, and where you stay I will stay. Your people will be my people and your God my God. Where you die I will die, and there I will be buried. May the LORD deal with me, be it ever so severely, if even death separates you and me.'"

Among Sacra's friends and family, "I can't think of a single person who said, 'Don't go back,'" Debbie told me.

"I'm proud of him for doing it," Decker said. "We rest on the sovereign goodness of God. We walk in with our eyes wide open. There was no guarantee he was going to survive—same with Kent and Nancy—but we all would have said this is a thing worth laying down your life for."

To lay down your life for people—people whom you don't know, who can't pay you back, and who might not even like you—is the hallmark of gospelbound care for the weak. If you put Sacra in a tunic, he would fit right in with the early Christians. During two infamous plagues that hit the Roman Empire, most people did all they could to avoid contact with the infected, including fleeing their cities and throwing the sick into the street as soon as the first symptom appeared.[20] But Christians, like Sacra, ran *toward* the disaster, not away from it.

In our Christianity-steeped culture, we honor that sacrifice. We praise the firefighters who ran into the doomed World Trade Center. We bang pots and pans for health-care workers who fought coronavirus in hard-hit New York hospitals. We make movies about superheroes who run toward danger in order to protect innocent bystanders.

Those are Christian instincts, introduced by a God who moved toward his hurting people, by a Savior who sacrificed his own life to rescue us, by a Spirit who plants that same desire in us. But you don't develop these instincts just through biblical and theological reading. You develop them by practicing them. You trust in God, and you take one step forward. Then another. And then another. Until doing the right thing becomes second nature.

Like Starr, Sacra keeps clinging to the one thing he knows God has told him to do—minister to people through medical missions at ELWA Hospital in Liberia. His life is a long arc bending toward mercy, toward obedience. It isn't complicated—in fact, it's the simplest thing in the world. He heard a call, and he'll answer it until he hears a different one.

Sometimes it works out great. God spared Sacra's life. He won a prize for his outstanding service.[21] The news media wrote stories about his heroic work.[22] In 2014, the Ebola fighters were named *Time*'s Person of the Year.[23]

But it doesn't always go that way.

Caring for the Weak Even When the Cameras Go Away

IT TOOK THE two of us a long time to write about the abortion protests of the late 1980s and early 1990s. We knew something had changed since then with anti-abortion activism. But we didn't know what. And we didn't know how. We couldn't figure out the right angle. Were the protesters right when they blocked access to clinics back then? If so, why don't we hear of people holding signs in front of Planned Parenthood clinics anymore? Or were the protesters fixated on the wrong solution? How could that be, when they were trying to stop murders? We wanted to learn from them to better inform pro-life work today. But we didn't know what the lesson was.

Turns out, we were confused because we didn't know the whole story.

One of the most famous early protesters was pastor, author, and speaker Randy Alcorn. He was arrested seven times for his protests, eventually spending a night in jail.

"I was in a holding cell with a guy in for attempted murder, at least one gang member, auto theft and a few guys who looked like psychopaths," Alcorn wrote in 1989.[24]

Alcorn was in for two days, punishment for standing in front of abortion clinic doors. The civil disobedience strategy was borrowed from Martin Luther King Jr. and named "rescuing" by Randall Terry, who founded Operation Rescue in 1986. (Motto: "If you believe abortion is murder, you must act like it is murder.")[25]

The evangelical pro-life movement was only a decade or two old, operating with an energy born of righteous anger. Most protesters stood in front of clinic doorways, though others lay in front of clinic employees' cars as they arrived, and at least one man chained himself to a heavy metal garbage can.[26] From 1977 to 1989, more than twenty-four thousand pro-life protesters were arrested at abortion clinics.[27]

The news coverage didn't help the pro-life cause. "400 Are Arrested in Atlanta Abortion Protests," the *New York Times* reported in 1988.[28] "Anti-Abortion Protesters Blockade Clinic in Va.," the *Washington Post* said a few weeks later.[29] "Huge Protest at Abortion Clinic Turns Violent," the *Los Angeles Times* reported in 1990.[30]

"At least 242 people were arrested Saturday after militant abortion protesters descended on a Los Angeles women's clinic during a violence-marred, seven-hour siege that capped a week of abortion rights protests in Southern California," the *Times* said. "The demonstration, organized by the national anti-abortion group Operation

Rescue, failed to shut down the Mid-Wilshire clinic. As hundreds of abortion rights activists cheered them on, police cleared a path to the entrance and security guards escorted staff and patients inside."[31]

For many abortion protesters, the negativity of the media coverage came as a surprise. After all, the nonviolent protests were borrowed from the civil rights movement,[32] which the national news media supported.[33]

"How the media broadcasted the civil rights movement versus the abortion protests had a significant impact on how the public saw it," said Clarke Forsythe, senior counsel at Americans United for Life. "They were generally positive about the civil rights sit-ins and disparaged the pro-life sit-ins."

The bias was clear enough to be documented by the *Los Angeles Times*. "Two major media studies have shown that 80% to 90% of U.S. journalists personally favor abortion rights," it reported. "Abortion-rights advocates are often quoted more frequently and characterized more favorably. . . . Columns of commentary favoring abortion rights outnumber those opposing abortion by a margin of more than 2 to 1 on the op-ed pages."[34]

It was true that a few abortion opponents did turn violent—though rarely in conjunction with a public protest. Lone actors killed seven abortion providers or supporters in the 1990s.[35] Clinics also reported fifteen bombs, ninety-six cases of arson, and one hundred acid attacks.[36]

More often, though, participants didn't even recognize the coverage of the events they attended. "The media portrayed us as screaming," said Kathy Norquist, whose husband spent several months in jail for protesting at an abortion clinic. "Certainly that wasn't what was happening."

"They said we were pulling women's hair," Alcorn said. "That had never happened, and if it had, I would've told that person to leave and not to come back."

What *was* happening? As pastor and activist Jerry Falwell and others threw their weight into politics, abortion was becoming a Republican rallying point. But newsrooms were heading in the opposite direction: In 1992, about 60 percent of staffers at prominent media organizations said they leaned left politically, compared with 33 percent in 1982–83.[37] Their stories followed; more than a third of journalists said media coverage helped Bill Clinton win the 1992 election, compared with 3 percent who said it helped George Bush.[38]

"The news was terrible," said Mike Reid, who was executive director of Portland Pregnancy Resource Center in the 1990s. "The [protesters] were portrayed to look like lunatics, and the news was so consistent with that portrayal."

You'd think the weight of negative coverage—especially when combined with increasingly harsh legal punishments—would quell the protests. And they did fade from the headlines.

But the pro-life movement didn't slow when the cameras swung away. Just the opposite: Over the past thirty years, Care Net and Heartbeat International and others have opened so many pregnancy centers that they outnumber abortion clinics three to one.[39] Organizations like Americans United for Life and National Right to Life have been working—often with increased focus on assisting women—to curtail abortion through state restrictions.[40] And the number of those who stand outside abortion clinics—which historically hovered between five thousand and fifteen thousand a year—has risen dramatically. In 2018, the number of protesters reported by abortion providers exceeded ninety-nine thousand—the most, by far, ever seen in the United States.[41]

But the lack of attention on pro-life work can lead some to believe it isn't happening at all.

"Dear Pro-Life friends: what have you *personally* done to support lower income single mothers?" tweeted Times of Israel's new media editor Sarah Tuttle-Singer, who is pro-choice. Clearly expecting no replies, she added, "I'll wait."[42]

She didn't wait long. Over the next six days, more than thirteen thousand people responded.

"Became foster parents, which led to adoption. Intentionally worked to build relationship with and support our son's birth mother. Helped her w/ buying furniture & more when she got out of prison and moved into low-income housing. Hosted & officiated her wedding a few years later," one person replied.[43] "Donated a well working car to a pregnancy support center, which was given to a single mom who chose life," another said.[44]

Other pro-life advocates reported donating diapers, paying for medical expenses, volunteering at pregnancy centers, mentoring, opening their homes so women could live with them, making meals, helping women find jobs, fostering, and adopting. One gave pro bono legal aid; another read ultrasounds for free.

"I truly do hope all the answers encourage you," replied one woman who also volunteered at a center helping mothers with physical wellness, babysat, donated to adoptions, drove moms to appointments, and befriended low-income single moms. "Most people serve and love quietly."[45]

Endurance When the Cameras Are Off

WE DON'T WANT to come down too hard on Sarah Tuttle-Singer. Her perspective—that Christians don't care about the weak or poor or abused—is increasingly common among nonbelievers. We could blame media for obsessive attention on the fringe and the negative. The two of us think that's a major factor in how the world perceives Christianity.

But there's also something else going on. I (Collin) didn't realize this until my conversation with Tom Holland. The historian explained to me how the West coped with the overwhelming trauma of World War II. Nazi Germany had rejected Christian values, namely, that all humans are born with dignity, being made in the image of God, and that the weak will ultimately overcome the strong in the coming kingdom. In the wake of Nazi defeat, a new morality emerged, Holland explained.

"In the wake of the Second World War and the defeat of Nazism, the shock to the West was so profound that, in a sense, there was no longer any need for institutional Christianity," he told me.

At first I couldn't understand. Why would the West reject Christianity, after the Nazis had rejected Christianity? Didn't they want to be different from the Nazis? It seemed like they should want to get back to Jesus. Indeed, Holland explained that, until World War II, Jesus had long been the moral lodestar for people in the West, even for those who weren't Christians.

But the trauma of war and genocide was so great that caring for the weak became the overwhelming priority in the aftermath. The story of Christianity faded behind the story of recovery. Out with Jesus as the moral model. In with a new moral standard.

"After the Second World War, the moral lodestar became Hitler," Holland told me. "All people had to ask themselves in the West was 'What is your sense of right and wrong?' People look at Hitler, and they decide, whatever he believes in, we believe the opposite."

You know how every ethical argument on Twitter seems to end with accusations about Hitler? Now you know why. Our culture has created a microwavable morality to assess any decision. Would Hitler do that? If he would, I won't.

The problem is that not every ethical situation can be mapped onto Nazism. You need a more comprehensive ethics if you want to endure while caring for the weak. You need a compass when you can't see your next step through the fog. You need a hand to hold when you're lost in the wilderness of unending pain. You need a cup of cold water when you've expended your last energy in the desert.

Without Jesus as the moral lodestar, caring for the weak devolves into an exhausting battle for limited resources. It becomes just another way to judge and condemn one another. If you're a pro-life activist, you may look down on those who only serve in food pantries. If you're involved in a prison ministry, you may dismiss those who run single mothers' ministries. In any area of service, you may raise an eyebrow at those who don't work as hard or give as much as you do.

That frustration can spread. You may end up irritated with the weak for not appreciating the sacrifices you're making. You might become frustrated because those parents aren't grateful for your free babysitting or because the unemployed don't show up for the jobs you secure for them or because the prisoner you're mentoring doesn't want to talk to you. You may end up angry with yourself, exhausted and burned out because you cannot save the people you're working with.

The remedy isn't to try to care for the weak *less*. It's to care for God *more*.

If God is your first love, then you'll be able to see the world—and the weak in it—more clearly. You won't aim to be anyone's savior. You'll know that those you're serving are broken people living in broken systems, just like you are. You'll know that, no matter how many hours you put in, you'll never get to the end of the need. You'll know that things will be put right only after Jesus comes back.

If you know that, you won't feel overly frustrated or discouraged when your efforts don't seem to make as big a difference as you'd like. You'll be able to serve patiently and joyfully, leaving the heaviness of the problems to the Lord.

You also won't need the poor or hungry to satisfy your desire for significance. If they don't thank you, you won't take it personally. If they don't change, you won't blame them for wasting your time but will trust patiently in God's working. You'll be able to care for them with patience and forgiveness and persistence, knowing that if they believe in God, their future is brighter than you can imagine.

And you'll have a reason to keep going—a reason deeper and more sustaining than "making the world a better place" and "trying not to be like Hitler." You'll give because God gave to you first. You'll operate out of your abundance, sharing the joy and patience and wisdom that were breathed into you. You won't need your service to fulfill you or give you meaning, because you'll be full of the meaning God has already given you (Ephesians 2:8–10).

When you hold the poor with an open hand, you won't be tempted to use them to further your own political agenda, to pad your résumé with service hours, or to portray a bighearted image on Facebook. You won't worry that their failures reflect on your competency. You'll rejoice in others' service because it won't take away from your own.

That's great news for Christians, anchoring us and buoying us at the same time.

Caution: Caring for *All* the Weak

You can't do it all. So sometimes it's tempting to limit your efforts so you don't burn out or to work on causes that aren't lost. You can't take care of the whole world, but you could maybe take care of your own family or tribe. And if you're going to volunteer, you might as well pick a good cause—one that looks nice on your résumé or Facebook page or one with grateful recipients to thank you or one with co-laborers who vote the same way you do.

In his parable of the Samaritan, Jesus responded to this tendency to care only for our own. After a man was beaten and robbed, leaders of his own religious community passed him by, writing him off as a lost cause that would only make them unclean. But a Samaritan—then an enemy of the Jews—stopped, helped, and paid for the man's continued care (Luke 10:30–37).

It was a radical example of care in Jesus's day, and it's no less extreme today. The Samaritan's concern for someone he didn't know—and who wouldn't like him if he did—seems almost dangerously crazy. Rationally, he should have crossed safely to the other side of the road, perhaps firing off a tweet about the dismal police presence or calling a congressman about the lack of affordable health care. That way he could have spoken for justice while protecting his time, energy, and bank account.

It seems ridiculous when you see it spelled out, but we see it all the time, don't we? We've done it ourselves. The social media tactics of adding profile picture ribbons or stickers to raise awareness, offering hot takes on government missteps, and jumping on a bandwagon of public shaming are so easy and quick. They gain us social approval and cost us almost nothing.

It's harder to gather supplies for a domestic violence shelter or raise money for a legal aid clinic. And it takes even more effort and energy to consistently show up at those places, building long relationships with people who can't pay you back and might even be mean to you.

In an impatient world, the slow, one-step-forward-two-steps-back work of helping someone struggle out of an abusive situation or get her GED can be exhausting. And then when that work is squandered—perhaps the person you're working with starts another fight or gets arrested again or makes another bad decision—it's demoralizing.

If you're doing that work without the Holy Spirit to affirm and encourage and guide you, it's easy to burn out. That any of our non-Christian friends keeps giving is a true testimony to the goodness of God's image in them.

Gospelbound Christians have an enormous advantage here. We aren't relying on human strength. We receive purpose from living in the Father's plan, direction from Jesus on what to do, and all the fruit of the Holy Spirit in order to keep going.

We serve, then, with supernatural grit—with resolute hope. Our patience is endless because we draw it from the Holy Spirit. Our grace is deep because it's his. Our faith is firm and our hope is bright because we are relying not on human frailty but on our eternally faithful God's universe-creating, world-sustaining power and promises.

If you know some gospelbound Christians (or if you are one), you've seen this in everyday life. Around the country, Christians drive the elderly to church, lead Bible studies for prisoners, and mentor children in inner-city schools. They open their homes to children in foster care, serve hot meals to rescue workers after natural disasters, and start support programs for opioid addicts.

In fact, research shows that the best predictor for financial generosity and volunteering is how often people attend worship services. (And it's not just that they give to their own churches. They're even more likely than secular people to give to nonreligious charities.)[46]

In a country that's drifting away from cultural Christianity—yet retaining the value of caring for the weak—the actions of thousands of faithful Christians are a bright witness.

Paul told the Christians in Rome that "we who are strong have an obligation to bear with the failings of the weak, and not to please ourselves" (Romans 15:1).

Let's take meals to and push wheelchairs for the physically weak. Let's teach patiently and reason gently with the intellectually weak. Let's listen to and support the emotionally weak. Let's share the good news of Jesus's death and resurrection with the spiritually weak. Because it doesn't get any weaker than being dead in trespasses. And that's where God sought and loved each one of us who believes (Ephesians 2:4–5).

"To the weak I became weak, that I might win the weak," the apostle Paul told the power-obsessed Corinthians. Gospelbound Christians care for the feeble and fragile because they see themselves the same way. Because their Savior cared for them in their weakness, they can never look down on someone who needs help. "I have become all things to all people, that by all means I might save some" (1 Corinthians 9:22).

CHAPTER 6

Gospelbound Christians
Set Another Seat at the Table

Contribute to the needs of the saints and seek to show hospitality.
—ROMANS 12:13

Nearly every evening, church members or neighbors drop by the Butterfield home for the evening meal and family devotions. That's right: Not just every once in a while. Nearly every evening.

"I homeschool my kids," Rosaria Butterfield told women at The Gospel Coalition women's conference in 2018. She's married to a Reformed Presbyterian pastor and lives in North Carolina. "So I'm probably like you. At five o'clock, when dinnertime is rolling around, I'm still beating my head against the table with a math lesson, and I have laundry all over the dining room table."

But her guests help her stuff it back into the dryer and set out the plates and cut up the vegetables. They talk through their days, hear how they can help people in the neighborhood, and offer prayer for those who sit around the table. There's always another seat around the Butterfield table, whether or not you believe in Jesus.

You'd never guess where Butterfield honed those hospitality skills—the gay and lesbian community of Syracuse, New York. More than twenty years ago, as a leftist lesbian English professor at Syracuse University, Butterfield watched AIDS creep into her community. The disease brought homosexual people together, and they formed a coalition around hospitality, Butterfield said. Each night of the week, a different couple opened their home to the community.

That hospitality was critical to a group of people on the margins. Many had been estranged from their families or were viewed with suspicion by society. Now even their health seemed to betray them. By coming together regularly for meals and conversation and encouragement, the gay community was forming its own family.

Butterfield learned many lessons in those years, but she practices a different kind of hospitality now with her husband, Kent. "What was happening in my lesbian community was a kind of liberal communitarianism," she said. "It was based on the idea that people are basically good. . . . We believed that part of appealing to the goodness of people was bringing them in and feeding them. We believed that all you needed was a meal and a hug and a shoulder to cry on."

Now she sees a much deeper need running through our lonely and polarized times. Resolute hope doesn't assume goodness but still offers love.

A few years ago, the Butterfields befriended a man who lived across the street. It wasn't easy, because he was reclusive—he didn't mow the lawn, owned a giant pit bull that sometimes got loose, and dismantled his doorbell after the Butterfields walked over as a family to introduce themselves.

But the Butterfields "genuinely believe that God doesn't get the address wrong," so they kept trying. They walked their dog with him, had conversations in the front yards, and talked him into coming over for Thanksgiving.

And then one morning, agents from the Drug Enforcement Administration knocked on the front door. Turns out, their neighbor was running a meth lab from his home. The Butterfields were floored ("How did we miss a meth lab across the street?") and felt vaguely guilty ("Did we do something wrong?").

"We prayed, and we talked about it, and we agreed that this is what it means to dine with sinners," Butterfield said. The Butterfields took in the neighbor's pit bull, visited the man in jail, and continue to write him letters. Over time, both the neighbor and the woman who'd been living with him gave their lives to Jesus.

The Butterfields didn't limit their love to the one neighbor. After the raid, they invited all the concerned and disgruntled neighbors over for coffee, then over for a cookout, then over regularly for meals. They talked about the crime scene tape, the neighbor's dog, and whether having an illegal drug lab in your neighborhood lowers property values. And Kent Butterfield talked about the brokenness of the world, how nobody there was better than a meth manufacturer, and how everyone needed Jesus.

"You want to know the problem with you Christians?" one neighbor asked eventually. "You're so open minded it's like your brains are falling out your ears."[1]

Open minded? That's probably not how most Americans would describe Christians today. But that's how gospelbound Christians can come across to their neighbors. They even set a seat at the table for the meth dealer across the street.

Isolated and Divided

THE NEED IS great for what the Butterfields call "radically ordinary hospitality"—radical because hardly anyone practices it, ordinary because you're inviting people into the everyday rhythms of your life.

Even before the coronavirus, Americans were feeling isolated. Three in five adults told Cigna researchers they were lonely in 2019, up from 2018 (54 percent to 61 percent). More people reported feeling like no one knows them well, feeling left out, feeling like their relationships with others aren't meaningful, and feeling like their interests and ideas aren't shared by those around them.[2]

COVID-19 did not help. Social distancing and sheltering in place limited connections with anyone outside our homes and threw off nearly everyone's routine. If you were living by yourself, it could have been an especially lonely time. Half of Americans told University of Chicago researchers they felt isolated in early 2020, compared with a quarter in 2018.[3]

On the other hand, if you were quarantined with family or friends, your relationships may have deteriorated.

"The stresses and strains of marriage and family life in the time of Covid-19 will send thousands of couples to divorce court," University of Virginia sociology professor W. Bradford Wilcox predicted in the *Wall Street Journal*. Especially at risk are couples who get their idea of romance from Hollywood. "The soul mate model—trumpeted in books like Elizabeth Gilbert's *Eat, Pray, Love*, not to mention countless songs and rom-coms—is the idea that marriage is primarily about an intense emotional and romantic connection between two people and should last only so long as that connection remains happy and fulfilling for both parties."[4]

Spending months cooped up with Mr. Right is a good way to discover he's not right all the time.

A marriage, if it was built on the shifting sand of how your spouse makes you feel, wasn't likely to stand the strain of the novel coronavirus and its aftermath. In fact, from April to June 2020, 20 percent of couples married five months or less filed for divorce, up from 11 percent in the same period of 2019.[5] (Notably, for many other couples, bonding through the stressful experience actually increased their likelihood of staying together.)[6]

Adding to the social stress was the partisan divide that split opinions on whether social distancing measures were helping a lot (three-quarters of liberal Democrats but only half of conservative Republicans said yes), whether a lack of testing was a major reason for new coronavirus cases (82 percent of liberal Democrats but only 31 percent of conservative Republicans agreed), and whether COVID-19 was spreading because people weren't following social distancing measures (72 percent of liberal Democrats but only 36 percent of conservative Republicans said this was true).

Your political party also influenced how much you trusted medical scientists to act in the best interests of the public, how seriously you thought the virus was threatening public health, and whether you thought COVID-19 spreads more easily than other infectious diseases.[7] I (Collin) don't think I've ever seen so many conspiracy theories spread so quickly, aided by too much time on social media and too little time around the table with diverse groups of friends.

Churches, many of them unable to meet and others separating members by six feet and masks, struggled under the stress of new questions with no clear answers. At the same time, strong opinions abounded.

"How to maintain social distance and limit crowd size, whether or not to require masks, to sing or not to sing, what to do with children, and so on—the whole conversation is fraught with potential for division," TGC senior editor Brett McCracken wrote in an article viewed more than 720,000 times. "If a congregation—and within it, a leadership team—is at all a microcosm of our larger society, it will likely contain a broad assortment of strongly held convictions. Some will be eager to meet in person and impatient to wait much longer to get back to normal. Others will insist it's unwise to meet at all until there's a vaccine. Plenty will fall somewhere in between."[8]

Crises can help us remember what's important and draw us together. But what if "we're all in this together" feels less like working together to solve a problem and more like being trapped in an eternal car ride with people who either drive too recklessly or scream every time there's a small bump in the road? The stress can make people want to protect themselves by pulling away even further.

But gospelbound Christians know that isolated and divided people need *more* time together, not less. They need comfort and encouragement, community and meaningful friendships. They need more than a meal and a hug and a shoulder to cry on—but not less.

They need you to set another seat at the table. So they can know their sin and the love of a Savior. So they can see right relationships modeled over soup and over time. So they can know about the intimacy of the Father shown by the Son and experienced through the Spirit. They need to know the constant presence of the Lord, to share deep friendships based on common belief, and to strive for a purpose worth giving their lives to.

God created us to do those things *together.* Sharing ideas over coffee and cake sure beats shooting social media arrows from the quiet of our own rooms. Laughing or crying with friends protects us from panicking in isolation. Distance deepens our divisions. The way forward is to know and be known by family and colleagues and neighbors and friends.

Setting another seat at the table isn't just an evangelism strategy (though it's especially good for that). It's the way we love our neighbors, disciple our kids' friends, and build partnerships. It's the way we thrive as the social, communal beings God created us to be.

Expansion of the Christian Family

CHRISTIANS DON'T ALWAYS do this well. The example set by Rosaria Butterfield can feel intimidating. We're more apt to shield our children from the meth dealer than to introduce them so they can talk about Jesus.

We Christians are known for our focus on the family, sometimes to the exclusion of everything else. It can seem that we care more about matching Sunday outfits and well-designed Instagram photos than the messiness of relationships outside our megachurches. And it can seem that our definition of the family—mom, dad, and two or three cute, well-behaved kids—doesn't leave any space for interactions with the single, the divorced, or the childless, much less the unmarried-but-living-together.

To be honest, building friendships—both inside and outside the church—is easier if you belong to a family unit. When I (Collin) pick up my son from school or take him to baseball practice, it's natural to fall into conversation and friendship with other parents. And the two of us applaud efforts to strengthen nuclear families at a time when so many forces—from media to activities to education—seek to pull them apart. But in the history of the church, Christians haven't stood out only because they value nuclear families. Through Christ, believers share a bond even stronger in some ways than the love of a mother for her child.

If that strikes you as odd, you're not alone. In fact, the closeness of the early Christians could be baffling and even off-putting. To the Romans, the language of "loving our brothers and sisters" sounded akin to incest, and the practice of sharing money and possessions with those who weren't relatives seemed like a good way to become poor.

A Christian view of family, like a Christian view of the afterlife, turned Roman expectations upside down. The Roman family—which contained multiple generations and the servants and slaves they held—was under the ultimate power of the male head of the household. He decided whether each baby would be kept or abandoned (likely to die or be raised for prostitution or slavery), whom his children would marry and whether they would divorce, and which family members would be banished or sold into slavery.

A Christian man, by contrast, led his family the way Christ led the church, by giving himself up for them. While Roman men were not expected to stay faithful to their wives, a Christian man was to love his wife as his own body (Ephesians 5:28). Roman men could divorce as they pleased, but Christians were expected to join for life (Matthew 19:6; 1 Corinthians 7:10–11). Instead of exasperating their children, Christian fathers were told to "bring them up in the discipline and instruction of the Lord" (Ephesians 6:4).

"Seek to show hospitality," Paul wrote to Roman Christians, and then he told them how:

> Bless those who persecute you; bless and do not curse them. Rejoice with those who rejoice, weep with those

who weep. Live in harmony with one another. Do not
be haughty, but associate with the lowly. Never be
wise in your own sight. Repay no one evil for evil, but
give thought to do what is honorable in the sight of
all. If possible, so far as it depends on you, live peaceably with all. . . . "If your enemy is hungry, feed him;
if he is thirsty, give him something to drink." (Romans
12:13–18, 20)

You can see, then, why these Christian families flourished. They
loved one another because they loved Jesus even more. They prior-
itized the nuclear family, but they always left room for one more seat
at the table. They searched for the person who didn't look like she
belonged. Adding more chairs strengthened not only their nuclear
families but also the community around them.

Gospelbound Christians show us that we can build stronger nuclear families even as we make them more hospitable to the growing
number of isolated and divided Americans who need a home.

Shrinking of the American Family

ONE REASON FOR America's growing isolation—and also, it seems, our
growing secularism—is that our families are shrinking.

While Roman families were vast and sprawling, including everyone from grandma to stepchildren, today's American families are
getting smaller and smaller. When our country was founded, the average household size was 5.8, according to Pew Research Center. By
2018, it was less than half that size—2.6.[9]

The reasons aren't hard to pin down: While annual marriage rates
have bounced around (down during the Depression, up after World
War II),[10] the percent of married Americans has been steadily dropping from a record high (72 percent in 1960)[11] to a record low (50
percent in 2017).[12] Those married couples are producing fewer children. In 1790, white women gave birth to an average of seven children; today that number is 1.6. Black women gave birth to an average
of 7.7 children in 1870 and 1.8 in 2018.[13]

In addition, trends like urbanization and industrialization mean
that fewer parents live with their adult children. In 1850, nearly 70

percent of those older than sixty-five lived with their children. By 2000, that number had dropped to 15 percent.[14]

I (Sarah) can see this change in my own family, and maybe you can too. My grandmother grew up with thirteen brothers and sisters; my father had four; I have two; my children have one. My father and several of his siblings lived within miles of my grandparents, while my cousins and I have scattered across the United States. I don't expect that my children will consider my location when making their eventual employment decisions—or even their college decisions.

Instead of setting more places at the family table, Americans have been steadily removing them.

This trend is closely correlated with declining Christianity in our country, American Enterprise Institute adjunct fellow Lyman Stone found.[15] Studies show that being married—and having children—increases religious behaviors. Those who are married are more likely to believe in God, attend religious services, pray, and read Scripture than people who either are living together or have never been married.[16]

Married Percentage and Index of Religiosity

Note: Index of adult religiosity is the average of estimated adult religious attendance, membership, and affiliation.

Source: Lyman Stone, *Promise and Peril: The History of American Religiosity and Its Recent Decline* (American Enterprise Institute, April 2020), 48, www.aei.org/wp-content/uploads/2020/04/Promise-and-Peril.pdf. Reprinted with permission from the American Enterprise Institute.

In fact, the correlation is so tight that when marriage rates in the United States increased from 1850 to the 1960s, so did religiosity.[17]

It's difficult to know, though, which comes first—the wedding or the church attendance. Are religious people more eager to get married? Are they, then, more likely to make lifelong commitments to each other? Or is there something about the institution of marriage, set out by God in the Garden of Eden, that prompts a person to know and worship God?

While it might be fun to know the answer, it isn't really necessary. Even if marriage sparks in people a desire for faith, we aren't going to roll out a "get married" campaign as an evangelism strategy. That's not going to solve America's growing boredom with religion.

Getting married doesn't save anyone. Jesus does. He just sometimes uses a generous marriage to pull people to himself.

Fitting Another Person in the Pew

DURING THE SINGING time at the beginning of the church service, Rebecca McLaughlin glanced behind her. She noticed a young woman standing in the back of the sanctuary, looking uncertainly around for a place to sit.

"Our first service is mostly composed of families. She was alone," McLaughlin recounted. "Our church is majority white. She was black. Many of us have been here for years, and she was new."

McLaughlin waved to her, indicating she should join their family. The woman, looking confused, didn't move.

"I felt embarrassed," McLaughlin remembered. "Then I asked myself, would I rather this woman came to our church and felt like we were overly friendly, or risk her coming and feeling like no one cared?"[18]

She left her husband and two children, walked back to the woman, and asked whether she'd like to come and sit with them. The woman, looking nervous, did. After the service, they talked for a bit before the woman left.

"I left that conversation thinking I might have screwed up," McLaughlin told me (Sarah).[19] Had she been overly friendly and off-putting? Had this woman just wanted to sit by herself? A few days later, McLaughlin got an email from her pastor, letting her know that a newcomer the previous Sunday had reported being "welcomed by a European lady with small children" and how much it had meant to her.[20]

McLaughlin is from England, and that's where she learned to extend enthusiastic hospitality at church. The UK doesn't have cultural evangelicals, so "Christians have a deep sense that it's on you to evangelize everyone you meet," she said. Christians know that at church "their first job is to look for newcomers and outsiders."[21]

To this day, McLaughlin and her husband, Bryan, spend about half their Sunday services separately, with one or both of them sitting beside a new person or a single person in the congregation.

"My first priority is strangers, because this may be their one shot to be welcomed into the church," she said. "Then I look for people who are alone for some reason—particularly those who have come by themselves or are different from me in age, race, or socioeconomic situation. If we're serious about the gospel making us a family of great diversity, we need to live into that."[22]

She and Bryan connect with new people by asking open-ended questions: "How was your week?" "What keeps you busy these days?" As they learn more about the person, they try to introduce him or her to a church member he or she has something in common with.

Even with lots of practice, it's not always easy or comfortable. Conversations across differences—especially educational differences—take work. But the McLaughlins' efforts are typically well received, and they love welcoming new people and building relationships in the congregation.

The American church "could miss thousands of people every week because we aren't looking out for those coming in," McLaughlin said. "According to the New Testament, our primary family unit is not the nuclear family but the church. And if we can't come close to practicing that on a Sunday morning, God help us the rest of the week!"

It's not that the McLaughlins don't love each other or don't think that worshipping as a family is important. (They have a family worship time at home each evening.) But they see God's plan for his larger family—one that isn't confined to biological children but is always ready to scoot down to fit another person in the pew.

I (Sarah) love talking to people, and I was intrigued by McLaughlin's habit. Maybe I could try that? Then COVID-19 hit, and it didn't seem like such a good idea. But when my church has had socially distanced or outdoor times of fellowship, I've almost always found a new person to talk to. (Since I'm relatively new to my church, this is easy to do.) I usually don't know whether the person is a first-timer or someone who's been going to this church far longer than I have. But a big smile and "How was your week?" work to start any conversation.

One exchange doesn't build a friendship. But it does make a connection, which makes the next conversation easier. A few weeks later, you and your new friend are a little closer to each other and to the church.

Shrinking of the American Classroom

It's easy for families to forget how intimidating it can be to walk into a church building alone. As we prioritize nuclear families in the American church, we can make those who don't have a spouse and young children feel isolated, awkwardly orbiting on the edges of organized church activities.

But there's another fault line that often divides churches—the choice of whether to send children to public schools or private schools or home schools. There isn't one right answer: strong, faithful Christians come from all types of educational backgrounds (and the two of us take different approaches). But that doesn't mean there is no difference between the options. In fact, according to Lyman Stone's research, changes in education are a key to understanding America's growing secularization.[23]

Throughout history, helping a child learn to spell, to add numbers, and to understand the past has been an act of inclusion, extending the hospitality of knowledge to another generation. Parents everywhere have recognized that education opens up a child's future opportunities. "Get wisdom, and whatever you get, get insight," Proverbs 4:7–8 instructs. "Prize her highly, and she will exalt you; she will honor you if you embrace her."

For most of history, education sat under the purview of the family or the church, which aimed to shape not only children's minds but also their spirits. Learning *how* to read would help you communicate. Learning *what* to read would order your thoughts and inspire your soul.

As it emerged in the Western world, formal education largely shared these assumptions. The great theologian Augustine noted that true wisdom stands on a two-part foundation: first, a knowledge and understanding of the Bible and, second, a broad study of everything else, especially "true and unchangeable" topics like logic and mathematics.[24] Through the centuries, students have memorized Bible verses and poems, read classic texts from Homer and Thomas Aquinas, and studied logical fallacies.

In the New World, literacy rates soared as Puritans taught their children how to read the Bible. *The New England Primer* taught students with rhymes like "In Adam's fall we sinned all" and "My book [Bible] and Heart shall never part."[25] The colonists founded colleges like Harvard and Yale with the purpose of educating ministers.

But gradually American schools began to detach from religion. In 1848, Wisconsin became the first state to prohibit the state's financial support of any sectarian school. Since most public schools were effectively Protestant, this was a blatant attempt to limit Catholic schools.

"What began as *discrimination* ended as *secularization*," Stone wrote in his study on declining religiosity.[26] Spurred by the Industrial Revolution, mass immigration, the scientific revolution, and the advent of the social sciences, the purpose of education began to shift.

Early in the twentieth century, influential educational reformer John Dewey argued against objective truth.[27] He believed education should be solely pragmatic and focused on helping humans adapt to their environment. Dewey's goal was to equip individuals for particular spheres of usefulness—business, medicine, housework, or manufacturing. This approach to education quickly became popular, so much so that progressive education has dominated the landscape in the United States since the 1920s.

"The questions in education went from 'What kind of citizen do we want?' to 'What do they need to be able to do, and how can we prepare them for that?'" said Keith Nix, who heads Veritas School in Richmond, Virginia. "Not only did we start to lose subjects like Latin, but we also started thinking differently about subjects like mathematics. If we think math is man-made, the question is 'What do I need it for?' rather than 'What is true and beautiful and good about math that I need to pursue?'"

What happened next was logical: when you decrease religious instruction, religiosity decreases. "Policy changes around religious schooling *have* been explored in other countries, most notably France and Turkey," Stone wrote. "These studies present clear findings: French educational changes in the late 19th century restricting Catholic education reduced religiosity. In Turkey, expanded compulsory, secular education, as opposed to Islamic schools, also reduced religiosity, especially for Muslim women."[28]

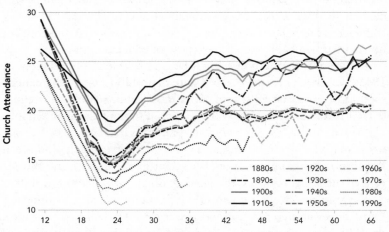

Average Religious Attendance per Year by Birth Cohort

Note: Years not available in General Social Survey data were filled in assuming similar progress through age as observed in cohorts for which data are available; age 12 religiosity was determined from retrospectively reported religiosity.

Source: Adapted from Lyman Stone, *Promise and Peril: The History of American Religiosity and Its Recent Decline* (American Enterprise Institute, April 2020), 43, www.aei .org/wp-content/uploads/2020/04/Promise-and-Peril.pdf. Reprinted with permission from the American Enterprise Institute.

In the United States, "the generations that attended public schools after the 1940s spent much of their life in schools that were far more secularized, and these are the generations during which religiosity has declined," Stone explained.[29]

It's common for Christians to blame skeptical universities or big, worldly cities for loss of faith among young adults. And when combined with delayed and declining marriage, these trends do work against transmitting religion to the next generation. So does not growing up with multiple generations, inside and outside your home, of older role models in the faith. But a much bigger factor, according to Stone, is how many years you went to a public middle school or high school.

"It is striking that religiosity declines so much between age 12 and 18, *before* children have left the home," he wrote.[30]

To be sure, many strong Christians grew up in public schools. I (Collin) became a Christian at age fifteen and worked out my faith evangelizing other students in my public school. Yet as we study the reasons religion continues to decline, we can't discount the effect of schools that assume there is no God, that pin virtues to what feels right instead of objective truth, that shape a child to be an economic producer instead of a God-glorifying image bearer.

"In other words, the content of education matters," Stone wrote. And not just for the children. The increasing amount of money spent on public schools may have spread a secular worldview so effectively that it has "even alter[ed] parental behavior and household environment."[31]

Gospelbound Christians have taught their children at home, sent them to public schools, or enrolled them in Christian schools. But whatever their choice, they know they can't outsource the full responsibility of education to others. Hospitality starts with our neighbors at home—our own children. It starts with helping our kids learn about how God created the earth, how the beauty of a mathematical proof points to God's design, and how history shows God's faithfulness amid human frailty.

But gospelbound Christians don't stop there. Like a big meal, education is meant to be shared. They know feeding one person and leaving another starving isn't right. And the classroom, like the family table during the holidays, always has room for one more chair.

So some of them did something about it.

Adding Another Desk to the Classroom

I (SARAH) SEND my children to a classical Christian school. I've been doing it for almost five years now, so I should be used to the gospel-centered learning environment and the depth of the curriculum. But I don't think I've ever seen an art show, watched a theater production, visited a science fair, or attended a year-end program without crying happy tears over the gift of the high-quality, soul-shaping, God-honoring education my children are getting.

My friends don't send their kids to our school, though, and it's hard to argue with them: It takes me an hour to drive there each morning, which is a lot more time than most people can spare. The tuition is expensive, which also means the student body isn't as socioeconomically diverse as it is in other places. And to some, *classical* sounds like code for "smart kids only."

So I really loved the story Russ Gregg told me.

On a Monday morning about twenty years ago, Gregg quit his job because of a sermon he'd heard the day before from his pastor, John Piper, about "venturing something for God that's a little bit crazy."

He left his position as development director for a Christian school in one of Minneapolis's wealthiest suburbs in order to launch a classical Christian school in one of the city's poorest, most violent neighborhoods[32]—where he, Piper, and others from Bethlehem Baptist Church were already living. (Two decades later, George Floyd would be killed a few blocks south of them.)

Without teachers, parents, a building, or financial support, Gregg was determined to love his neighbors as he loved himself. So he sought to give them the best education he could think of—a school like the one his own kids attended.

Since the early 1980s, classical Christian schools have been popping up across the country. Instead of Dewey's social studies, which center on the child (learning about my family, my community, my state, my region, my country), classical Christian schools teach history chronologically (from ancient Egyptian pyramids to the Greeks and Romans to the Middle Ages to the modern era). Instead of learning to read by memorizing the shapes of words (called "whole-language learning"), classical schools teach phonics. They dust off classic literature and Latin flashcards, implement Socratic discussion and school uniforms. They teach the fruit of the Spirit and shape the souls of children to seek and enjoy God.

In fall 1993, there were ten such schools in the United States. By 2003, there were 153. Today more than 325 schools are members of the Association of Classical Christian Schools (ACCS), and they educate more than fifty thousand students a year. The total number of students receiving a classical Christian education each year is higher and harder to calculate, since it includes both non-ACCS schools and home schools. Experts place the number somewhere between two hundred thousand and three hundred thousand students nationwide.

Children are taught objective truths: *God is real. There are facts we can know for sure. Truth does not change with circumstances or popular opinion.* Teachers also seek to cultivate goodness in students' lives. "One of the number one values of Hope Academy is . . . to cultivate virtues—the fruits of the Spirit," Gregg said. "What do we do if we have a student bullying another student? There's good news from the gospel both for the bully and also the one being bullied that could cause repentance and bring about reconciliation."

He said Hope encourages high parental involvement, which can be hard in the inner city. "Many schools have decided it's hopeless to engage the families," Gregg said, "but we have bucked against that trend and gone to some extraordinary lengths to engage and involve parents."

Every year, teachers visit the home of each child in their class. Parents are required to come to school two Saturdays a year, where they attend workshops on how to support their children's education. Hope also provides parental report cards to let them know how they're doing.

"In our neighborhood, about 15 percent of parents go to parent-teacher conferences," Gregg said. "Here it's 97 percent on the first day, and the other 3 percent get it done the next week."

That's because Hope asks them to keep their children home until the conference is rescheduled. "New families don't believe we'll follow through, but we do," he said. "We find that all of us need accountability."

Leaning on parents for involvement fosters a community of love, something that prospective parents find more attractive than academic strength, Gregg said.

"Being a college prep school is too small of a goal," classical school principal Keith Nix said. "When we come together and talk about the kind of schools we're building, we return to the question 'What kind of citizen and human being and Christian will they be at age thirty? Forty? Sixty? What kind of old men do we want these fifth graders to be?'"

Those questions change everything, Nix said.

"One way the devil can get in is to get us too focused on something that is good but not best," said Christopher Perrin, a national leader in the classical education movement and cofounder and CEO of Classical Academic Press. "If we focus on the good of curriculum and neglect Christian love, we'll destroy everything, because we'll have made the secondary thing primary."

One of classical education's biggest challenges has been the stereotype that it's exclusive, kept for wealthy children with high IQs. But classical educators point to the success of Hope as proof that classical education isn't just for the privileged elite. In twenty years, Hope has grown from thirty-five students in a church basement to five hundred students in a seven-story school building.

Among Hope's nine classes to date, 98 percent of students have graduated. In fact, almost every graduate (98 percent) was accepted at two- or four-year colleges, with a few receiving full-ride scholarships to private liberal arts colleges.

"This is in a community where half of my neighbors aren't even graduating from high school," Gregg said. "The ones who do graduate read at an eighth-grade level." Three-quarters of his students are from low-income families, yet their math and reading scores are three times those of the neighboring public schools.

What's more, these students are accomplishing it on only $10,000 a year—a relative bargain compared with the $14,000 a year Minnesota spends on each of its public school students.[33]

Of course, in a school where the median household income is less than $28,000 a year, $10,000 remains far too high a price to pay for tuition. That's why all Gregg's students are on a scholarship model, he said. Parents pay what they can afford on a sliding scale; for many, it works out to around $600 a year, and the rest of the cost is picked up by sponsors.

These five hundred students require a lot of sponsors, especially with the school's excellent 88 percent retention rate.

"Every year, we need to find forty to fifty more partners who say, 'I really do want to change the inner city in the most powerful way possible by giving this child a great, God-centered education,'" Gregg said. But they're doing it. And when they set up a COVID fund to help parents—many of whom are service workers who lost their jobs during the shutdown—almost $100,000 came in.

The money is great. The test scores are even better. But Gregg is most encouraged by the "promising fruit" among students in their desire to follow Christ.

"On the very night our city was being destroyed in the [George Floyd] riots, we had our annual dinner for the high school seniors," Gregg said. Hope's class of 2020 met on Zoom to celebrate their graduation and hear individual tributes from their teachers. At the end of each one, the teacher told them, "Hope Academy has covenanted with your family to prepare you as a kingdom citizen. Now is your time to work for justice and economic opportunity and racial harmony and joy in the community. Remember that Jesus came not to be served but to serve."

"We heard that refrain twenty-one times," Gregg said. "As we were praying, we were all thinking, *Our city needs these future leaders now more than ever before*. It was one of the most poignant moments. I'll never ever forget that."

Gregg has his fair share of worries, chief among them religious freedom and students who show up far behind academically. But all things considered, he's optimistic. "Giving students the tools to become lifelong learners—that's the kind of education I want for my neighbors."

A gospelbound Christian like Gregg sets more seats at the table for the children in his neighborhood. He knows that education, rightly understood, is not elite or exclusive. Education is meant to open doors and welcome people in. It should be used not to shuttle children into narrow career tracks but to connect them with their Creator and the wide world around them.

Sharing that worldview with others is an act of generous hospitality.

Historical Inhospitality

Family status divides us. Education decisions divide us. We've seen the rotten fruit of both divisions, not only for church unity but also for the spiritual health of our country.

But perhaps the most visible and heartbreaking fracture has been over race. What should be the easiest barrier for Christians to overcome has proved to be one of the hardest, at least in the United States.

From the beginning, Christianity has been open to all who believe— regardless of race, political group, or country of origin. Jesus told the disciples to "go therefore and make disciples of all nations" (Matthew 28:19). When the Holy Spirit came at Pentecost, the disciples spoke "in other tongues" to "devout men from every nation under heaven," including Mesopotamia, Asia, and Egypt (Acts 2:1–12).

"Many of us associate Christianity with white, Western imperialism," Rebecca McLaughlin wrote in *Christianity Today* under the title "The Most Diverse Movement in History."[34] But Christianity's spread from the Roman Empire reached Asia and Africa before coming to Europe and America. "Most of the world's Christians are neither white nor Western, and Christianity is getting less white and less Western by the day," she wrote.[35] She's right. Christianity has circled the globe, able to thrive in every culture. About a third of the world's population now identifies as Christian, according to Pew Research Center.[36]

Majority Religion, by Country

Countries are shaded according to the majority religion.

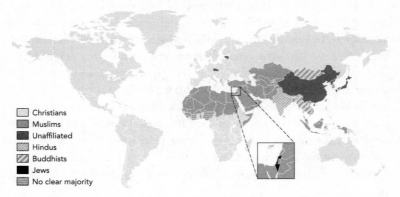

Christians
Muslims
Unaffiliated
Hindus
Buddhists
Jews
No clear majority

Note: Nine countries have no clear religious majority: Guinea Bissau, Ivory Coast, Macau, Nigeria, Singapore, South Korea, Taiwan, Togo, and Vietnam. There are no countries in which adherents of folk religions make up a clear majority. There are also no countries in which followers of other religions (such as Baha'is, Jains, Sikhs, Shintoists, Taoists, followers of Tenrikyo, Wiccans, or Zoroastrians) make up a clear majority. Source: Adapted from "The Global Religious Landscape," Pew Research Center, December 18, 2012, www.pewforum.org/2012/12/18/global-religious-landscape-exec. Used with permission.

The global body of Christ brings together people who are rich and poor, young and old, men and women, of every color and culture. In it, God has designed a vibrant, unique, purposeful community that transcends all other communities.

But our churches don't always look like that. Martin Luther King Jr. called 11:00 a.m. on Sunday morning "the most segregated hour of Christian America."[37] As late as 1998, only 4 percent of Protestant congregations were officially multiracial (which means at least 20 percent of congregants belong to a different ethnicity than the majority).[38] When it was time to go to church, Christians in America often shut the doors to others instead of opening them.

But gospelbound Christians want to open those doors wider to all.

Opening the Church Doors

It started off small, so small you'd never guess what was coming.

Two pastors in Iowa—Rod Dooley of the predominantly African American Oakhill Jackson Community Church and Daniel Winn of the predominantly white Cedar Rapids Family Church—met to pray together. Then they did it again. And again, until they were praying together every week.

The next step was also small—and completely normal. Every once in a while, they'd switch pulpits. Eventually they decided to do an Easter service together. Both churches were healthy and growing, and at the joint choir rehearsal the Thursday before Easter 2017, Dooley told Winn about his search for a bigger building.

"Everything we're looking at is either too small or too big," Dooley explained.

Before he could talk himself out of it, Winn shot back, "You know, it wouldn't be too large if we merged our churches together."

It wasn't an impulsive suggestion. "I had been thinking for a long time about merging our churches," Winn said. "But I knew that was a crazy thing." *Daniel, you're out of your mind*, he told himself. *He's not going to go for that.* And for a beat, there was dead silence.

"Are you serious?" Dooley asked.

"One hundred percent," Winn answered.

"I've actually been thinking that myself," Dooley said. "But I wasn't going to bring it up to you."

That's because healthy churches don't merge. Especially not if they're both growing. Especially not if one is white and one is black. Especially not if both senior pastors are planning to stay. When I (Collin) heard this story after speaking in Cedar Rapids, I had to ask a couple of times for clarifying details. This kind of thing just doesn't happen. Or at least I didn't think it did.

The setting is also unexpected: With a population of 133,000, Cedar Rapids is the second-biggest city in Iowa (after Des Moines). Settled primarily by white Europeans who built farms instead of cities, Iowa wasn't a viable option for most African Americans migrating north during the twentieth century. At the time of the 2010 census, Cedar Rapids was 85 percent white.[39] So it's not surprising that the same year—when Cedar Rapids had eighty-eight evangelical, seventy-five mainline, and eighteen Catholic churches—it had just two black Protestant congregations.[40]

One of them was Dooley's church. Dooley is a bivocational pastor. In the early 2000s, he was combining youth pastoring with his full-time job in human resources at Rockwell Collins. That meant he saw the needs of a wide swath of Rockwell's eight-thousand-plus employees.

"He had a grander vision—of black, white, Indian, Chinese together," said LaShunda McFarland, who joined the church when she was in high school. "That is something God put on his heart."

When he moved from youth pastor to lead pastor, Dooley started talking about reaching out to the whole town.

"We live in a predominately white city," Dooley said of his desire to show hospitality to his whole city. "If we were going to grow, we had to reach [the white] community as well. That was always on our heart."

His congregation was game—most of them worked in predominantly white companies or went to predominantly white schools or lived in predominantly white neighborhoods, so it didn't seem too hard to add some diversity to their worship. But white Cedar Rapidians weren't walking in the door.

"I'd never bring my family to your church," one white Rockwell colleague told Dooley honestly. "It's all African American."

"We became frustrated," Dooley said. "I felt like, 'God, I know you're calling us to do this, but it's just not happening.'"

About five miles away, Winn was feeling the same thing at the predominantly white Cedar Rapids Family Church. "My vision was to create a diverse church in Cedar Rapids," said Winn, who had begun his ministry at a racially diverse church in Des Moines. "We had become somewhat diverse but probably weren't even 5 percent African American. I wanted to see more progress."

It felt like God was asking for something that neither church could deliver. And the city would keep seeing churches divided along the same lines as every other social group in town.

At the time, Oakhill Jackson was outgrowing its space. The congregation was pushing 125 and running more and more programs. "We also had multiple levels in an old building but no elevator," Dooley said. "We knew if we were going to continue to grow, we needed to do something different."

One location looked promising, but it fell through. Others were too big or too small or didn't work for the church's needs. "God brought a bit of frustration to the process," Dooley said.

It was that frustration he was sharing with Winn before the Easter service, prompting Winn to toss out the perhaps-unprecedented, clearly impossible idea of combining two healthy, growing churches.

When their wives approved, the two pastors took their crazy idea to their elders.

The two elder boards "went through our bylaws and statements of faith," Winn said. "And there were a couple of things that came up." For example, not everyone was on the same page regarding the gifts of the Spirit given through healing or speaking in tongues. Some couldn't get on board with once-saved-always-saved theology. And not everybody agreed on the chronology of the end times.

"The gospel needs to be held in a closed fist—we cannot let go of some things," Winn told his elders. "But some other things, like healing, we can hold in an open hand. Not everybody is going to believe the same, but I'm not going to drive ministry based on it."

And in fact, doctrinal questions weren't worrying the congregation so much as cultural questions. "We knew early on there was going to be differences there," Winn said.

"Mostly when you hear two churches have merged, it's really one acquiring the other," Dooley said. "That's not been the case here."

But it could have been. Because even though Oakhill Jackson had grown to around 125, Cedar Rapids Family was pushing past 250.

And instead of the churches finding a new building, Oakhill Jackson moved into the larger space of Cedar Rapids Family. And the culture of the town and the state—like Cedar Rapids Family—is overwhelmingly white. It would have been easy for Oakhill Jackson to be swallowed up—to be acquired.

"In all honesty, it was like, 'Wow, Rod, you guys are making the greater sacrifice here,'" Winn said. Early in the process, he learned that, in many multiethnic churches, the white culture is still dominant. And Dooley told him black church culture is so distinct because it was one of the few places African Americans could lead without white interference.

For Dooley's congregation, the idea of driving fifteen minutes down the road to join with a white church got more approval than you'd expect. "There were definitely some people who were skeptical," he said. A handful of people didn't make the transition. "But overall, we had overwhelming support."

The combined church—named New City Church because both churches wanted to help renew the city—kept all the previous ministries. From the beginning, Dooley and Winn were careful to balance Sunday mornings, each pastor taking the pulpit every other week. (About eighteen months later, they planned to each teach a series at a time.) They kept both music leaders. And they included gospel and contemporary Christian songs in each service.

For the original congregations of New City, life is better together—when someone sets another seat for you at the table.

The folks from Oakhill Jackson still tell one another old stories over coffee in the back, and so do folks from Cedar Rapids Family. But they're also getting to know one another—now they serve in children's ministry together and gather for small groups together and play softball together. They're dreaming together about using the old Oakhill Jackson building to set up an outreach center.

And they're watching God bring them new growth. More than 130 new families have begun attending since New City opened in January 2018. "We're seeing people's lives being transformed," Winn said. In July 2019, they baptized nine teenagers of different ethnicities. When the teens shared their testimonies, "there wasn't a dry eye in the house."

"People are interacting with people they never would have before," Dooley said. "In the first few months, it wasn't uncommon to have grown men from both churches coming up to us after the service with tears in their eyes, saying, 'This is so great.'"

That's because the churches were finally walking into the vision they both had of "renewing the city by helping people find authentic relationship in Jesus."

"We aren't just doing this for diversity's sake but for the gospel's sake and for Christ's sake," Winn said. He hopes that the church can be an example to the community—which has noticed what they're doing[41]—in how Christians behave toward one another. When the world doesn't see Christians working together regardless of race or politics, we shouldn't be surprised that it concludes that the power of the gospel can't solve today's problems of loneliness and division.

But New City Church and other multiethnic churches around the country are intentionally expanding to reflect the family of God. Sometimes the integration goes well. Sometimes it fails. It's always messy and never easy. But gospelbound Christians aren't giving up.

By 2012, a Baylor study found that 12 percent of Protestant churches were multiethnic.[42] By 2019, other preliminary research showed that the number had grown to 23 percent among evangelical Protestant churches.[43] It's small, but it's a start.

Expanding the Kitchen Table, the Classroom, and the Church Pew

In an increasingly anxious, isolated, and lonely time, generous hospitality is exactly what we need to see. If the church is going to recapture the country's attention, it's going to need to look different from our divided states of America.

We'll need strong families that eat together and set places for strangers. We'll need schools that teach all sorts of students they've been made by a Creator to glorify him in their pursuit of truth. We'll need churches that make everyone just uncomfortable enough that it feels like a family reunion.

The gospelbound Christian life—of the Butterfields, of the McLaughlins, of Hope Academy, of New City Church—is so hospitable that it's odd. And in a time of smaller households and unknown neighbors, that oddity is appealing.

Hospitality starts small, with smiling at someone at church, praying for someone who sits alone, or noticing that new neighbors have moved in. It grows with an intentional next step, the one that's a little uncomfortable—taking cookies to the neighbors or striking up a conversation with someone you don't know. And then another step—inviting someone over for dinner or asking someone out for coffee.

The more you practice hospitality—on purpose, even when it feels awkward—the more natural it will become, and the more you'll be able to care for others. Maybe eventually you'll have a group of college students over for pizza every Friday, invite a foreign exchange student to live in your spare bedroom, or consider foster care or adoption.

Gospelbound Christians are the families with the open door, the teachers who shape every child's soul to seek God, the church members who talk to visitors who don't look like them. And those are just a few examples—gospelbound Christians are also building friendships with prisoners and sitting with the outcast kids in the lunchroom. They're inviting high school kids to youth group, inviting hungry people to the church food pantry, and inviting the recluse across the street over for dinner. And they're inviting everyone to the cross, where Jesus welcomes all who repent and believe.

The beauty of the gospel is that grace swings the door wide open. There's always another seat at the table.

CHAPTER 7

Gospelbound Christians
Love Their Enemies

*If your enemy is hungry, feed him; if he is thirsty, give him something
to drink.*

—ROMANS 12:20

In 2019, Pew Research Center asked single Americans whether
they'd mind dating someone who didn't vote the way they did.

Turns out, they did mind. A lot. Nearly a quarter of single Republicans said they wouldn't date a Democrat, while 43 percent of Democrats said they wouldn't date a Republican. More than 70 percent
of Democrats indicated they wouldn't consider dating someone who
had voted for President Donald Trump.

This romantic aversion has grown from what Pew calls "modern
historic highs" in political polarization.[1] Splits in opinion between
the political parties broke records under Barack Obama and kept
widening under Trump. Democrats and Republicans are less likely
to agree on just about everything—immigration, government aid
to the poor, racial discrimination, military strength, environmental
regulations—than they used to.

The gap between political parties "dwarfs other divisions in society,
along such lines as gender, race and ethnicity, religious observance or
education," Pew reported.[2] It's also grown more acrimonious—more
than half of both Democrats (55 percent) and Republicans (58 percent)
have a "very unfavorable" opinion of the other party, compared with
about 20 percent of both parties in 1994.[3]

A significant number of Republicans and Democrats see one another as more closed minded, unpatriotic, dishonest, lazy, and immoral than other Americans. Majorities of both parties said the other party is "too extreme in its positions."[4]

There are all kinds of speculation as to why polarization is growing. It could be the lack of a foreign enemy to unite against (such as the Soviet Union during the Cold War) or the simultaneous collapse of traditional news media and proliferation of fast and fake news

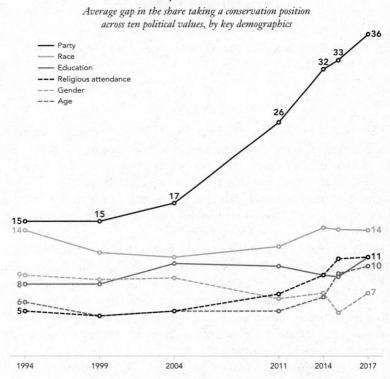

As Partisan Divides over Political Values Widen, Other Gaps Remain Modest

Average gap in the share taking a conservation position across ten political values, by key demographics

Legend:
— Party
— Race
— Education
--- Religious attendance
--- Gender
--- Age

Note: Indicates average gap between the share of two groups taking the conservative position across ten values items. Party=difference between Rep/Lean Rep and Dem/Lead Dem. Race=white non-Hispanic/black non-Hispanic. Education=college grad/non-college grad. Age=18–49/50+. Religion=weekly+ religious service attenders/less often. Source: "1. Partisan Divides over Political Values Widen," Pew Research Center, October 5, 2017, www.pewresearch.org/politics/2017/10/05/1-partisan-divides-over-political-values-widen. Used with permission.

online. Polarization is almost certainly affected by the way Americans have self-sorted both by party (for example, there are few pro-abortion Republicans or pro-life Democrats left) and by geography (after you move, you tend to start agreeing politically with those around you).[5]

Regardless of how we got here, it's increasingly difficult for Americans to get along. Our perceived biggest enemy isn't communism or Nazism or even terrorism. It's one another. These days, even a common enemy such as COVID-19 isn't enough to bring us together. It just splits us further apart.

How can we fix this tendency to blame one another? A few ideas have been tossed around: Hold citizen assemblies to find common ground.[6] Hold fewer elections so we don't have to talk about politics as often.[7] Make voting mandatory so politicians are forced to consider a moderate middle as well as their passionate base.[8]

On an individual level, some suggest avoiding political discussions,[9] taking breaks from the news, and stepping away from social media.[10] And certainly there is value in guarding your words, stewarding your time wisely, and being careful with the news sources you choose. I (Collin) have observed that polarization, not to mention anger and anxiety, correlates strongly with time spent watching cable news, listening to talk radio, and browsing social media.

But we've been shown an even more excellent way. "Love your enemies and pray for those who persecute you," Jesus said in Matthew 5:44.

Paul repeated him in Romans 12:14: "Bless those who persecute you; bless and do not curse them." Then he followed with instructions (verses 16–21):

- "Live in harmony with one another."
- "Repay no one evil for evil, but give thought to do what is honorable in the sight of all."
- "If possible, so far as it depends on you, live peaceably with all."
- "Beloved, never avenge yourselves, but leave it to the wrath of God, for it is written, 'Vengeance is mine, I will repay, says the Lord.' "
- "To the contrary, 'if your enemy is hungry, feed him; if he is

> thirsty, give him something to drink; for by so doing you will
> heap burning coals on his head.' "

- "Do not be overcome by evil, but overcome evil with good."

Gospelbound Christians aren't supposed to personally punish their enemies (even those who set themselves up against God),
scream at their enemies, or even avoid their enemies. Jesus—the only
perfect human and our example—didn't do any of those things. In
fact, he didn't even stop at holding his tongue or turning the other
cheek. Jesus healed people who would never believe, exhausted himself teaching people who would never understand, suffered for people who would never know or care who he was.

He loved his enemies.

So, how do we do that too? Is it even possible in our polarized
times?

We think it is. And we can start by overcoming evil with good.

Overcome Evil with Good

It took five hours for someone to pull together enough courage to
tell missionary Gladys Staines that her husband and two young sons
were dead.

Graham Staines, fifty-eight, had been working with leprosy patients
in India since he was twenty-four years old. He cared for the sick,[11]
preached the gospel, worked on Bible translation,[12] and tried to look
after the neighboring poor while also running the leprosy home. He'd
met Gladys not in Australia, where they were both from, but in India,
where they were both working. The Staines were committed to staying
in India as long as God wanted them to:[13] their three children—born in
Calcutta—learned to play cricket and spoke the native Odia language.

Every year, Graham gathered with other Christians in the small
village of Manoharpur for teaching and fellowship. In 1999, he took
his two sons—Philip, ten, and Timothy, six—along with him. As they
usually did on trips to primitive areas, Graham and his sons crawled
into their station wagon to sleep for the night.

A few hours later, a mob of Hindu extremists, angry about Christian conversions, surrounded the vehicle. Later there would be in-
quiries into and arguments over how closely the leader, Dara Singh,

was working with an extremist group connected to the Hindu nationalist government. Over the past year, Christian persecution had ramped up dramatically; in 1998, more crimes were perpetrated against Christians than in the previous fifty years combined.[14]

"I was first told that the jeep had been burned," Gladys said afterward. Five hours later, friends broke the news. "They were shaking like crazy," Gladys said. "Finally one of the women said, 'Gladys, I don't want you to be like a stone, but I want you to be strong for [her thirteen-year-old daughter] Esther.'"[15]

Gladys knew then that her husband and sons were dead—but not yet how brutal the killings had been. The mob doused the vehicle with gasoline and lit it in the middle of the night while Graham and the boys were sleeping. When they awoke and tried to escape, the mob kept blocking the way, swinging sticks, breaking the windows, and deflating the car's tires. When the charred bodies were recovered, all three were huddled together.

Gladys immediately found Esther and told her, "It seems like we've been left alone. But we will forgive."

"Yes, Mummy, we will," Esther answered.[16]

And they did. When reporters asked whether she was angry, Gladys told them she wasn't. Instead, she shared the gospel of Jesus Christ.

"Of course we are deeply shocked," she said at the funeral. "We are deeply hurt. . . . And still my prayer and desire is that these people who took my husband's life will be touched by that same love so that they will never do this to any other person."

"I praise God that he chose my father, that he thought my father was worthy," Esther told reporters at the funeral.[17]

The news of their loving response headlined newspapers all over India—and then all over the world. It was a major story in the West. Gladys and Esther drew attention again when they chose to stay in India[18]—even though some tribal people hid Dara Singh for a year before he was caught by police.[19] Even though the Orissa High Court commuted his death sentence to life in prison and released eleven of his twelve accomplices.[20] Even though the Supreme Court upheld Singh's commutation to life in prison by explaining that Singh was "teach[ing] a lesson" to Christian evangelists.[21]

Through it all, Gladys kept right on working with the leprosy patients her husband had loved. Eventually she'd be awarded both the Padma Shri—the fourth-highest civilian award in India—and the Mother Teresa Memorial Award for Social Justice.[22]

"God enabled me to forgive, but it doesn't take away the sadness and the grief that's there," Gladys explained in 2019, when a film about her family debuted in Australia. "It's not a matter of moving on—it's moving forward. It's not a matter of saying time heals. Time of itself can't heal, but God works through situations to bring joy out of sorrow."[23]

One spot of joy has been watching Esther, who studied to become a doctor, married, and had four children. (Gladys now lives close to their family in Australia.) Another source of joy has been setting up the fifteen-bed Graham Staines Memorial Hospital.

But her biggest reason for joy is seeing people come to faith in Christ.

Graham "taught about Christ. He shared about Christ through the deaths, in a sense," Gladys said. "I have heard of many, many, many people who've said, 'Their God is real. I want to be Christian.' How many people will we see in heaven directly related to those events? We will never know. And I just praise God for that."[24]

Gospelbound Christians love their enemies by overcoming evil with good. Because our story isn't over, even in death. Only this strategy can never fail. So long as God rules and eternity awaits, evil will never triumph.

Trust in God's Ultimate Justice

UNTIL JESUS RETURNS, Christians will face opposition in this world. "In the world you will have tribulation," Jesus promised in John 16:33. Those who boldly live out their faith—by moving to India to care for lepers, by protesting at an abortion clinic, by working for racial justice—will attract enemies.

But it's not as if only gospelbound Christians face opposition. Satan is the father of lies, and he uses them to spread chaos. Unfaithful spouses, broken families, fights among friends, organizational splits, escalating differences at work—even if you don't trust in Christ, you're not safe from Satan's attacks. He isn't a kind master to anyone.

Even for Christians, Jesus's command to love our enemies seems impossible. How could Gladys and Esther spend years working with and raising money for the Indian people? For that matter, how could the Amish community in Pennsylvania donate money to the widow and three children of the school shooter who killed five of their young girls in 2006?[25] How could Elisabeth Elliot love the Ecuadorian tribe that killed her husband, Jim, and take up his cause and take them the gospel?

This response—to work for the good of your enemy—is both baffling and beautiful. And you can't do it on your own.

"It was God who gave me that strength," Gladys said.[26] She held on to Romans 12:19, which says, "Vengeance is mine, I will repay, says the Lord." She released her desire for justice to God so completely that she didn't stress about the hunt for the killers, worry about the trial, or even read all the reports.

Loving our enemies doesn't mean accepting injustice. It means we care too much about justice to trust it entirely to humans who don't always catch the right people, try them fairly, deliver just sentences, or carry them out to completion. While gospelbound Christians eagerly seek justice on earth, they ultimately trust in God's justice in the new heavens and the new earth. They may work doggedly for a better justice system, but they also know that when it fails, God will not. We trust he will right all manner of wrong in his time.

Gladys sees a bigger picture. She knows that God will handle the justice for her family. She also knows that Dara Singh is a human being made in God's image. She knows he is lost. And she knows he isn't her biggest enemy.

Because she knows that Satan wars against God. But God's victory is secure, and justice will be delivered. Gladys and Esther will see the rest of their family again. And everything will be made right.

Since final justice cannot be denied, gospelbound Christians can truly love their enemies, whether or not they ever ask our forgiveness. But it's easier to love your enemies if you know a little more about them.

....

Understand the Enemy

IN 2018, JONATHAN Haidt—professor of social psychology at New York University's Stern School of Business, ethnically Jewish, politically left leaning, and religiously atheist—stood on the main stage of the Council for Christian Colleges and Universities (CCCU) conference.

"I was born to be the sort of person who is opposed to your mission," he told about 1,200 college leaders. "Within two years of my bar mitzvah, I started calling myself an atheist. And not just an atheist, but one of those atheists that sees religion—Christianity especially—as the opponent, as the enemy, because they believe creationism and we scientists believe in evolution."

Several things changed his mind, Haidt said. Not to convert to Christianity—he's still an atheist—but to drop his hostility toward it.

"I got my first teaching position at the University of Virginia," he told the CCCU. His Christian students "radiated a kind of sweetness, a kind of warmth and gentleness and humility that I hadn't seen before," he said. "It was really lovely." He saw the same "warmth and openness and love" from evangelical churches he visited as part of a class on moral communities. "It was really beautiful, and it touched my heart. And when your heart is open, then your mind is open."

As one who studies morality, Haidt was also impressed with the Bible ("among the richest repositories of psychological wisdom ever assembled") and with the actions of Christians ("religious conservative Americans are . . . more generous with their time and money [than secular Americans]").[27]

"I started realizing that the scientific community at that time . . . was really underestimating and misunderstanding religion," he said.

His book *The Righteous Mind: Why Good People Are Divided by Politics and Religion*—"the most important book in years," Ethics & Religious Liberty Commission president Russell Moore once tweeted[28]—caught the CCCU's attention. I (Collin) have probably never recommended another book as often as this one. In two interviews with Haidt, he has struck me as you'd expect from his writing: inquisitive, open minded, convicted, and generous. During the nearly constant social and political turmoil of the last decade, I have returned again and again to his work to help me understand and even empathize with critics across the spectrum. Haidt's book is laced with evolutionary explanations, but it's not hard to see God's design in what he has discovered.

Haidt argued that people make most of their decisions emotionally rather than logically. He's done this himself. In the early nineties, he spent three months in India on a Fulbright fellowship, watching women serve men in silence in a "sex-segregated, hierarchically stratified, devoutly religious society." As a twenty-nine-year-old liberal atheist, he struggled with this culture—but only for a few weeks.

"I *liked* these people who were hosting me, helping me, and teaching me," he wrote in *The Righteous Mind.* "Wherever I went, people were kind to me. And when you're grateful to people, it's easier to adopt their perspective." Haidt began to open to their interpretation of reality—where men weren't oppressors of helpless female victims but all were part of an interdependent family, where "honoring elders, gods, and guests, protecting subordinates, and fulfilling one's role-based duties were more important" than personal autonomy and equality.[29]

In this, Haidt himself exemplifies his "rider and elephant" analogy. If our emotions are like an elephant, reason is a rider perched on top. Most of our decisions are gut reactions, our intuition as strong and unwieldy as an elephant. Our reasoning comes later to justify our decisions, and only through hard work can the rider get the elephant to switch directions.

Haidt isn't the first to argue that emotions usually trump reasoning. The Bible is full of warnings about what we love. "The heart is deceitful above all things, and desperately sick; who can understand it?" Jeremiah 17:9 says. "Keep your heart with all vigilance, for from it flow the springs of life," Proverbs 4:23 says. "I have the desire to do what is right, but not the ability to carry it out," Paul wrote in Romans 7:18.

Turns out, we aren't primarily rational beings who explain our arguments to one another until one side or another prevails. Instead, we are profoundly driven by our emotions, our affections, and our intuitions.

How does this knowledge help Christians love their enemies? Because, in the loss of shared culture shaped by the Bible, non-Christians are less likely to believe in God or even to want to believe in God. They're not even likely to know what they're missing. As

Christian values fall out of favor, the country's peer pressure is shifting. Historically, being a Christian or belonging to a church was the socially approved path. These days, people associate the church with fanatical Trump support or repressed sexuality.[30]

If Haidt is correct, then it won't necessarily be the most cogent arguments that win the day. Because that's not why the tide began to shift against Christianity in the first place. Effective evangelism will need to help skeptics *want* to want to believe. And the key to that strategy can be seen in the lives of Gladys and Esther Staines. Live such a peaceful and compelling life that, by watching you, some *want* to believe.

"Keep your conduct among the Gentiles honorable," Peter wrote in 1 Peter 2:12, "so that when they speak against you as evildoers, they may see your good deeds and glorify God on the day of visitation." He continued in verse 15, "For this is the will of God, that by doing good you should put to silence the ignorance of foolish people."

There's a time and place for arguments. Evangelism by definition speaks the good news about Jesus Christ. But when we understand those who don't believe, we recognize that arguing might not be the best place to start. You might be surprised to learn what they actually think, when you're willing to ask. And in doing good, you may find common ground.

"An obsession with righteousness . . . is the normal human condition," Haidt wrote.[31] He told the CCCU, "Human beings evolved to be religious. It's in our nature. . . . There is a God-shaped hole in the heart of each man."

It's a remarkable statement for an academic atheist.

"If there is a God-shaped hole in everyone's heart, regardless of how it came about, then it matters how that hole gets filled," he said. "If you fill it with a community that values service and decency and responsibility and caring for your family and caring for others . . . then things will go well for those people and for the community and for the country."

He was alluding to his moral foundations theory—or the six values he believes are common across time and cultures:[32]

- Care/harm. (We want to help those who are hurting and punish those who are cruel.)

- Fairness/cheating. (We want to work with people who won't exploit us, and we shun cheaters.)
- Liberty/oppression. (We are sensitive to—and don't like—attempts to bully or dominate.)
- Loyalty/betrayal. (We reward those who are trustworthy and avoid or hurt those who betray us.)
- Authority/subversion. (We keep order by forming social hierarchies.)
- Sanctity/degradation. (We give certain objects—say, a crucifix or a communion chalice—what Haidt called "irrational and extreme value,"[33] which serves to bind us together socially.)

Using multiple surveys, Haidt found that political liberals don't give much credence to the last three values. Even in the first two, which conservatives and liberals both hold highly, the interpretations cause fractures. While both parties prize care, they disagree on crime (Should we focus on rehabilitating criminals or on protecting victims?) and abortion (Do we prioritize the mother or the child?). And while both prize fairness, liberals tend to value a fair division of resources, while conservatives value a fair opportunity to earn those resources.

No wonder it feels like the right and left are talking past each other. American politics is set up perfectly for this battle of self-righteousness between the left and the right.

As Christians, it's helpful to remember that we are not the only people with moral convictions. All God's image bearers can feel an acute sense of right and wrong, even if they're wrong about what's right. We cannot treat our neighbors as if they are amoral; they aren't. In fact, they're just as likely to believe *us* to be immoral, especially when it comes to our beliefs about sexual ethics.

Taking time to really listen or even to find common ground—"Hey, we both care about protecting the vulnerable from the virus *and* from economic devastation"—is a great place to start. But listening to one another and being kind, while helpful, doesn't completely solve the difficulty between liberals and conservatives. Because each side is fighting not just for its values but also for its tribe.

"Hiving [living in community] comes naturally, easily, and joyfully to us," Haidt wrote in *The Righteous Mind*.[34] But drawing lines to create inclusion also creates exclusion—being close friends with some people means you aren't close with others, joining one church means you aren't a member elsewhere, living in one country means you aren't a resident of another.

And that "we are not them" reality means our gut reactions—our elephants—are always leaning toward our community and away from others. So when a political or theological issue crops up—say, the environment or immigration or masks or infant baptism—we're wired to agree with our clan right off the bat and then look for reasons to support that decision.

This is why Republicans were incensed by Democrat Bill Clinton's affair with his intern but blasé about Donald Trump's serial harassment of women. It's why Democrats weren't worried about Clinton but put conservative Supreme Court nominee Brett Kavanaugh on trial for a less substantiated accusation. It's why members of both parties swing around on whether we should obey or protest our government, whether federal spending is too much or not enough, and whether the Supreme Court should strike down laws or defer to Congress.

Haidt's message caught the attention of Biola University president Barry Corey. In 2016, a California state senator proposed stripping colleges of their financial aid unless they lined up with a liberal stance on sexuality. Schools would be unable to teach that marriage is between a man and a woman or to limit bathrooms by biological gender. Biola and other Christian colleges protested, and the issue grew heated. Eventually the bill was amended. But Corey wasn't satisfied. He knew what he was trying to do, but he didn't know how he was coming across to the other tribe.

He contacted Evan Low, chair of the LGBT caucus in the state assembly. "How can we do things better?" Corey asked Low. "We aren't changing our core [stance], but we've probably made some mistakes along the way. How can we do better?" The two explained what happened next in a piece for the *Washington Post*. Corey visited Low's office in the state capitol, and Low visited Biola to see Corey and meet faculty, staff, and students. They grabbed dinner to discuss their differences. Gradually they dropped their defenses.

As they wrote in their *Washington Post* article, "It's amazing how quickly biases can be overcome when real relationships are prior-itized, when you realize the person you once thought an adversary is in many ways like you, with a story and passions and fears, and a hope that we can make the world a better place."[35]

It's not as if a pleasant meal made all their disagreement disappear. They still have different views about human flourishing and justice. But they recognized many areas where they actually agree, from helping minority students to fighting sexual assault to making college affordable. And they recognized that they would accomplish much more on these common causes if they worked together, despite their differences.

Corey didn't have to reach out to Low. It would've been a lot easier to write him off, to figure he'd always be a thorn in the side at best, a powerful enemy at worst. If Corey had taken a more antagonistic approach, he might have been able to rouse donors into giving a lot of money for his school and legal fees.

But Corey knows that Christ calls him to love those the world calls his enemy. And that means seeing him as Christ does and understanding him. By spending time together, eating together, and finding some common ground, Corey and Low moved from being opponents to being, if not close friends, then people who respect each other. They can call each other if they have questions. They can explain their views and know they'll be heard. They can work together in areas where they agree.

They can do this because they've seen and heard each other. And because at least one of them is taking the long view. That's the final way the two of us have seen gospelbound Christians love their enemies.

Take the Long View

SAM NKOMO WAS sixteen and heading to one of the most important school exams he'd take—the math test that would help determine whether he would continue with school. But as the South African got off the train at his stop, dressed in a school uniform and carrying his school bag, he was pulled aside by police.

"I couldn't understand—why are they stopping me?" he remembered. But now, nearly five decades later, he knows. "They wanted me to produce [my] pass."[36]

Nkomo was black in South Africa in 1970, a time when everyone who wasn't white needed travel papers to be in the city of Johannesburg. But Nkomo was young and a student—he didn't think he needed papers. He was wrong.

"I was locked up at a police station," he told me (Sarah). He tried to reason with a white officer, explaining that he needed to get to his exam. He couldn't retake it.

"He wouldn't listen to me," Nkomo said. Eventually "I was released with the warning [to] make sure I get a reference book as quick as possible. Otherwise, next time they find me, I'm gonna go to jail" or be deported. That would almost be worse—Nkomo was Zulu and would have seventy-two hours to leave Johannesburg. He would be sent more than five hours away to the province of Natal, where his ancestors originated. He knew no one there now.

Nkomo raced to school. He was forty-five minutes late for the examination and shouldn't have been allowed to take the test until the next year. But his principal smuggled him in, and Nkomo rushed through.

"That was my first taste of apartheid," Nkomo said. His first conscious taste, that is, because Nkomo had been choking down apartheid since he was born. He had to use separate facilities from whites.[37] He went to black schools, where the education wasn't just inferior—it was designed to train black students for menial jobs or servitude. He wasn't allowed to own land, vote, or marry a white woman. Any pushback was dangerous—Nkomo's brother was assassinated in 1991 by a police operative (a civilian with a police-issued revolver) for teaching history "the way it should be taught"—that is, without a positive spin on apartheid.

"I was full of hatred, and I was very bitter at that time," Nkomo said. "The pain is still there of that incident. It will never go away. . . . [But] I am not bitter now because I have accepted Christ as my Lord and Savior." He credits his parents and Sunday school teacher with grounding him in his faith and showing him how to love his enemies. The lesson took so well that Nkomo is now a member at Christ Church Midrand, a half-black, half-white church in Johannesburg.

Christ Church Midrand was planted in 1994, the same year apartheid was overturned. But multiculturalism wasn't built into its DNA. At the beginning, the church was almost entirely white. Through steady attention to race and an eagerness to embrace all cultures, however, it's now 50 percent black.

"It is one of the great joys of my life to be part of this multiracial, multilinguistic church," said founder and lead pastor Martin Morrison. It wouldn't be a stretch to add "miraculous." Because not only is Morrison white—his grandfather's cousin was D. F. Malan, a Dutch Reformed Church minister who led the National Party that legally introduced apartheid in 1948.

Malan's administration wasted no time in sorting the population into four categories (whites, blacks, mixed black and white, and Indian/Asian) and implementing laws that forbade marriage or sexual intercourse between the races, required travel papers for all non-whites, and forcibly moved thousands of black people into small, undeveloped "homelands" far away from urban areas. In order to find employment, black men could receive passes to live and work in the city, but they had to leave their families behind.[38]

These injustices didn't go unnoticed or unchallenged by the rest of the world. The United Nations' first declaration opposing apartheid came in 1950;[39] over the next four decades, it would create a Special Committee Against Apartheid, mandate a South African arms embargo, encourage an oil and cultural/sports embargo, and declare South Africa's constitution invalid. But South Africa's most famous critic was Nelson Mandela, a native son who spent twenty-seven years in jail for his opposition to the government.[40] He was released in 1990 by F. W. de Klerk, Malan's successor as head of the National Party.

De Klerk was Malan's polar opposite, working with Mandela to write a brand-new anti-apartheid constitution (for which the duo shared a Nobel Peace Prize).[41] When Mandela was elected president in 1994, de Klerk was his second-in-command. But South African whites and blacks didn't meld as quickly or as closely as Mandela and de Klerk did. In the past twenty-five years, black income has gone up, but inequality remains (the top 10 percent of earners take home half the money; the bottom 20 percent get 2.7 percent).[42] Land redistribution has been promised, but the actual practice is slow and controversial.[43] The imbalance has led to frustration, which sometimes turns to violence. White farmers are facing increasing attacks,[44] perhaps egged on by extremist politicians.[45] Other whites are targets for robbery or rape.[46]

And in the middle, Morrison built a church.

Like Nkomo, Morrison didn't even notice apartheid until he was older, though his introduction was gentler—through studying law at the university. He sought out black friends at the largely white school, then spent time working in the black Soweto area of Johannesburg. Eventually Morrison and his wife ended up in Midrand—a suburb of Johannesburg. Surrounded by fields and cattle, they started Christ Church Midrand in a hotel just as apartheid was ending. Six adults and two children came.

"I hadn't read any books on church planting, and I think I got it all wrong," Morrison told me (Sarah). I (Collin) met Morrison through his work with The Gospel Coalition Africa. On such a massive continent with so many cultures and needs, Morrison has earned trust among a diverse collection of leaders. It probably helps that he's in no hurry, and he isn't doing this to make himself famous. His long-term strategy for flourishing African churches resembles the basics he practices in church planting—preaching the gospel and starting Bible studies. More than twenty years later, Christ Church Midrand is home to about 1,200 souls—about half white and half black.

"We were 95 percent white when we started . . . and I was the white minister," he said. "God in his goodness sent us some wonderful black Christians, and we automatically drew them in because they were part of the neighborhood and that's what the Bible teaches—that you must love your neighbor."

The integration happened gradually. "Just like anybody else, they were given opportunities for service, and for ministry, so that when other black people came in, they saw black people take part in leading the prayers, in running the Bible studies, on staff," he said.

The church also addressed race early and often, both in sermons and in small groups. Morrison carefully chooses the racial mix of those who make the announcements, read, pray, and serve communion. He is also intentional about those who lead Sunday school, youth groups, and Bible studies. And at least one of the songs each week is in Zulu or Sotho or Xhosa—sometimes youth worker Blaque Nubon even raps.[47] "You are saying to black people, 'These are some of the songs you sing in black churches. We're going to sing them because this is your church,'" Morrison said.

He addressed race head-on in a two-part series in January 2016, when national tensions were high after a white woman called blacks "monkeys" on social media.[48] "I was brought up with all the privileges of being white in this country," Morrison told his congregation. "It's wrong for me to say I understand. I don't understand what the ravages of 350 years of apartheid have been to black people in our country. White people like me tend to forget."

"What we are talking about is not unique to South Africa," he said. "It's Hitler and the Jews. It's the Hutus and the Tutsis. It's apartheid. It's ISIS and Christians. It's the Serbs and the Croats. It's the Poles and the Russians. It's the Greeks and the Turks."

It's also in every human heart. "Part of our sinfulness is that we see ourselves as superior to other people," he told his church. (In fact, he's a little skeptical of people who say they aren't racist.) But there is a cure. "It's found in Christ," Morrison said. "It's found in facing the truth, it's found in believing the truth, and it's found in acting the truth."

That means acknowledging racism, repenting, and affirming the dignity of every person, he said. In South Africa, that can look like greeting people in their native language, calling people by their given name even if it's difficult to pronounce, and spending time getting to know one another. It means committing to change, to loving enemies with the long view in mind.

Because there is often a cost to loving your enemies. Sometimes it's the other Christians who will hate you for it. Morrison's reconciliation with one group meant estranging another. Several white people left Christ Church over the sermon series. "I'm very sad they are leaving," Morrison told his congregation. "But I'm not sad about what I said. If the Bible and the gospel doesn't affect every area of life, then we are not getting it right."

When the apartheid laws were tossed out in 1994, "it was freedom not just for black people but for white people," Morrison told me (Sarah). "We could be freed from our racism and from our oppression." It opened the door for churches like Christ Church Midrand, which Morrison counts "a wonderful joy."

"I wouldn't leave this place for a million dollars because of the joy, the richness of being part of this family," he said. While he cautions against too much satisfaction—"I really don't want anyone to get any ideas that we have arrived"—they've sure come a long way.

"We have seen a change in the past twenty years in our country," said Lutic Mosoane, who works with youth at Christ Church Midrand. Still, "we would never have seen something like Christ Church Midrand if it wasn't for the gospel."

Years ago, when planting his church, Morrison took the long view. So did Nelson Mandela. He knew that governments aren't changed in a moment. A man of deep Christian faith,[49] he waited twenty-seven years in prison, slowly studying for his law degree even though he didn't know whether he'd ever be released.

When his turn in power finally came, he didn't punish his white enemies but worked for restoration and reconciliation. As a result, Morrison could plant a church that was open to both whites and blacks, and today Nkomo can worship alongside the same race that killed his brother and constrained his own life. They see one another not as enemies but as brothers and sisters in the Lord.

So, be patient, gospelbound Christians. The arc of history is long. It's rare that deep rifts or painful wrongs can be quickly overcome. It's unusual for long fights to be resolved in a hurry. Wherever you are in your reconciliation, ask God to help you take one more step. His way may not be fast (at least as we experience it), but it is right and good.

Love Your Enemies by Loving Jesus More

REMEMBER ANANIAS? HE's the guy who went to Saul after Saul heard Jesus's voice and was blinded by light on the road to Damascus. When God told him where to find Saul, Ananias protested.

"Lord, I have heard from many about this man, how much evil he has done to your saints at Jerusalem. And here he has authority from the chief priests to bind all who call on your name" (Acts 9:13–14).

The annals of church history don't include many enemies of Christ more vicious than Saul of Tarsus. Ananias thought he understood Saul, but he didn't yet see him as Christ saw him. Ananias couldn't take the long view—he was just trying to survive the persecution.

It's telling that God didn't ask Ananias to persuade Saul to become a Christian. Ananias wasn't supposed to argue with Saul about doctrine. It's not likely anyone could have outdebated Saul, anyway—he was a student of the famous rabbi Gamaliel.

No, when Ananias went to his enemy Saul—a man who had come to Damascus specifically to hunt and hurt Christians—God had already done the work. He'd already done the saving. Ananias was responsible not for changing Saul's mind, just for putting the warmth of his hands on Saul's face.

Can you think of someone you'd call an enemy? A former friend? An unfair boss? An ex-spouse? No matter how much you have been hurt by someone, no matter how far apart you are on the political spectrum, no matter how much someone has done to lose your respect—Jesus invites you to love that person.

He's not being unfair or unkind. He's not asking us to give up on justice. He's not demanding that we lie down and let people run over us.

What he's really asking us to do is to love *him*.

Because while almost all people love those who love them (Luke 6:32), it's nearly impossible for anybody to love somebody who is really annoying or who constantly lies or steals or who deliberately hurts people.

Unless we love Jesus more. The more we dwell on the kindness and justice and protection of God, the less we feel we have to secure those things for ourselves. And the more we can release to his sovereign control—the unfair test grade, the unfaithful spouse, the depraved abuser—the more our hearts can see our enemies as Christ does: sinners who need a Savior.

John Piper told us that he's a lot less worried about being taken advantage of than he used to be. His car has been broken into, his sons' bikes stolen out from under them. Last summer, a boy asked whether he could cut the grass. Piper said yes—he always does when a kid wants to work. But later the boy came back with a friend and tried to jimmy the window open. "[We] were sitting five feet away, watching them do it," he said. "I opened the door, and they bolted.

"I used to pride myself that I could see through lies and get people to contradict themselves when they were asking for money," he said. "But gradually the Lord made it clear to me that at the judgment day there will be no rewards for shrewdness but only for love. And Jesus's commands to turn the other cheek and to give your cloak as well as your shirt and to go two miles, not just one—all of that showed me that being taken advantage of is normal.

"Jesus cares as much about killing my selfishness as he does about who gets what money," he said. "The issue for me is, Will I be content in him so that being taken advantage of is no big deal?"

It also helps to remember that we, too, are sinners who need a Savior. We, too, are someone's enemy. We've hurt people with the words we've said and the things we've done. We've cheated people, lied to people, manipulated people. We're guilty—not of the same crimes, perhaps, but guilty nonetheless.

Remembering our own sin and how much God has sacrificed to make us righteous deepens our love for him. And with his love—the love the Spirit grows like fruit in us—we can love our enemies.

That's the truth Gladys Staines holds on to as she makes her way through life without her husband and her sons. That's the truth Sam Nkomo remembers as he sits with his white brothers and sisters in the pews of Christ Church Midrand. Even the atheist Jonathan Haidt has shown us a better way than the polarization that poisons our relationships. We're not better than our enemies. We don't need to snark at them on Twitter or talk badly about them to our friends or give them the silent treatment.

Because we have a God who loved us first, we can love even our enemies.

CHAPTER 8

Gospelbound Christians
Give Away Their Freedom

Thanks be to God, that you who were once slaves of sin have become obedient from the heart to the standard of teaching to which you were committed, and, having been set free from sin, have become slaves of righteousness.

—ROMANS 6:17–18

The morning of May 20, 2000, dawned damp and gray over a grassy field in Memphis, where a portable city had sprung up overnight. Thousands of muted tents stood in wet rows; fog made everything hazy.

About forty thousand college students had arrived for the fourth Passion Conference, its first outdoors. It was a day they wouldn't forget, one they describe with words like *special* and *holy* and *weight of glory.*

Even people who weren't there remember it, because that day John Piper gave his famous seashells message.[1]

"The sermon was formative for our generation," said Matt Capps, now a senior pastor in North Carolina. "Only time will tell if it marks Christian history the way sermons like [Jonathan Edwards's] 'Sinners in the Hands of an Angry God' did. But in our generation, at least in my circles, if you mention the seashells illustration, everybody knows what you're talking about."

Piper spoke in the early afternoon, around 1:00 p.m. Students sat on jackets or garbage bags on the wet grass, fanned out around a wooden stage.

"You don't have to know a lot of things for your life to make a lasting difference in the world," Piper began. You don't have to be smart or good looking or from a good family. "You just have to know a few, basic, glorious, majestic, obvious, unchanging, eternal things and be gripped by them and be willing to lay down your life for them."

Five minutes in, he laid out the comparison nobody forgot:

> Three weeks ago, we got news at our church that Ruby Eliason and Laura Edwards were killed in Cameroon. Ruby Eliason—over eighty, single all her life, a nurse. Poured her life out for one thing: to make Jesus Christ known among the sick and the poor in the hardest and most unreached places.
>
> Laura Edwards, a medical doctor in the Twin Cities and, in her retirement, partnering up with Ruby. [She was] also pushing eighty and going from village to village in Cameroon. The brakes give way, over a cliff they go, and they're dead instantly. And I asked my people, "Is this a tragedy?"
>
> Two women, in their eighties almost, a whole life devoted to one idea—Jesus Christ magnified among the poor and the sick in the hardest places. And twenty years after most of their American counterparts had begun to throw their lives away on trivialities in Florida and New Mexico, [they] fly into eternity with a death in a moment. "Is this a tragedy?" I asked.

The crowd knew the answer, calling out "No!"

"It is not a tragedy," Piper affirmed. "I'll read you what a tragedy is."

He pulled out a page from *Reader's Digest*: "'Bob and Penny . . . took early retirement from their jobs in the Northeast five years ago when he was 59 and she was 51. Now they live in Punta Gorda, Florida, where they cruise on their 30-foot trawler, play softball, and collect shells.'"

"*That's* a tragedy," he told the crowd. He also said,

> There are people in this country that are spending billions of dollars to get you to buy it. And I get forty minutes to plead with you—don't buy it. With all my heart I plead with you—don't buy that dream. . . . As the last

chapter before you stand before the Creator of the universe to give an account with what you did: "Here it is, Lord—my shell collection. . . . And I've got a good swing. And look at my boat."

Advice on retirement doesn't seem like the right fit for a crowd of college students. But Piper's next line "Don't waste your life" exploded out, sparking a book, a study guide, tracts, and even a rap song.[2]

"It changed my perspective about not just retirement but what I'd do with my career," said Justin Converse, who was then twenty-four. He would go on to work a few years in advertising for clients like Hilton Hotels before joining Dennis Rainey's FamilyLife ministry, then Nancy DeMoss Wolgemuth's *Revive Our Hearts* radio program. "I'm probably never going to 'retire,'" he said. "I want to do something with my life beyond fifty, sixty, seventy that makes a difference, whether that's volunteering at a soup kitchen or mentoring kids or whatever that looks like."

Sagemont Church lead pastor Matt Carter feels the same way. "I was in the crowd. That sermon ended all my dreams of retirement," he tweeted a few years ago.[3] Paul Coleman, then nineteen, called the message "a crucial building block that helped me see it was worth it to live for Jesus." Today he's the lead pastor of DeepWater Church in South Carolina. Chad Huddleston had just finished his freshman year of college and was sitting in the middle of the crowd. "That was probably one of the most impactful sermons of my life," he said. Several years later, Huddleston and his wife left to do mission work in China.

Marian Jordan Ellis was sitting in the back, a twenty-seven-year-old volunteer and a new Christian. She spent the next two weeks on a trip to Israel with Passion Conference founder Louie Giglio. "It was like a fork in the road," she said of the conference and trip. "Either you're going to live for the glory of God or for yourself. And I had already been living for myself, so I knew I had to go the other direction. Because who wants to waste their life, right?" She began teaching the Bible to her Christian high school students, then headed back to seminary before starting This Redeemed Life. Now she teaches the Bible to young women all across the country.

It doesn't make sense. Piper's message should've been met with blank stares or rolling eyes. Because young people aren't usually long-term planners. The younger you are, the harder it is to make an educated guess about what's coming. To a college student, retirement seems a million years away—far too distant to consider seriously.

But many of the young adults who heard that message were so struck by it that they remember what part of the field they were sitting on. And twenty years later, they're still determined to work for the Lord until they die. I (Collin) did not attend, but I must know at least a dozen friends who did, and they're serving others all around the world.

Even more surprising, their parents felt the same way. "I've had probably more fifty-somethings thank me for that book than young people," Piper told me (Sarah). "The couple that went to Punta Gorda were fifty-nine and fifty-one—that's what stung. These were people in their prime deciding to play for the rest of their lives. . . . I think I have had as many fifty-somethings [as young people] thank me for rescuing them from the folly of retirement."

Folly? Our culture holds retirement as the ultimate good—the reward for decades of grinding through nine-to-fives. It's when we're finally free—free from work, free from worrying about money, free to travel, free to spend all day sipping drinks on the beach. Giving up the hard-earned freedom to do whatever you want is exactly the opposite of every commercial aimed at older folks.

So, why would Christians, both younger and older, give away the freedom of retirement?

Freedom from Constraints

AMERICANS LOVE FREEDOM. Every year, we set off fireworks to celebrate our country's independence, and every day, we hang our national identity on it. We protect the freedom to choose almost anything—your religion, your school, your church, your career, your location. You can freely choose your spouse, then nearly as easily choose a no-fault divorce. You can choose to get pregnant; if you change your mind, you can choose to end the pregnancy. You can choose your gender or to be genderless. You can choose to sleep with one person or a hundred people, of whichever gender (or lack of gender) you prefer.

Sometimes it seems like we're limited only by our own past choices. Maybe you have heard this from an older adult (or have said it to someone younger): "I'm so envious of you. You've got your whole life ahead of you. You have so much freedom. You can do whatever you want."

People say this because you haven't yet tied yourself to a career track or a spouse or a mortgage. To independent Americans, a fresh start, unhampered by mistakes or commitments, is as free as we'll ever get. We watch movies about it, sing songs about it, write books about it. Everything from age-defying makeup to plastic surgery to Viagra speaks of our desire to recapture the vitality and freedom of youth.

By many standards, today's American youth are the freest in history. They're less likely to be tied to a mortgage—more are living at home with their parents for longer than previous generations did.[4] They're less likely to be committed to a spouse and more likely to have cohabitated with a significant other,[5] which means they were free to leave if things turned sour. They're less likely to be responsible for childcare, as the birth rate has been dropping since the 1960s.[6] Thanks to growing affluence and developments in technology, they also have more educational and career choices than anyone else in history.

By comparison, the self-control of Christianity looks outdated. To a generation committed to throwing off any constraints, things like commandments and laws and right behavior sound backward at best, abusive at worst. I (Collin) don't remember my 1990s youth group obsessing over sexual purity and presenting a dangerously narrow view of sex. But judging by the backlash from my peers, many of them resent their churches for the way abstinence before marriage was taught.

It's cliché, but sex and drugs (if not rock and roll) are still the markers of youthful rebellion. Only it doesn't look as if millennials and Gen Z are enjoying that freedom.

Sex and Drugs and Rock and Roll

THE FIRST OPIOID addictions started with doctors' prescriptions for painkillers. In finding freedom from physical pain, thousands of Americans inadvertently stepped into a prison of addiction. As opioids moved to the streets, they quickly became the most popular drug of choice, primarily because they work so well to offer a numb freedom from all sorts of pain.

In 2016, "we had twenty-six overdoses in four hours in Huntington," West Virginia pastor Chris Priestley told me (Sarah). Huntington's population is about forty-five thousand. "They ran out of ambulances."

Priestley first ran into opioids when he worked with youth in Charleston. The kids he talked to at the skate parks were using the drugs after they got into a fight or got a bad report card. Reaching for pain pills "was a consistent pattern," he said.

But opioid addiction is nearly impossible to kick, as I have learned from talking with experts.[7] When someone uses opioids, his or her brain produces more opioid receptors, which feel uncomfortable when they're empty. And when the brain floods itself with dopamine during opioid hits, it stops producing its normal amount of dopamine. But the body needs that regular dopamine, which makes the craving for opioids even stronger. (The brain changes are even more stark in those whose prefrontal cortex hasn't yet matured—so anyone younger than twenty-five.)[8]

The number of Americans dying from drug overdoses—especially from the opioid fentanyl—rose sharply after 2015.[9] Thanks to opioids, overdosing on drugs is now the most common cause of death for people younger than fifty.[10] This path of escape leads right to death.

What about sex, then? The change in values from generation to generation has been pronounced. Rebelling against the monogamy of their parents, the boomers freed sex from marriage. Eighty percent of boomer women had sex outside marriage by the time they were twenty-five. Millennials were even more free: 89 percent of women had sex outside marriage by age twenty-five.[11]

Millennials and Gen Z also freed sex from human relationships. Pornography use has skyrocketed, both from easier access (you can watch on your phone instead of finding magazines in the dark back room of a convenience store) and from less stigma (in one survey, those ages thirteen to twenty-four said that watching porn was more acceptable than not recycling). Ninety-three percent of boys and 62 percent of girls first view porn before their eighteenth birthday; 57 percent search out porn at least monthly.[12]

But freeing sex from the boundaries of marriage—or even real-life relationships—doesn't make it better. Filmed sex scenes are unrealistic and can leave viewers disappointed with actual partners or anxious about actual situations.[13] Sexual pleasure affects the brain in much the same way as cocaine, which means the more you use porn, the more you'll need to use to feel the same satisfaction.[14] Porn users report less real-life intimacy, altered sexual tastes, and attachment problems.[15]

In the end, the generation that has access to free birth control, has no prejudice against premarital (and sometimes even extramarital) sex, and can legally obtain abortions is having less sex than any other generation in the last sixty years.[16]

Perhaps they should've listened to their grandparents. In 1988, a *Rolling Stone* article reported that the sexually free boomer generation "considers more permissive attitudes toward sex a change for the worse."[17] And three-quarters of the generation that used the most drugs[18] said they'd disapprove of their children experimenting with drugs. (Of those with children, 94 percent said they'd disapprove.)

"It's not so much that they want to deny the next generation the freedom to experiment," reporter David Sheff explained. "It's more that they acknowledge the high toll exacted for the experimentation."[19]

The Bible puts it this way: "When you were slaves of sin, you were free in regard to righteousness. But what fruit were you getting at that time from the things of which you are now ashamed? For the end of those things is death" (Romans 6:20–21).

Nobody wants to be a slave of alcohol or pornography or painkillers. Nobody likes to be addicted, unable to control his or her own impulses. People chase those vices as ways to be free. But they don't free you at all.

So what will?

Finding Freedom in Constraints

Of anyone or anything, God is the most free. He can always do what he wants, when he wants, where he wants. He isn't tied down by lack of money or space or time. He isn't paralyzed by indecision or slowed down by lack of imagination.

"All of our freedom derives from his," wrote Reformed University Fellowship campus minister Derek Rishmawy.[20] We can see this in Scripture: "You were called to freedom, brothers," says Galatians 5:13. "Live as people who are free," says 1 Peter 2:16. "You have been set free from sin," says Romans 6:22.

But true freedom isn't found in coloring outside the lines. Just the opposite.

"God demonstrates his freedom—the freedom of sovereign love—in making a choice, a covenant, binding himself to a people in condescending love," Rishmawy wrote. "Analogically, we find our greatest freedom in making an actual choice instead of just keeping our options open. Freedom is found in choosing the particular, not choice in general."[21]

God chose us to be his children. He tied himself to us. "I will not leave you or forsake you," he said over and over again (Deuteronomy 31:8; Joshua 1:5; Hebrews 13:5). So it makes sense that we would also find our freedom in covenantal love—loving both God and others (Matthew 22:37–40).

Common sense tells us that those who do their homework earn better grades. Those who faithfully show up to work earn the favor of their bosses. Those who invest in others build better friendships. I (Collin) tell new members at my church, many of whom are looking for community, that they'll get everything they want if they just show up consistently. It's not a secret formula. Committing to something—that is, giving up your freedom in favor of gaining something of value—will eventually gain you more than continually keeping open a range of choices or an escape hatch.

As far as it can, research bears this out. We know constraints increase creativity.[22] Married people report better relationships—and better sex—than partners who aren't married.[23] Those who commit to a four-year college are more likely to graduate with a bachelor's degree than those who plan on transferring partway through.[24]

Gospelbound Christians, then, reflect God by going all in on commitment. "You were called to freedom, brothers," Paul wrote to the Galatians, then went on to tell them, "Only do not use your freedom as an opportunity for the flesh, but through love serve one another" (5:13).

"Live as people who are free," wrote Peter, "not using your freedom as a cover-up for evil, but living as servants of God" (1 Peter 2:16).

As human beings, we are not free like God is. We are constrained by time and money and space. We don't know the future. We do get tired. We can't see our way around some problems, can't imagine what's coming next. Because we are created beings, we are limited.

But acknowledging that limitation gives us the freedom to live with joy inside it.

"Do you not know that if you present yourselves to anyone as obedient slaves, you are slaves of the one whom you obey, either of sin, which leads to death, or of obedience, which leads to righteousness?" Paul wrote in Romans 6:16–18. "But thanks be to God, that you who were once slaves of sin have become obedient from the heart to the standard of teaching to which you were committed, and, having been set free from sin, have become slaves of righteousness."

Being a slave of righteousness means you can do the right thing. It means you can think well. It means you can be generous and kind, speak with graciousness, enjoy life. It means your conscience is clear. It means you don't need to worry, because your trust in God is firm.

The more you submit yourself to God and know and follow and worship him, the more you'll be able to trust your own Spirit-led impulses. You'll be free to make the right choices. Your temper won't be as quick; your words won't be as sharp. Your self-control will be stronger. You'll like yourself more. If there's anything I (Collin) could convey to youth today, it's this point. You don't find yourself by looking within and following your impulses. That's like freeing a toddler to eat whatever he wants and choose his own bedtime. We all need guidance. We all need an authority we can trust to look out for us— that friend or mentor who loves us so much that she tells us when we need to call our mom or take a different job or apologize to someone. Love supersedes freedom.

A good friend helps you see right through the world's promises that money or houses or sex or drugs will set you free and make you happy. In fact, you might even give up your retirement—or, if you're really smart, your entire life—for something that will *actually* set you free and make you happy.

Freedom from the World's Promises

JON FIELDER COULD'VE had a job anywhere.

He graduated summa cum laude from the prestigious Williams

College, then with honors from the elite Baylor College of Medicine. He followed with a residency in internal medicine at Johns Hopkins University, where he was named the top intern in his class.

Fielder would have been "at the top of his profession in the United States," said Mark Gerson, his college roommate who was just that—cofounding a successful peer-to-peer business learning community of top professionals. But while he was in medical school, Fielder came to Christ. Immediately serious about his faith, he took a year off to work with Mother Teresa's organization in Calcutta. He hadn't left the achievement lane, but now his energy was aimed in a different direction.

"I spent the long hours of my internship surfing missionary websites, such as they were—they weren't that advanced back then," he told us. "I was looking for a place to go when I finished my training."

He found one. A few months after he finished at Johns Hopkins, Fielder proposed to his girlfriend and (the next day) moved to Kenya.

Except for the engagement, the timing couldn't have been better. Fielder was "intensely interested" and trained in infectious diseases, and Africa was racked with one of the worst. AIDS deaths worldwide would peak in 2005 at about two million;[25] nearly three-quarters of them were in sub-Saharan Africa.[26]

In Kijabe, Kenya, the mission hospital didn't have enough staff or supplies or funding. Fielder was the only one there who knew how to treat HIV, but there wasn't enough money for the drugs he needed. He worked ten- to twelve-hour days, spent a year away from his fiancée, and was on call in the intensive care unit for two years without a substantial break. He worked with a pharmacy that kept inventory "less than perfectly," and he started an HIV program with staff who weren't trained in HIV care. He did his continuing education not with conferences in Boston or New York but with old textbooks and later with an internet connection and online journals.

"I once used an old textbook to mix peritoneal [abdominal] dialysis solutions for a patient whose kidneys had shut down as a complication from pregnancy," he told me (Sarah).

"What?" I squawked, amazed and a little horrified. "How did that turn out?"

Not much ruffles Fielder. "She survived," he said calmly.

Had Fielder stayed in the United States, he would likely have commanded a superior salary. He would've probably worked in a top-notch facility with skilled colleagues and a wide range of treatment options for patients. His prestige and income would've gained for him a type of freedom—to buy what he wanted or to vacation where he liked.

In rural African medicine, "the challenges are tremendous," he said. "Discouragement stems from witnessing so much early suffering and death, especially as a result of potentially treatable diseases. 'Why was this condition not diagnosed earlier?' 'Why did it take so long for the family to bring the patient to the hospital?' Because they had no money, of course."

He's worked with African patients who lack twelve dollars for an urgent surgery or fifty dollars for a needed diagnostic test. He's seen a patient with pneumonia die twenty minutes after the power cut out, because there was no fuel for the backup generator and the oxygen concentrator stopped working. "It can be totally demoralizing," he said.

So Fielder goes back to Matthew 25:31–46, Jesus's story of sorting the sheep and the goats based on how they treated "the least of these my brothers" during life. When he gets discouraged, he holds on to a passage from Fyodor Dostoyevsky's *The Brothers Karamazov:* "I predict that even in that very moment when you see with horror that despite all your efforts, you not only have not come nearer your goal but seem to have gotten farther from it, at that very moment—I predict this to you—you will suddenly reach your goal and will clearly behold over you the wonder-working power of the Lord, who all the while has been loving you, and all the while has been mysteriously guiding you," one character tells another.[27]

It's a twist on the endless, exhausting circling of trying to find yourself: if you're following God, he's guiding you through the wandering. And someday—sometimes even while you're here on earth— you'll see with blinding clarity the beauty of what he was doing.

Fielder can see some of that beauty already. By partnering with Gerson, he has been able to financially support thirty-eight mission hospitals in sixteen countries where health care is both scarce and desperately needed. The compassion and persistence of mission hospitals and doctors are "a powerful witness," he said. "Our partners contribute to the Great Commandment as well as to the Great Commission. Many minister in unreached areas or to unreached groups.

The facilities nurture the Christian faith of their staff. And they show to all the love and compassion of Christ in a world too often devoid of simple mercy."

Like Fielder, those doctors traded the prestige and comfort of practicing in the United States for the deprivation of a developing country. Doing so severely limited their choices, and in many ways, they can feel trapped in the dirt and distress. But by committing to something, by giving up their freedom to go hard after serving God and neighbor, they're gaining something far more valuable. They have the love and respect of the people who know them best.

Fielder's "energy and discipline are incredible," said Jonathan Mwiindi, who came on as a pharmacist at Fielder's hospital in 2003. "He doesn't work because he has nothing else to do but because he's driven to. All he sees is he's where God wants him to be and where he can have the most impact."

"He's the best person I know—a man of deep faith with complete determination to serve God by serving his children," Gerson said. "He makes you realize how much one person properly oriented can accomplish."

Fielder is a gospelbound Christian, and he can see right through the world's promises of freedom. That makes it easy for him to choose God's way.

Freedom *for* Loving God and Neighbor

WHEN YOU UNDERSTAND the emptiness and confusion of the world's version of freedom, the security and purpose in following Christ become that much more attractive. But gospel freedom isn't just *from* something—such as from false promises. We're also set free to move *toward* something.

The first thing we move toward is a deeper love of God—one that takes our hearts, souls, minds, and strength (Luke 10:27). And the second is a deeper love for our neighbors. Sometimes this means moving to meet them where they are.

Maybe you know of a congregation like College Park Church. The two of us love to share about this church. You hear a lot of negative stories out of megachurches. We've reported plenty of this bad news ourselves. But College Park doesn't feel self-satisfied, as if they've figured everything out. They're eager to share what God has taught them through trial and error. And that makes them a useful model for other churches that want to grow in love and effectiveness.

College Park sits in the first suburb north of Indianapolis. Carmel (originally named Bethlehem by Quakers back in the 1830s)[28] was ranked America's best place to live by CNN Money in 2012,[29] then by Niche in 2017 and 2018.[30]

Seven out of ten Carmel residents have graduated from college. Most own their own homes, the median value of which is more than $330,000. Their median household income tops $116,000.[31] Before a July 2020 shooting left one victim dead, no one had been killed there since a man shot his ex-wife and then himself in 2014.[32]

College Park fits in well, with 2,400 members, a gorgeous new sanctuary, and a nearly $14 million annual budget.[33] The church offers livestreamed church services, small groups (you can search for the one geographically closest to you), and online directions on how to donate stock.

But if you drive about thirty minutes south, you'll find a neighborhood that police used to call "the swamp." In Brookside, garbage is piled up in the alley. Windows are broken and boarded up, and lawns are overgrown. More than a third of houses here are abandoned.[34] In the wider area—called the Near Eastside—residents earn a median income of about $29,000 and less than 25 percent of adults have a college degree.[35] And the homicide rates have made it one of the most dangerous neighborhoods in Indianapolis.[36]

It's been that way for a while. Twenty-five years ago, when College Park asked the mayor which part of their city needed the most help, he pointed to Brookside. The church started a Saturday kids' church in a local community center in the mid-1990s, but the need seemed greater elsewhere. College Park spent the next ten years focusing on other countries.

"We wanted to go where people had never heard the name of Jesus," urban outreach pastor Dale Shaw said. "But we had a blind eye to some of the needs in America." It wasn't until a congregational survey in 2006 that the leadership realized their weakness on local missions and tapped Shaw to beef up the effort. He figured they'd focus on Brookside—after all, they already had that kids' church there.

Shaw wasn't naive; he knew it wasn't going to be easy. The set-up—a wealthy megachurch from the suburbs reaching back into the city—does not lend itself to easy success. Even with patience and hard work, the cultural and socioeconomic barriers often prove too hard to cross. He'd seen other churches try and fail and try and fail. So he relied heavily on bringing together a free legal clinic, a ministry for low-income mothers, a classical school with a heart for underprivileged neighborhoods, and a furniture-making company that employs homeless or formerly homeless men. He also leaned heavily on the relationships the kids' church had been building over the years and the knowledge the staff had of the neighborhood.

Before long, College Park's efforts in Brookside began to bear fruit. In fact, it looked like a textbook example of principles advocated in the award-winning book *When Helping Hurts*—listening and building relationships, grassroots ministries springing up in response to actual needs, long-term development instead of quick relief, centering everything around the gospel and the need to live biblically.

"I love the layers," said Kelly Altman, head of the classical Christian school in Brookside. "There are moms who attend [the moms' group] and dads who work at [the furniture business] and children who attend [the school]. There is an opportunity to redeem what has been broken for many years because there are so many layers around it. That's invaluable for families—that there is such strong partnership and so many people cheering them on."

The most influential cheerleaders are peers—members of churches that were already there as well as the men and women from the neighborhood who have already believed the gospel and begun to stabilize their lives. But the B-team cheerleaders are College Park members who started the moms' group and furniture business and who work at the legal clinic and school. They are also passionate, because nothing is more attractive or invigorating than watching the Spirit of God at work. ("I told my husband I would do this for free," Altman said.)

From the beginning, the thirty minutes from College Park to Brookside seemed like a long trip, especially since part of the ministry of the moms' group—called Heart Change—is picking up mothers who don't have their own vehicles. "You'd be driving to their homes and have to go around four cop cars just to get to the house," said Sarah Shaw, Dale's wife. Doing that over and over "defanged it. These are just people, and so many of them are young and isolated."

Heart Change volunteers went with moms to the bank, to the doctor, to the kids' schools. They attended baby showers and parent-teacher conferences and court proceedings. Eventually Sarah and founder Cindy Palmer began to joke with each other, "Boy, it sure would be easier if we lived down here."

And then somebody did. Dori Morton—who was involved with Heart Change—and her husband, Frank. "They fell in love with it," Dale Shaw said. "They said they had found more friends in one year than they did in twenty in [their suburb]."

Cindy and Sarah got a little more serious. "Look," their husbands said to each other. "It doesn't have to be forever. We could try it." A week later, Sarah found the house she wanted. When she and Dale walked in the first time, he felt "nauseated." It was falling apart, full of junk, and smelled horrible.

It's not that way now. The Shaws bought the place and gutted it; by the time I (Sarah) stayed over in the Shaws' home, it was a charming 1913 house with an open floor plan, a fireplace, and a screened-in porch off their second-floor bedroom. From it, I could see both their well-kept backyard and the scrap metal piled in the neighbor's.

Another College Park couple moved in and then another. When we went for a bike ride, Dale kept pointing out families who were from College Park or who were connected with efforts the church was supporting. It seemed like he knew *everybody*.

Today there are twelve College Park families living within a few blocks of one another and more thinking about making the move. "They're not just cosmetically fixing the houses—they're making them nice," said Todd Ralston, who has lived in Brookside since the early seventies. The Shaws now live two doors down from him.

"You look at it, and it stands out, like, 'Wow. I didn't know the street could look like that,'" Ralston said. "That is very uplifting. Even if it's one house or two, that can change a whole block." (And Dale Shaw makes sure it's just a house or two—he's mindful of spacing, making sure church members aren't gentrifying the neighborhood.)

But the advantages are deeper than stable home ownership and better-kept lawns. "Most of our moms only experience community when they're in class with us," Cindy Palmer said. "Most of these women live in isolation. Many are afraid that if anyone comes in your house, they're seeing what you have so they can come and steal it, or to see how you're living so they can report you to the [Department of Child Services]." Now that Heart Change women are living in the same neighborhood, they walk together—and with Heart Change mentors—on Tuesday evenings. They have coffee on Saturdays. They sit and talk on one another's porches.

By the end of 2016, a media report called the Brookside neighborhood "one of Indy's most improved neighborhoods," where "crime and drug activity are both down."[37]

"It's amazing to see how this place has changed," said Indianapolis police spokesman Aaron Hamer, who patrolled in Brookside when he joined the department eleven years ago. (He attends the College Park Fishers congregation.)

It's a great story—and one that churches could emulate. But it's not perfect. The blocks with College Park homes feel moderately safe (no bars on the doors or windows), but someone dumped the bodies of three decomposing dogs a few streets over.[38] In the past few years, a man was shot dead in the middle of the afternoon,[39] a drug dealer was found riddled with bullets,[40] and at least three children were hit by bullets—while they were *inside* their homes.[41]

But "we think the gospel has the power to light up the whole neighborhood," Dale Shaw said. He's already seen it, in the smiles and waves of neighbors, in the kids giving speeches at school and the men praying before work at the furniture company, in the funeral he did for a neighbor in which he laid out the gospel message. He sees it in the houses themselves, with their fresh paint and cut lawns and bright flowers. And he sees it in himself, in his prejudices that have been challenged and his heart that has been softened.

"God is on the move," he said. "He keeps changing us."

That's a common sentiment. "I can see people in poverty, and I'm not intimidated by that anymore," Heart Change volunteer coordinator Kris Schneider said. "I can talk to them. I love the relationships I've formed with the women here and what that does for me and my heart." Her heart change can hardly be overstated. Schneider and her husband have adopted two children of a Heart Change mother who could no longer parent.

"We see through a glass darkly—we cannot get a full picture," Altman said. "God does far more with our 'yes' than we could ever do by plan or intent. It's definitely a privilege to be here—sometimes I feel like I need to pinch myself."

Altman and Schneider are giving up their freedom—to relax, to watch television, to travel extensively, to focus on themselves. The Shaws and the Palmers are giving up their freedom—to live in safety, to have a beautiful-looking block, to have fewer worries about neighbors fighting or dealing drugs.

They're trading it for a level of community and purpose they never would've found in their old neighborhoods. They realized that physical safety doesn't guarantee spiritual flourishing. They found joy in commitment to others rather than in a futile and anxiety-inducing attempt to protect themselves from any discomfort. Their lives have been changed—for the better—by downward mobility.

Freedom to Follow God Wherever He Leads

It's possible God is calling you to live in an underprivileged neighborhood in your own town. Or it's possible he's calling you to the mission field. Or he might be calling you to work in the halls of power in Washington, DC, to befriend neighbors in a comfortable suburb in Houston, or to minister to celebrities in Beverly Hills.

The point of giving up your freedom isn't that you always get left with the worst or hardest option. It's that you always choose to follow God. You trust his love and design for you enough that you're willing to go where he leads you.

Sometimes that's through Harvard Law School and a Supreme Court clerkship to a job at one of the most prestigious law firms in the country. And sometimes that's to years of caring for a wife with chronic illness.

Meet twins Alex and Brett Harris. They wrote *Do Hard Things: A Teenage Rebellion Against Low Expectations* when they were teens themselves.[42] Get up early, they told readers. Step out of your comfort zone. Do more than what's required. Find a cause. Be faithful. Go against the crowd. Be better than your culture expects.

The Harris twins, then eighteen, were leading by example. They worked through the summer to finish their (home school) high school at sixteen, then clerked with the Alabama Supreme Court. They organized a statewide grassroots political campaign. They started a blog, launched the Rebelution movement (the website has more than forty-seven million page views), wrote their book (which has sold more than five hundred thousand copies), and spoke at conferences.

They didn't slow down when they turned twenty. The twins enrolled at Patrick Henry College, took first place in the moot court nationals, and wrote another book.[43] They dated and married their wives, cared for and buried their mother, and chose directions for their careers. Since then, God has taken Alex and Brett, now thirty-two, in starkly different directions that illustrate the Lord's mysterious plans and purposes as he calls us to lay down our freedom and follow him.

"We do hard things, not in order to be saved, but because we are saved," Brett told me (Sarah). "Our willingness to obey God even when it's hard magnifies the worth of Christ, because in our hard obedience we're communicating to the world that Jesus is more valuable than comfort, than ease, than staying safe."

When you're younger, the hard choices aren't always big ones or always between right and wrong—opting to read rather than watch TV, to study rather than play video games, to join the debate team rather than the basketball team. But "doing hard things in one season prepares you to step into the next with momentum and purpose," Alex said. Turns out, they both needed all the preparation they could get.

Brett works with the Rebelution movement but has spent most of his time caring for his wife, Ana, who suffers from Lyme disease. Over the years they have moved multiple times searching for answers—including a long stint camping in the desert to detox from mold. Along with keeping track of doctors' appointments and medical options, Brett cooked for her, bathed her, carried her up the stairs, and, during her sickest months, worked with her through the panic attacks induced by the bacterial infection in her brain.

Suffering with Ana sometimes got so bad that he just felt "utterly helpless," Brett said. "And in that moment you either self-destruct or you throw yourself on God's mercy. You cannot look intense suffering in the face without making the choice between faith and cynicism. It either hardens you or melts you."

As Brett and Ana cried out to Jesus, they found freedom in accepting their life as it is for now. "This is not some big distraction. This is not some huge detour. This is the path God has for us, and it leads somewhere good. It could even be our defining moment."

God has not abandoned them. In fact, he has prepared Brett through the discipline of doing hard things. When their mother, Sono Harris, was diagnosed with cancer, Alex and Brett were sophomores in college. That summer, Brett was one of her primary caregivers. The difficult months he spent with her helped prepare him for caring for his wife. "You don't choose what you're going to bear down the road, and if you haven't worked the muscle [of doing hard things], it's going to crush you," he said. "That's what I see happening to many others."

Sometimes exercising that muscle just plain wears you out. "Caretaking can make you weary, because you're thinking, *This is not what I wanted my life, my marriage, to be like*," Brett said. Ana's pain has been excruciating, and staying on top of her treatment has been exhausting.

"I don't want my wife to have to go through this," he said. "I didn't want to go through this. It's easy to focus on the feeling that this is not the life I want, rather than on the reality that this is the life God has for me."

Remembering the story of Joseph—and God's faithfulness over a lifetime—refocuses him. "Joseph's story looked pretty bleak for a while, but God was working in his heart and preparing him for future service," Brett said. "His story reminds me that my plan for my life is not as good as God's plan."

Loving Ana and laying down his life for her are obviously what God wants him to do, Brett said. "What keeps me going is knowing that this is what I'm supposed to be doing. This is not an interruption of God's plan for my life. This is his plan for my life, at least for a season. And at the end of the day, I know this is what I will wish I had done."

As an attorney, Alex also finds faithfulness in small tasks the most difficult. "The things people don't praise you for, that don't earn the same level of admiration from your peers, are harder, but those are usually the more important things," he said. As a law student, a law clerk to Judge Neil Gorsuch and Supreme Court Justice Anthony Kennedy, and now an attorney, Alex has had to make daily choices to prioritize time with his wife, Courtney, and their young daughter.

You can't "do it all" and do a good job, he said. But you can do everything God has called you to do. And so far, the Harris brothers offer living proof.

"I feel like Alex's and my stories thus far are two different testimonies to the power of doing hard things and rebelling against low expectations," Brett said. "Alex is demonstrating the incredible momentum that you can have, and the level of competence and character that can be achieved, if you start pursuing them at a young age."

Brett's life, on the other hand, illustrates the need to do hard things in order to prepare for the brokenness of our world. "Quiet faithfulness, laying your life down daily for another person—that is what God calls us to as believers," Alex said. "It's incredibly hard, and it's not glamorous, but it brings glory to God. And that's exactly what Brett is doing."

Both twins were ready because for years they'd been choosing to expect more of themselves for the sake of God and their neighbors. They know that God calls gospelbound Christians to give up their freedom so they can partake in his glory. And they find joy in his service.

Whom Will You Serve?

Giving up your freedom doesn't sound appealing, unless you remember you never really had any to begin with—at least not in the way we often imagine freedom. Even those with millions of dollars and hours of uncommitted time are bound by worries and threats and exhaustion.

We're all tied down not only by our mortality but also by the God-shaped hole inside our hearts. We all worship something, which means we all serve something. Some of us are serving money. Others are serving "keeping the options open." And others are serving comfort or ambition.

Realizing that truth will help you make the only decision that really matters: Whom or what will you serve? Gospelbound Christians are bound to God. They are serving the One who made them, who guides them, who provides for them. The work they're called to is almost always difficult. But it's always—*always*—worth it.

You might be called to give up your freedom in order to give birth to, foster, or adopt a child (or a bunch of them). You might be called to give up your weekends to work in a food pantry or volunteer at a pregnancy clinic. You might be called to give up your free time to babysit for a single mom or have a long conversation with a neighbor. You might even be called to give yourself up to a different job, a different town, or a different country.

These choices might not come naturally in an anxious age obsessed with freedom—until you realize that anxiety and freedom are linked. You weren't made to maximize pleasure through endless choice. We don't celebrate the person who reaches the end of his life free of commitments. We honor the person who's given her life to lifting others, to making the world a little more just—and thus free—for all.

Giving away our freedom means disciplining our minds and hearts to turn first to the Lord, to see the world as he does. When we do that, "we know that our old self was crucified with him in order that the body of sin might be brought to nothing, so that we would no longer be enslaved to sin," as Paul wrote in Romans 6:6–8, 10. "For one who has died has been set free from sin. Now if we have died with Christ, we believe that we will also live with him. . . . For the death he died he died to sin, once for all, but the life he lives he lives to God."

And "if the Son sets you free," Jesus said, "you will be free indeed" (John 8:36).

No Apology Needed

Talk has never been cheaper—because we have too much of it. It's a matter of supply and demand. We produce an unprecedented volume of content through talk radio, social media, websites, and cable news. We consume more and more while working out and washing dishes and relaxing before bed and commuting to work and school. But how can anyone keep up? And how can anyone know whom to trust?

Amid this glut, Christians have put a lot of emphasis on getting our message right and getting it out. Much money and hope have been invested in developing better arguments that will convince our neighbors to trust Jesus. We write smart books on apologetics, on defending the faith. We develop helpful courses. We publish thoughtful podcasts. The church has improved in how we teach the truth. But what if God wants more from us? And what if our time and place demand another priority?

The apostle Paul might be considered our patron saint of apologetics. We admire his innovative preaching from Mars Hill in Athens in Acts 17. And we quote his letter to the Corinthians: "We destroy arguments and every lofty opinion raised against the knowledge of God, and take every thought captive to obey Christ" (2 Corinthians 10:5).

Some may take that verse and head straight to Facebook to destroy arguments and every lofty opinion raised against the knowledge of God! Someone is wrong on the internet! But what reason did Paul give for why we take every thought captive? So that we might obey Christ. God intends our belief to result in godly behavior. It's easier in many cases to speak the truth than to live the truth. Sometimes, in our zeal to defend God, we stretch the truth or slander our opponents. We end up needing to apologize for our apologetics. Sadly, you don't need to look long to find Christians willing to lie because they think their lies will advance the truth.

But such a disconnect would not have made sense to Paul. Elsewhere he likewise married truth and obedience in a curious phrase: "obey the truth." You see it in Romans 2:6–8:

> He will render to each one according to his works: to those who by patience in well-doing seek for glory and honor and immortality, he will give eternal life; but for those who are self-seeking and do not obey the truth, but obey unrighteousness, there will be wrath and fury.

We tend to think of truth as an exclusively cognitive category. It's a matter of orthodoxy, right belief, rather than orthopraxy, right behavior. But Scripture doesn't draw such a sharp distinction between truth and obedience. They're both necessary. You can't have one without the other. If you're lying for the sake of truth, you're not working for God.

We know that Paul reserved some really harsh words for preachers who change or reject his message. That seems to be the context for his using the phrase "obeying the truth" in Galatians 5:7. The so-called circumcision party had distorted the truth by saying that Gentiles must obey the law and be circumcised. Obeying the truth, in this case, means enjoying the freedom of the gospel, received by faith.

But listen to what he said to the teachers who have the right message but not the right behavior (Romans 2:21–24). He condemned the preachers who say stealing is wrong but still steal and those who condemn adultery while they commit adultery. This is hypocrisy. Their words don't match their actions. They're playacting. They boast in the law, but according to Paul, they dishonor God by breaking the law. And in verse 24 he quoted the condemnation of Isaiah 52:5: "The name of God is blasphemed among the Gentiles because of you."

This passage tells us that we can preach the right message but if we don't obey the truth, we hinder others from believing God. That's sobering. Churches get a lot of unfair criticism. But we probably all know churches that would not make anyone want to be a Christian. They twist the teaching of Jesus and his gospel message, and they condemn

others for doing what they themselves practice. They're not characterized by faith, hope, or love. They may take the name of Jesus, but they
don't look or sound like him. When we meet people who grew up in or
visited these churches, we want to apologize to them on behalf of other
Christians. We wish they could enjoy the safety, freedom, and love of a
church where God's people obey him. Our hearts ache for friends who
never knew God's love even when they knew God's people.

But there's another side to this story. And it should encourage us.
Paul implied that if we obey the truth, we will encourage others to
follow God. You don't need to argue. You don't need to perfect an answer to every possible objection. You don't need to answer every er-
roneous comment on Facebook. You don't need to say or do anything
special except to live out the power of the Spirit, who dwells in you.

When we live in the light, no apology is needed.

Outlive Our Neighbors

ONE OF THE most capable and determined apologists of the twentieth
century was Carl F. H. Henry. You can still find and own all six vol-
umes and all three thousand pages of his landmark work, *God, Revelation, and Authority*. If anyone believed in the power of arguments and
in the urgency of writing, it was Henry, who also served as the first
editor of *Christianity Today* magazine. And this great theologian often
practiced evangelism with strangers. Imagine sitting next to him on
one of his many flights around the world as an ambassador for World
Vision. Rarely did he enter a debate he couldn't win, even going so
far as to take on the titanic intellect of theologian Karl Barth in one
famous exchange.

But Henry didn't necessarily think good arguments would make
the world believe in Jesus. He didn't put all his eggs in the basket of
apologetics. He believed the modern mind would turn to Jesus when
skeptics saw Christians obey the truth. Listen to what he wrote in his
1947 classic, *The Uneasy Conscience of Modern Fundamentalism*:

> The evangelical task primarily is the preaching of the
> Gospel, in the interest of individual regeneration by the
> supernatural grace of God, in such a way that divine re-
> demption can be recognized as the best solution of our

problems, individual and social. This produces within history, through the regenerative work of the Holy Spirit, a divine society that transcends national and international lines. The corporate testimony of believers, in their purity of life, should provide for the world an example of the divine dynamic to overcome evils in every realm. The social problems of our day are much more complex than in apostolic times, but they do not on that account differ in principle. When the twentieth century church begins to "out-live" its environment as the first century church outreached its pagan neighbors, the modern mind, too, will stop casting about for other solutions.[1]

There's a whole lot going on this passage. Henry affirmed that our first task as Christians is to tell people the good news about Jesus. It's always necessary to use words when preaching the gospel. People won't conclude just from watching your life that Jesus is the Son of God, that he died and rose for sinners, and that he is coming again soon to renew the heavens and the earth. You must tell them this good news and call them to repent of their sin and believe.

When they believe, Henry observed, this individual regeneration will produce "a divine society" that displays "the divine dynamic" in and for our troubled world. Basically, our unbelieving friends and families should be able to look at us and see something different and compelling. They should see how the bonds of the Spirit bring together people who don't normally get along. They should see people making peace across the borders of our violent age. They should see us love one another in ways that don't make sense apart from the blood of Christ. Henry wasn't setting any new expectation here. He was echoing the teaching of Jesus from John 13:34–35:

> A new commandment I give to you, that you love one another: just as I have loved you, you also are to love one another. By this all people will know that you are my disciples, if you have love for one another.

They will know we are Christians by our love. So, what happens when we don't love one another? When we don't set an example for the world? Henry wrote in the aftermath of the Second World War.

The great Christian nations of the West had not once but twice unleashed unprecedented violence on one another. Is it any wonder the Western church declined in this so-called Christian century, which had started with such hopefulness? What hope could Christians offer the world while they killed one another in the trenches of Verdun and the forests of Bastogne?

Yet Henry remained hopeful that the church could chart a different course. Christians could still outlive their neighbors. After all, they had done so in the early church. Early Christians had little to no political power, yet in the power of the Holy Spirit, they turned the world upside down. Not even persecution could dissuade many pagans from forsaking false gods and worshipping Jesus instead. They realized nothing and no one else could solve their problems. Though Christians did not set out to conquer the Roman Empire, their practice of evangelism and ethic of love effected the greatest social change the world has yet known. If God was for them—and if he is for us—then who can be against us?

Maybe the problems today in a nuclear age are more complex, Henry admitted. But so long as humanity's central problem remains alienation from one another and from God in sin, the cross of Christ remains the only ultimate solution to the problem of evil and death. The world will realize and embrace this solution when it sees born-again Christians "obey the truth" in love for one another.

Crisis of Confidence

NEARLY SEVENTY-FIVE YEARS after Henry wrote this little book, we once again face a crisis of confidence in the power of the gospel to change societies. We sense that we're losing the arguments in the public square. We've lost ground in sexual ethics and religious liberty. Youth show much less interest in Christianity compared with their grandparents. We see Christians lose their jobs for believing the Bible. We see universities refuse to recognize Christian ministries so they cannot meet on campus. We fear that an unfavorable election or Supreme Court decision could inhibit our ministry or even silence our preaching. We almost sense the need to apologize for our beliefs, as if catching them from us would be harmful to our neighbors' health.

But is our situation any more dire than Henry's? He had lived through the two greatest disasters in world history and was writing this book just two years before the Soviet Union would complete its first successful nuclear test. Following this fateful day in 1949, a Communist and atheist state bent on world domination would develop the capability of destroying the planet with a single command. Can you imagine the fear and anxiety? Yet Henry saw the Lord raise up evangelical preachers and churches to lead a mass-scale revival in mid-twentieth-century America, an era of unprecedented church attendance, when Billy Graham and Martin Luther King Jr. shaped the national conscience.

In the same way, we see a different story unfolding today. We see Christians boldly championing Jesus in ways the world finds intriguing. We see open doors for the gospel in some of the most unlikely places, from strip clubs to the Arabian Peninsula. We see a world starving for meaning and purpose and hope—and finding all that and more in the gospel. We see a compelling apologetic emerging as Christians outlive their coworkers and families and friends with resolute hope.

We're not saying it's easy. It's true that, in many places and many ways, it's hard to identify as a Christian. Indeed, it's always been hard in some way or another. It was hard in Henry's day. It was hard in the days of Jesus and Paul.

And it was hard in the second century. Scholars of this dynamic period of church history have identified a number of clues for why the church grew even amid continued opposition to Christianity after the death of the apostles. Larry Hurtado, the late scholar of second-century Christianity, described these believers' lived apologetics as accessible and odd:

> A successful religious movement must retain a certain level of continuity with its cultural setting, and yet it must also "maintain a medium level of tension" with that setting as well. That is, a movement must avoid being seen as completely alien or incomprehensible. But, on the other hand, it must also have what I mean by distinctives, distinguishing features that set it apart in its cultural setting, including the behavioral demands made upon its

converts. There has to be a clear difference between being an insider to the group and an outsider.[2]

"Accessible and odd" is how the two of us like to think of gospelbound Christians. They're different from the world but in a way that makes you want to follow their lead. Another scholar of second-century Christianity, Alan Kreider, echoed Hurtado. Church leaders from this era wrote landmark theological and apologetic works to define and defend the faith. But Kreider contended that it was example, more than argument, that compelled many Romans to believe in Jesus:

> It was not primarily what the Christians said that carried weight with outsiders; it was what they did and embodied that was both disconcerting and converting. It was their habitus—their reflexes and ways of life that suggested that there was another way to perceive reality—that made the Christians interesting, challenging, and worth investigating.[3]

That's another good phrase to describe gospelbound Christians and their resolute hope: "disconcerting and converting." When anxiety levels have spiked and happiness has declined, why shouldn't Christians be disconcerting? This is not the time when Christians should be trying to fit in. Yes, we should do everything we can to make the gospel comprehensible—that is, so that our neighbors can understand. But we should not seek to make them comfortable in their fear and anxiety. For the sake of Jesus Christ, gospelbound Christians show a better way in faith and love. Only their lived apologetics can expose the lie that more, louder arguments will finally win the day.

If we don't set this example, to what alternative will the world turn?

Small Actions Add Up

BASED ON WHAT we see on social media and in political campaigns, the world believes that if you'll just hate your enemies a little more, you can finally defeat them. This isn't so much a new revelation as the default human condition. So we're not the first Christians to face this challenge. Consider the example of African American Christians.

It's nothing short of a miracle that the United States did not erupt in a second, far deadlier civil war one hundred years after the first one ended. Even so, African Americans suffered violence and sometimes even death as they demanded the rights due to them as men and women made in the image of God and subject to the protection of the US Constitution.

The fact that such a war never broke out owes much to Christian leaders like Fannie Lou Hamer, who endured a brutal beating by white police officers in 1963. Her supposed crime? She wanted African Americans to be able to vote. Hamer loved her enemies enough to seek justice on earth and warn them of God's ultimate justice. In an exchange with her jailer's wife, Hamer told her to read Proverbs 26:26: "Though his hatred be covered with deception, his wickedness will be exposed in the assembly." She warned the jailer himself that he would one day stand before God and give account for his actions.

As a Christian, Hamer preached the gospel and modeled the example of Jesus. She embodied 1 Peter 2:22–23: "He committed no sin, neither was deceit found in his mouth. When he was reviled, he did not revile in return; when he suffered, he did not threaten, but continued entrusting himself to him who judges justly."

Hamer's lived apologetic challenged white authorities who honored Jesus with their lips while their hearts were far from him (Isaiah 29:13). She loved them enough to warn them of God's wrath. She loved them enough to leave vengeance to God (Deuteronomy 32:35). Her example today endures as a Christian model for a world that doesn't know how to end the cycle of violence and recrimination.

And she's not alone. Alongside Hamer's call for justice, we've seen Christians extend forgiveness to their enemies. Their stories stand out precisely because the world doesn't understand, even as it is unexpectedly captivated by this love. Recall the shocking 2015 murders at Emanuel AME Church in Charleston, South Carolina, where twenty-one-year-old white supremacist Dylann Roof sat through a Bible study in the famed historically black church before gunning down nine of the attendees. Remember that the grieved community never sought revenge against Roof or his relations. Wouldn't the world have judged them justified in doing so? Isn't that the natural human response? How would you have responded if a stranger had studied the Bible alongside your mother or grandfather or husband

and then stood up and shot your family member in cold blood? If we're honest, we probably would not have offered love and forgiveness to the killer.

"It should shock us when we encounter a situation in which a victim *doesn't* take revenge," pastor Vermon Pierre observed after this mass shooting. "When someone chooses to forgive, we are watching someone pay an enormously heavy and personal cost. Historically, the black church has arguably paid this bill more than most other communities in America. We should never take this forgiveness for granted. We should marvel and thank God every time we see it."[4]

Hopefully, you will never suffer the way Hamer or the Charleston Nine did. But you won't need to go looking for your own hardship. In life, enemies always find you. How will you treat them? If justice and vengeance belong to God, you can afford to love them. Jesus told us to love our enemies and pray for those who persecute us (Matthew 5:44). All of us can love the people who love us back. But the world takes notice when we love the people who hurt us and cannot or will not love us back.

Some of the gospelbound Christians we've highlighted might feel out of reach to you. They're doing harder things than you can ever imagine attempting. But we don't want you to be discouraged by their example. We want you to see in the lives of Hamer and the Charleston Nine that Jesus will never leave or forsake you, no matter what comes your way. That's why you don't need to be fearful or anxious. You can take that next step of resolute hope in faith and love. It might be small, and only a few people may ever know. Setting a seat at the dinner table for your neighbor. Saying no to sexual temptation. Volunteering at the food bank. Listening to and learning from someone who doesn't look like you. Praying for joy when the pain doesn't go away. Upholding your wedding vows. Working hard in a job you don't always love.

But small actions add up to a much better world than what you see portrayed in media aimed at making you fear and loathe the world God loves (John 3:16). We tend to spend a lot of time worrying about things, like elections and court decisions, that we cannot control. And then we respond with actions, such as complaining on social media, that cannot make much difference. We hope that in this book you've learned from the lived apologetics of gospelbound Christians how you can trust Jesus no matter what happens in the news, no matter whether the polls show Christian beliefs waxing or waning.

Win the West?

MANY OF THE best minds in the church today have focused their attention on the problem of what to do in Western nations that have turned away from their Christian formation. Some of them you've already met in this book as we've studied their work. Longtime New York City pastor Tim Keller described the challenge this way:

> We are entering a new era in which, in many places in the West, there is not only no social benefit to being a Christian, but an actual social cost to espousing faith. Culture is becoming more actively hostile toward Christian beliefs and practices. Semi-biblical, generically religious beliefs in God, truth, sin, and the afterlife (the "religious dots") are disappearing in more and more people as culture produces people for whom Christianity is not only offensive, but incomprehensible. Therefore, we must find ways of evangelizing people who lack the "religious dots" and would never think of coming to church.[5]

Carl Trueman has brilliantly explained how the last several centuries have delivered us to this point. Even acknowledging challenges unique to our post-Christian age, Trueman sees much resemblance to the second century, the times of the early Christians. It's daunting to imagine facing that level of opposition in our lifetimes.

> The second-century world is, in a sense, our world, where Christianity is a choice—and a choice likely at some point to run afoul of the authorities.
>
> It was that second-century world, of course, that laid down the foundations for the later successes of the third and fourth centuries. And she did it by what means? By existing as a close-knit, doctrinally bounded community that required her members to act consistently with their faith and to be good citizens of the earthly city as far

as good citizenship was compatible with faithfulness to Christ. How we do that today and where the limits are—these are the pressing questions of this present moment and beyond the scope of this volume. But it is a discussion to which I hope the narratives and analyses I have offered here might form a helpful prolegomenon.[6]

Trueman wrote those words at the end of his book on the modern self. We hope our book, in turn, has been able to show what that good citizenship and Christian faithfulness look like today. Probably not many of the gospelbound Christians we've profiled could describe why the West has turned against Christianity. Probably not many of them have closely studied the second century either. But they're still showing us the way of resolute hope in hostile cultures. They expect to fight for faith amid this world that put Christ to death on the cross.

It's easy to think in our communications age that we can or should break through the growing skepticism toward Christianity with better, stronger, louder arguments. Or that if we can apologize for strange and hurtful things Christians have done, we'll find friendly audiences for the gospel. Both approaches could be warranted, depending on the situation.

But when we look at where and how the church is acting and growing around the world, the two of us see much cause for rejoicing and much reason for confidence. We see resolute hope in Jesus Christ. We see gospelbound Christians—rooted in unchanging truth, looking forward to Christ's glorious return.

We don't see Christians cowering as they await the next court decision. We don't see them overly worried about offending their neighbors. We see them loving their enemies, caring for the weak, suffering with joy, and living with honor. We see them giving away their freedom, embracing the future, and setting another seat at the table. We see them following Jesus and calling others to follow him too. We see them embodying an apologetic for the gospel, demonstrating the fruit of faith as they explicitly invite others to believe in Jesus.

When talk is cheap, our actions speak. And no apology is needed.

Introduction:
Why You're Anxious and Afraid

1. What makes you anxious? What keeps you up at night?

2. Read Ecclesiastes 1:9. In what ways does it feel like American culture is in the midst of immense upheaval? At the same time, how is it true that there's "nothing new under the sun"?

3. Where do you typically get most of your news? How does it affect the way you view the world?

4. Read Philippians 4:8. How could you better honor God in your thought life—by what you put in, the way you train yourself to think, and what comes out?

5. When you think of Bible stories or even Christian biographies, how do stories of real people encourage your faith? Why do we need to hear and share these stories with one another?

6. Read 1 Peter 1:13. How can this verse affect the way you read the news?

7. Read Matthew 6:25–33. What do these verses teach us about God and his involvement in the world? How could you apply the truth of this passage to your upcoming week?

Chapter 1:
Resolute Hope

1. Consider what you are hoping for this week. In what ways is your hope fixed on earthly outcomes? In what ways is it focused on spiritual and eternal outcomes?

2. Read Psalm 33:17, Proverbs 21:1, and Isaiah 20:5–6. As you consider these verses, how can Christians engage in politics, both locally and nationally, while avoiding putting their hope in political outcomes? What would that look like in practice?

3. Read Isaiah 40:27–31, and consider these questions: In what ways does considering ourselves powerful stifle our dependence on God? How does an understanding of our weakness and dependence on God increase our strength? Could it be that proximity to power is not a strength but actually a hindrance to genuine Christlike faith and action?

4. Read Hebrews 12:11. Can you think of a time you were disciplined and were grateful for it? Or should have been disciplined and were not? What is the difference between God's discipline of his children and God's punishment for sin?

5. How would thinking big (about God's love and faithfulness) and thinking small (about how to help your family or next-door neighbor) ease your anxiety?

6. Read Psalm 77, and consider God's faithfulness to you in the past. How could remembering God's faithfulness improve the way you work or rest or clean the house or run errands?

Chapter 2:
Gospelbound Christians
Embrace the Future

1. What emotions do you feel when you think about tomorrow? About next year? The next ten years?

2. Read Ezekiel 28:26, Luke 13:29, and Romans 6:5. What emotions do you feel when you think about living in the new creation? What are you most looking forward to?

3. In your everyday life, do you tend to lean toward nostalgia (wishing for or remembering a perfect past) or progressivism (wishing or working for a perfect future)? What are the benefits of that way of thinking? What are the dangers?

4. Read Philippians 1:20–26. For Paul, both death and life lead to a win. C. S. Lewis wrote, "Aim at Heaven and you will get earth 'thrown in': aim at earth and you will get neither." How could this counterintuitive truth help you prioritize your tasks? Your time?

5. John and Keri Folmar are giving away the best years of their lives. The Summit Church is giving away some of its best leaders and part of its budget. How can you identify your best? Are there ways to offer that best to the Lord?

6. Americans don't often think about the afterlife. Logically, if our existence ends when we die, how would we expect people to live? Do you see people living like that? Are there reasons—other than being a Christian—that a person would live in view of eternity?

7. Read John 14:1–4. How can you better orient your daily life to your certain future with God? How does being certain of your future change the way you mow the lawn? Spend your weekends? Raise your kids?

Chapter 3:
Gospelbound Christians
Live with Honor

1. Can you think of a time when you achieved a goal but found that you didn't feel as amazing as you thought you would? Or that the amazing feeling didn't last as long as you'd hoped?

2. Read Hosea 8:7. Our decisions have consequences—what we sow, we reap. Is living with honor compatible with constantly keeping your options open, not committing to anything in case something better comes along? Do you live this way?

3. *Honor* is an old-fashioned word, but we know many people keeping their commitments, valuing others, and making the right choices even when it's hard. Can you think of an everyday example of how we could work with honor? Parent with honor? Be a church member with honor? Be a friend with honor?

4. The Lord is always honorable. Read Psalm 34:8, Psalm 100:5, and Psalm 135:3. Rachel Gilson said to always consider what God is saying from the source of his character. Can you think of some things God says that people think are arbitrary or cruel? How does considering his goodness change how we understand his commands?

5. If unhindered sexual encounters or enormous wealth fails to bring joy or lasting satisfaction, why does our society keep chasing those things? Why are people pursuing what can be found instead in the gospel?

6. No activity is neutral before God—not sending emails or participating in meetings or changing diapers. God is sovereign over all those things, and doing them with honor gives him glory. How does that change the way you view your mundane, everyday tasks? How does a person do laundry to the glory of God? Write a memo? Invest a retirement account?

7. It's tempting to try to live honorably by trying extra hard. But gospelbound Christians aren't trying to earn honor. They behave honorably because they're already made honorable through Jesus. When we feel like putting people down or making the wrong choice because it's easy, we need to ask God for help. What are some ways we can remember to do that? Are there people who can hold us accountable? Habits we can practice?

Chapter 4:
Gospelbound Christians
Suffer with Joy

1. Read Matthew 5:11. The Bible doesn't define the scope of what we should consider Christian persecution. Would

you consider a pastor questioned by police in China to be persecuted? What about a Christian in Nigeria who is killed in a civil war? What about a baker who is sued for refusing to bake a cake for a same-sex wedding? What about someone who is teased at the office because he or she won't go out drinking after work?

2. What is it about the prosperity gospel that we find so attractive?

3. It's often easier to handle things if we can see them coming. Read 2 Timothy 3:12, 1 Peter 4:12–14, and 1 John 3:13. Why do we feel scared of persecution? What's the worst thing that could happen to us?

4. If we aren't suffering, does that mean we're doing something wrong? That we're not being Christian enough?

5. Read Romans 5:3 and Romans 12:12. Rather than feeling fear or anger, Paul tells us to find joy in our sufferings. Have you ever done that? How is that possible? How did John Perkins do it? How do Chinese Christians do it?

6. Suffering reminds us that we're caught between heaven and earth, between the "already" and "not yet." How can that reminder comfort us?

7. How could a Christian photographer who is being taken to court for refusing to photograph a same-sex wedding suffer joyfully? How could a person who is unfairly targeted by police suffer joyfully? How could a person in a difficult work or home situation suffer joyfully?

8. We know that suffering doesn't automatically produce righteousness—sometimes it produces pride or self-pity. How can we endure suffering faithfully, in a way that leads us deeper and deeper into Christ?

Chapter 5:
Gospelbound Christians
Care for the Weak

1. Has there been a time recently when you've been frustrated by weakness, either in yourself or in others? What made it so disappointing?

2. Read Matthew 26:11. People are poor not just financially but also physically, emotionally, and spiritually. We're all needy in some areas, and we all need the gospel. What are some of the needs you see in people around you? In yourself?

3. Our inability to fix poverty can be frustrating. John Piper said, "My job is faithfulness. God's is fruitfulness." How would believing this statement affect *how* you work? What would you do more of? Less of?

4. As long as we live in a sinful world, we'll never get to the end of the problems, as IJM and Rachelle Starr illustrate. But they keep working, tackling challenges one at a time. What challenges seem overwhelming to you? Is there a single step you could take—volunteering on a weekend or cooking a meal for someone or making a phone call—that would begin to help?

5. Running toward the hurting is an instinct developed not just through Bible and theological reading but through practice. Rick Sacra moved toward the Ebola outbreak in a dramatic way. But years before, his first step was to physically come close to those who needed his medical skills. Are there people you know who are hurting? How can you physically move toward them? If you can't think of anyone, how could you find someone who needs help?

6. Read Exodus 22:22, Deuteronomy 10:18, and Isaiah 1:17. The unborn are perhaps the weakest of all. Protesting abortion is important, but we know Christian help doesn't end there. Is your church a welcoming place for single moms? How could you reach out to support and serve more of the women who chose life for their children?

7. Gospelbound Christians are able to serve with supernatural grit because they love God more than anything else and because he supplies their meaning and energy and direction. What habits can you cultivate that will deepen your love of the Lord?

Chapter 6:
Gospelbound Christians
Set Another Seat at the Table

1. Do you know your neighbors? What are a few ways you could reach out to them or get to know them better?

2. Read Romans 12:13–18. How have you seen people doing this in real life? Consider a time you've felt lonely or isolated. Was there a Bible verse or truth that you used for comfort? Was there a person who reached out to you?

3. The Christian life is communal. How could you engage more with other believers in order to solidify your faith and theirs?

4. Do new people often come into your church? What are some ways your church could be more welcoming to outsiders?

5. Read Proverbs 22:6. We often blame secular universities for undermining the faith of young adults—and sometimes they do play a part. But researcher Lyman Stone found that religiosity actually declines while children are in middle school and high school. Do you know students in those years? How can you encourage them in their faith? How can your church do so?

6. Hospitality starts small, with smiling at someone at church, praying for someone who sits alone, or noticing that new neighbors have moved in. It grows with an intentional next step, the one that's a little uncomfortable—taking cookies to the neighbors or striking up a conversation with someone you don't know. And then another step—inviting someone over for dinner or asking someone out for coffee. Which steps can you take this week?

Chapter 7:
Gospelbound Christians
Love Their Enemies

1. We don't usually use the word *enemies* to describe people we disagree with. But that doesn't mean we consider them

friends. Can you think of ways that we identify those we think of as "other"?

2. With God's help, Gladys Staines overcame the most horrendous evil with good. But forgiveness doesn't take away the grief, she said. "It's not a matter of moving on—it's moving forward. It's not a matter of saying time heals. Time of itself can't heal, but God works through situations to bring joy out of sorrow." Have you seen this in your life or in the life of someone close to you? Conversely, have you seen situations where someone chose not to forgive?

3. Read Romans 12:19. Loving those who have hurt us doesn't mean we dismiss the wrong they've done. It means we care too much about justice to leave it up to humans. Can you think of some injustices that will be made right only in heaven?

4. Loving your enemies is easier if you understand them. Jonathan Haidt has argued that people are primarily driven by emotions and group identity. If that's true, how can you begin to understand those you disagree with?

5. Read 1 Peter 2:11–15. One way to effectively evangelize is to live such a peaceful and compelling life that, by watching you, people *want* to believe. Have you ever met someone whose conduct made you want to grow closer to Jesus? What are some adjectives that describe those people or their behavior? What is it about a peaceful life that attracts people to it?

6. Biola University president Barry Corey and California state assembly member Evan Low forged an unlikely friendship by focusing on things they had in common and treating each other with respect. Do you have a strained relationship with someone because of differences of opinion or values? How could you focus on the things you have in common? When differences need to be addressed, how could you do so from a place of calm and love, leaving the results up to God?

7. Read Matthew 5:43–45. Sometimes it feels like our disagreements or rifts with family members or colleagues will

never get any better. It may help to remember that God asks you not to restore relationships but to love and pray for people. God alone can change hearts and fix what is broken. Are there a few people you can add to your prayer list?

8. In South Africa, an entire government perpetuated injustice, targeting its own citizens as enemies. We know that every society is full of sin and often pits people against one another based on things such as race, socioeconomic status, education, geography, or political party. How can we be working to change the way our culture privileges some groups over others, making people feel like enemies? What does God call us to do while we're waiting for him to come and make things right?

9. Read Romans 15:1. Piper said he's a lot less worried about being taken advantage of than he used to be. How would this mindset change the way you interact with the cable company that overcharged you? With the person who stole your identity? With the child (maybe even your own) who broke something in your home? With the emotionally needy friend who constantly demands reassurance and attention?

10. What could we focus on today that would help us rest in God's providence and care? What can help us release our relationship worries to him?

Chapter 8:
Gospelbound Christians
Give Away Their Freedom

1. How does John Piper's speech shift (if at all) the way you think about retirement? How could retiring from your day job open new opportunities for serving?

2. "Sex and drugs and rock and roll" sounds like freedom. So do eating only junk food and not wearing a seat belt and having an affair. Why is much of what people consider freedom so bad for them? What are they seeking freedom from?

3. Read Galatians 5:13 and 1 Peter 2:16. We are called to be free. But like God, "we find our greatest freedom in making an actual choice instead of just keeping our options open," Derek Rishmawy wrote. "Freedom is found in choosing the particular, not choice in general." We're often paralyzed by too many choices. How can we make good decisions?

4. Research shows that constraints increase creativity, that married people have better relationships and better sex than partners who aren't married, and that those who commit to a four-year college are more likely to graduate than those who plan on transferring partway through. Are there areas in your life where you should make a commitment? How would that decision benefit you?

5. Read Romans 6:16–18. Everyone is a slave to something—even freedom can keep you enslaved to keeping your options open and refusing to commit. What does it look like to serve righteousness? If you served righteousness tomorrow morning, how would that affect the way you spent your time, the way you did your work, and the condition of your heart?

6. Gospelbound Christians aren't just freed *from* sin—we're freed *for* the purpose of loving God and neighbor. What are some ways you might be able to serve if you weren't tied to behaviors that perpetuate sin or waste time?

7. "Doing hard things in one season prepares you to step into the next with momentum and purpose," Alex Harris said. What are some choices you can make—spending time with God rather than sleeping in, reading rather than watching TV, focusing on conversation with your spouse rather than scrolling your social media feeds—that would move you toward self-discipline for the sake of God and others?

ACKNOWLEDGMENTS

We are deeply grateful to the following people:

The gospelbound Christians who have told us their stories. We can't share them all, though if you're interested, you can read more at TGC.org. But we are delighted by every instance of God's Spirit at work in and through his people. The Lord is neither silent nor still—he is busy and active. We see evidence of this work over and over again.

The gospelbound Christians who *haven't* told us their stories. For every story we hear, there are thousands we don't—Christians who are loving their enemies, setting another seat at the table, and caring for the weak all over the globe. We're looking forward to hearing those stories in heaven someday and to giving God glory for the millions of ways he was working that we didn't even notice.

Our TGC team. We're honored to work with gospelbound Christians who love Jesus, laugh a lot, and keep pushing our standards higher (Proverbs 27:17). We love you guys.

Paul Pastor, who helped us give bones to the book.

Our families—Lauren, Carter, Elise, Adam, Noah, Luke—who have captivated our hearts. To share our lives with you is a gift beyond imagination. We love you.

God, the Creator and Sustainer, who amazes us with his creative and perfect care. What a joy to get to report on what he's doing!

Could we with ink the ocean fill,
And were the skies of parchment made;
Were every stalk on earth a quill,
And every man a scribe by trade;
To write the love of God above
Would drain the ocean dry;
Nor could the scroll contain the whole,
Though stretched from sky to sky.

—FREDERICK M. LEHMAN, "THE LOVE OF GOD"

NOTES

Introduction:
Why You're Anxious and Afraid

SOME MATERIAL FROM the introduction has been adapted and updated from the following previously published article: Sarah Eekhoff Zylstra, "Ask and You Shall Evangelize," The Gospel Coalition, November 14, 2018, www.thegospelcoalition .org/article/ask-shall-evangelize. Quotations from the interviews that occurred for this article are not cited separately here.

1. Talia Lavin, "Age of Anxiety," *New Republic*, February 26, 2019, https:// newrepublic.com/article/153153/age-anxiety.
2. Jean M. Twenge, "Time Period and Birth Cohort Differences in Depressive Symptoms in the U.S., 1982–2013," *Social Indicators Research* 121, no. 2 (April 2015): 437–54, https://link.springer.com/article/10 .1007/s11205-014-0647-1.
3. Holly Hedegaard, Sally C. Curtin, and Margaret Warner, "Suicide Mortality in the United States, 1999–2017," NCHS Data Brief, November 2018, 1, www.cdc.gov/nchs/data/databriefs/db330-h.pdf.
4. Julie Ray, "Americans' Stress, Worry and Anger Intensified in 2018," Gallup, April 25, 2019, https://news.gallup.com/poll/249098/americans -stress-worry-anger-intensified-2018.aspx.
5. Ashley Kirzinger et al., "KFF Health Tracking Poll—Early April 2020: The Impact of Coronavirus on Life in America," KFF, April 2, 2020, www.kff.org/coronavirus-covid-19/report/kff-health-tracking-poll-early -april-2020.
6. Paige Winfield Cunningham, "The Health 202: Texts to Federal Governmental Mental Health Hotline Up Roughly 1,000 Percent," *Washington Post*, May 4, 2020, www.washingtonpost.com/news/powerpost/ paloma/the-health-202/2020/05/04/the-health-202-texts-to-federal -government-mental-health-hotline-up-roughly-1-000-percent/

5eaae16c602ff15fb0021568/?itid=ap_paigewinfield%20cunningham&
itid=lk_inline_manual_12.

7. William Wan, "The Coronavirus Pandemic Is Pushing America into a
    Mental Health Crisis," *Washington Post*, May 4, 2020, www.washingtonpost
    .com/health/2020/05/04/mental-health-coronavirus.

8. Nicholas Bogel-Burroughs, "8 Minutes, 46 Seconds Became a Symbol in
    George Floyd's Death. The Exact Time Is Less Clear," *New York Times*,
    June 18, 2020, www.nytimes.com/2020/06/18/us/george-floyd-timing.html.

9. Alyssa Fowers and William Wan, "Depression and Anxiety Spiked
    Among Black Americans After George Floyd's Death," *Washington Post*,
    June 12, 2020, www.washingtonpost.com/health/2020/06/12/mental
    -health-george-floyd-census/?arc404=true.

10. Friedrich Nietzsche, *The Gay Science*, trans. Thomas Common (Mineola,
    NY: Dover, 2006), 155.

11. "The Age Gap in Religion Around the World," Pew Research Center,
    June 13, 2018, www.pewforum.org/2018/06/13/why-do-levels-of
    -religious-observance-vary-by-age-and-country.

12. Derek Thompson, "Three Decades Ago, America Lost Its Religion.
    Why?," *Atlantic*, September 26, 2019, www.theatlantic.com/ideas/
    archive/2019/09/atheism-fastest-growing-religion-us/598843.

13. Tim Keller, "North American Mission: The Outward Move," The Gos-
    pel and Our Cities Conference, Chicago, IL, October 18, 2018, www
    .facebook.com/watch/live/?v=462093247614418&ref=watch_permalink.

14. Tim Keller, "Why Tim Keller Wrote a Prequel to 'The Reason for
    God,'" interview by Matt Smethurst, The Gospel Coalition, September
    20, 2016, www.thegospelcoalition.org/article/why-keller-wrote-prequel
    -to-reason-for-god.

15. Thompson, "Three Decades Ago."

16. "'Nones' on the Rise," Pew Research Center, October 9, 2012, www
    .pewforum.org/2012/10/09/nones-on-the-rise.

17. Dalia Fahmy, "Key Findings About Americans' Belief in God," Pew Re-
    search Center, April 25, 2018, www.pewresearch.org/fact-tank/2018/04/
    25/key-findings-about-americans-belief-in-god.

18. "In U.S., Decline of Christianity Continues at Rapid Pace," Pew Re-
    search Center, October 17, 2019, www.pewforum.org/2019/10/17/in-u
    -s-decline-of-christianity-continues-at-rapid-pace.

19. "'Nones' on the Rise"; "In U.S., Decline of Christianity Continues."

20. "In U.S., Decline of Christianity Continues."

21. Ed Stetzer, *Christians in the Age of Outrage: How to Bring Our Best When
    the World Is at Its Worst* (Carol Stream, IL: Tyndale, 2018), 27.

22. Ed Stetzer, "InterVarsity 'Derecognized' at California State University's
    23 Campuses: Some Analysis and Reflections," *Christianity Today*, Sep-
    tember 6, 2014, www.christianitytoday.com/edstetzer/2014/september/
    intervarsity-now-derecognized-in-california-state-universit.html; Yonat
    Shimron, "Duke University's Student Government Rejects Young Life

over LGBTQ Policies," Religion News Service, September 13, 2019, https://religionnews.com/2019/09/13/duke-universitys-student -government-rejects-young-life-over-lgbtq-policies.

23. Justin McCarthy, "U.S. Confidence in Organized Religion Remains Low," Gallup, July 8, 2019, https://news.gallup.com/poll/259964/ confidence-organized-religion-remains-low.aspx.

24. "Americans Have Positive Views About Religion's Role in Society, but Want It Out of Politics," Pew Research Center, November 15, 2019, www.pewforum.org/2019/11/15/americans-have-positive-views-about -religions-role-in-society-but-want-it-out-of-politics.

25. Andrew Beaujon, "There's No Good Data on How Many Christians Are in Newsrooms," Poynter, April 12, 2013, www.poynter.org/reporting -editing/2013/theres-no-good-data-on-how-many-christians-are-in -newsrooms.

26. Sarah Eekhoff Zylstra, "1 in 3 American Evangelicals Is a Person of Color," *Christianity Today*, September 6, 2017, www.christianitytoday .com/news/2017/september/1-in-3-american-evangelicals-person-of -color-prri-atlas.html.

27. Michael Barthel, "5 Key Takeaways About the State of the News Media in 2018," Pew Research Center, July 23, 2019, www.pewresearch.org/ fact-tank/2019/07/23/key-takeaways-state-of-the-news-media-2018.

28. Elisa Shearer, "Social Media Outpaces Print Newspapers in the U.S. as a News Source," Pew Research Center, December 10, 2018, www.pew research.org/fact-tank/2018/12/10/social-media-outpaces-print -newspapers-in-the-u-s-as-a-news-source.

29. Elizabeth Grieco, "One-in-Five U.S. Newsroom Employees Live in New York, Los Angeles or D.C.," Pew Research Center, October 24, 2019, www.pewresearch.org/fact-tank/2019/10/24/one-in-five-u-s -newsroom-employees-live-in-new-york-los-angeles-or-d-c.

30. Paul Bond, "Ratings Skyrocket for Cable News amid Wall-to-Wall Coronavirus Coverage," *Newsweek*, March 23, 2020, www.newsweek .com/ratings-skyrocket-cable-news-amid-wall-wall-coronavirus -coverage-1493836.

31. Elisa Shearer and Elizabeth Grieco, "Americans Are Wary of the Role Social Media Sites Play in Delivering the News," Pew Research Center, October 2, 2019, www.journalism.org/2019/10/02/americans-are-wary -of-the-role-social-media-sites-play-in-delivering-the-news.

32. Elisa Shearer and Katerina Eva Matsa, "News Use Across Social Media Platforms 2018," Pew Research Center, September 10, 2018, www .journalism.org/2018/09/10/news-use-across-social-media-platforms -2018/#most-social-media-news-consumers-are-concerned-about -inaccuracy-but-many-still-see-benefits.

33. Stuart Soroka, "Why Do We Pay More Attention to Negative News than to Positive News?," *British Politics and Policy Blog*, May 25, 2015, https:// blogs.lse.ac.uk/politicsandpolicy/why-is-there-no-good-news.

34. Marc Trussler and Stuart Soroka, "Consumer Demand for Cynical and Negative News Frames," *International Journal of Press/Politics* 19, no. 3 (2014): 360–79, https://journals.sagepub.com/doi/abs/10.1177/1940161 214524832.

35. Andrew Perrin and Madhu Kumar, "About Three-in-Ten U.S. Adults Say They Are 'Almost Constantly' Online," Pew Research Center, July 25, 2019, www.pewresearch.org/fact-tank/2019/07/25/americans-going -online-almost-constantly.

36. Michael Luo, "The Urgent Quest for Slower, Better News," *New Yorker*, April 10, 2019, www.newyorker.com/culture/annals-of-inquiry/the -urgent-quest-for-slower-better-news.

37. Anya Kamenetz, "Americans Like Their Schools Just Fine—but Not Yours," NPR, August 23, 2016, www.npr.org/sections/ed/2016/08/23/ 490380129/americans-like-their-schools-just-fine-but-not-yours.

38. Carroll Doherty, "Key Findings on Americans' Views of the U.S. Political System and Democracy," Pew Research Center, April 26, 2018, www .pewresearch.org/fact-tank/2018/04/26/key-findings-on-americans -views-of-the-u-s-political-system-and-democracy.

Chapter 1:
Resolute Hope

1. Personal interview by Sarah Eekhoff Zylstra, January 29, 2020.
2. See George Yancey, "Is There Really Anti-Christian Discrimination in America?," The Gospel Coalition, August 19, 2019, www.thegospel coalition.org/article/anti-christian-discrimination-america.

Chapter 2:
Gospelbound Christians
Embrace the Future

SOME MATERIAL FROM this chapter has been adapted and updated from the following previously published articles: Sarah Eekhoff Zylstra, "How Southern Baptists Trained More Disaster Relief Workers than the Red Cross," The Gospel Coalition, November 17, 2017, www.thegospelcoalition.org/article/how -southern-baptists-trained-more-disaster-relief-volunteers-than-the-red-cross; Sarah Eekhoff Zylstra, "How Reformed Churches Are Growing on the Arabian Peninsula," The Gospel Coalition, September 4, 2018, www.thegospelcoalition .org/article/growing-reformed-churches-arabian-peninsula; Collin Hansen, "From D.C. to Dubai: Meet Keri Folmar," The Gospel Coalition, September 8, 2011, www.thegospelcoalition.org/article/from-d-c-to-dubai-meet-keri-folmar; Collin Hansen, "Spiritual Oasis in the Middle East," The Gospel Coalition, November 28, 2011, www.thegospelcoalition.org/article/spiritual-oasis-in-the -middle-east; Sarah Eekhoff Zylstra, "How One Baptist Church Has Seven-

Times More Missionaries than Anyone Else," The Gospel Coalition, April 10, 2018, www.thegospelcoalition.org/article/sending-from-the-summit-how-one -baptist-church-has-seven-times-more-missionaries-than-anyone-else. Quotations from the interviews that occurred for these articles are not cited separately here.

1. "On Evangelism and Soul-Winning," Southern Baptist Convention, June 1, 2016, www.sbc.net/resource-library/resolutions/on-evangelism -and-soul-winning.

2. Glenn Stanton, "FactChecker: Misquoting Francis of Assisi," The Gospel Coalition, July 10, 2012, www.thegospelcoalition.org/article/fact checker-misquoting-francis-of-assisi.

3. Trevin Wax, "When John Stott Confronted Billy Graham," The Gospel Coalition, May 8, 2013, www.thegospelcoalition.org/blogs/trevin-wax/ when-john-stott-confronted-billy-graham.

4. Cliff Satterwhite, quoted in Mickey Noah, "Hugo, 20 Years Ago, Was Disaster Relief Catalyst," Baptist Press, August 26, 2009, www.baptist press.com/resource-library/news/hugo-20-years-ago-was-disaster-relief -catalyst.

5. "RELIEF: Hurricane Andrew Established Florida Baptist's DR Ministry in Jesus' Name," *Florida Baptist Witness*, September 6, 2012, www.blue toad.com/article/RELIEF%3A_Hurricane_Andrew_established_Florida _Baptist%E2%80%99s_DR_ministry_in_Jesus%E2%80%99_name/ 1170924/125447/article.html.

6. Fred de Sam Lazaro, in "Hurricane Katrina Faith-Based Relief Efforts," PBS Religion & Ethics NewsWeekly, September 2, 2005, www.pbs.org/ wnet/religionandethics/2005/09/02/september-2-2005-hurricane -katrina-faith-based-relief-efforts/12722.

7. "Disaster Relief Ministry Promo Video 2014," MN-WI Baptist Convention Disaster Relief, www.facebook.com/MWBC.DR/videos/164588 3025430906.

8. Will Durant, *Caesar and Christ: A History of Roman Civilization and of Christianity from Their Beginnings to A.D. 325* (New York: Simon & Schuster, 1972), 59–60.

9. Thomas Kidd, "How Many Christians Were There in 200 A.D.?," The Gospel Coalition, September 22, 2017, www.thegospelcoalition.org/ blogs/evangelical-history/how-many-christians-were-there-in-200-a-d.

10. Steven D. Smith, *Pagans & Christians in the City: Culture Wars from the Tiber to the Potomac* (Grand Rapids, MI: Eerdmans, 2018), chap. 7.

11. Kidd, "How Many Christians Were There?"

12. Justin Martyr, quoted in Durant, *Caesar and Christ*, 611; *Encyclopaedia Britannica*, s.v. "Justin Martyr," www.britannica.com/biography/Saint -Justin-Martyr.

13. Attilio Mastrocinque, "Creating One's Own Religion: Intellectual Choices," in *A Companion to Roman Religion*, ed. Jörg Rüpke (Malden, MA: Wiley-Blackwell, 2011), 379.

14. "Perpetua: High Society Believer," *Christianity Today*, www.christianity today.com/history/people/martyrs/perpetua.html.

15. C. S. Lewis, *Mere Christianity* (New York: Touchstone, 1996), 119.

16. John Folmar, "Testimony: John Folmar," in *The Underestimated Gospel*, ed. Jonathan Leeman (Nashville: B&H, 2014), 192.

17. Folmar, "Testimony," 192–93.

18. Tahira Yaqoob, "How Missionaries Transformed Abu Dhabi Health-care," *National*, November 5, 2010, www.thenational.ae/uae/health/how-missionaries-transformed-abu-dhabi-healthcare-1.482263.

19. Tahira Yaqoob, "Focus: With the Oasis, a New Era Was Born," *National*, July 26, 2008, www.thenational.ae/uae/focus-with-the-oasis-a-new-era-was-born-1.228994.

20. "Dubai History," Emirates, www.emirates.com/english/discover-dubai/dubai-history.

21. "United Arab Emirates," in *World Factbook*, Central Intelligence Agency, April 2020, www.cia.gov/library/publications/the-world-factbook/attachments/summaries/AE-summary.pdf.

22. "Belief in God," Pew Research Center Religious Landscape Study, 2014, www.pewforum.org/religious-landscape-study/belief-in-god.

23. "Belief in Heaven," Pew Research Center Religious Landscape Study, 2014, www.pewforum.org/religious-landscape-study/belief-in-heaven.

24. "Americans Describe Their Views About Life After Death," Barna Group, October 21, 2003, www.barna.com/research/americans-describe-their-views-about-life-after-death.

25. "Americans Describe Their Views."

26. Bob Smietana, "Americans Believe in Heaven, Hell, and a Little Bit of Heresy," LifeWay Research, October 28, 2014, https://lifeway research.com/2014/10/28/americans-believe-in-heaven-hell-and-a-little-bit-of-heresy.

27. "Americans Describe Their Views."

28. Quoted in Andrew Sullivan, "What Do Atheists Think of Death?," *Atlantic*, May 16, 2010, www.theatlantic.com/daily-dish/archive/2010/05/what-do-atheists-think-of-death/187003.

Chapter 3:
Gospelbound Christians
Live with Honor

Some material from this chapter has been adapted and updated from the following previously published articles: Rachel Gilson, "Are You Willing to Obey Before You Understand?," interview by Collin Hansen, *Gospelbound* podcast, The Gospel Coalition, April 21, 2020, www .thegospelcoalition .org/ podcasts/ gospelbound/

you-willing-obey-before-understand; Sarah Eekhoff Zylstra, "How a Mortgage Company Is Loving Its Neighbors," The Gospel Coalition, June 12, 2018, www .thegospelcoalition.org/article/mortgage-company-loving-neighbors; Sarah Eekhoff Zylstra, "Redeeming Your 401(k)," The Gospel Coalition, February 12, 2020, www.thegospelcoalition.org/article/redeeming-your-401k. Quotations from the interviews that occurred for these articles are not cited separately here.

1. Becket Cook, *A Change of Affection: A Gay Man's Incredible Story of Redemption* (Nashville: Nelson Books, 2019).
2. Cook, *A Change of Affection*, 88.
3. Cook, *A Change of Affection*, 93.
4. "Youth: The Hippies," *Time*, July 7, 1967, http://content.time.com/ time/subscriber/article/0,33009,899555-4,00.html.
5. IDER, "You've Got Your Whole Life Ahead of You Baby," Glassnote Entertainment, 2018.
6. Lexico, s.v. "honor," www.lexico.com/en/definition/honor.
7. "Transgender People and Bathroom Access," National Center for Transgender Equality, https://transequality.org/sites/default/files/docs/ resources/Trans-People-Bathroom-Access-July-2016.pdf.
8. "Employment Nondiscrimination," Movement Advancement Project, www .lgbtmap.org/equality-maps/employment_non_discrimination_laws.
9. Ed Stetzer and Marty Duren, "California's Religious Liberty Moment—Coming to a State near You," *Christianity Today*, June 24, 2016, www .christianitytoday.com/edstetzer/2016/june/californias-religious-liberty -moment-coming-to-state-near-y.html.
10. Frankie Graziano, "Should Transgender Students Be Allowed to Compete in Women's Athletics?," NPR, March 3, 2020, www.npr.org/2020/ 03/03/811504625/should-transgender-students-be-allowed-to-compete -in-womens-athletics.
11. Rachel Gilson, *Born Again This Way: Coming Out, Coming to Faith, and What Comes Next* (Charlotte, NC: Good Book, 2020), 62.
12. Rachel Gilson, "I Never Became Straight. Perhaps That Was Never God's Goal," *Christianity Today*, September 20, 2017, www.christianity today.com/ct/2017/october/i-never-became-straight-perhaps-that-was -never-gods-goal.html.
13. Gilson, "I Never Became Straight."
14. Gilson, "I Never Became Straight."
15. Gilson, *Born Again This Way*, 103.
16. Matthew Rueger, *Sexual Morality in a Christless World* (St. Louis, MO: Concordia, 2016), chap. 1, Kindle.
17. Ana Swanson, "144 Years of Marriage and Divorce in the United States, in One Chart," *Washington Post*, June 23, 2015, www.washingtonpost.com/ news/wonk/wp/2015/06/23/144-years-of-marriage-and-divorce-in-the -united-states-in-one-chart; W. Bradford Wilcox and Lyman Stone, "The Happiness Recession," *Atlantic*, April 4, 2019, www.theatlantic.com/ideas/ archive/2019/04/happiness-recession-causing-sex-depression/586405.

18. Wilcox and Stone, "The Happiness Recession."

19. Christopher Ingraham, "The Share of Americans Not Having Sex Has Reached a Record High," *Washington Post*, March 29, 2019, www.washingtonpost.com/business/2019/03/29/share-americans-not-having-sex-has-reached-record-high.

20. Kate Julian, "Why Are Young People Having So Little Sex?," *Atlantic*, December 2018, www.theatlantic.com/magazine/archive/2018/12/the-sex-recession/573949.

21. Belinda Luscombe, "Porn and the Threat to Virility," *Time*, March 31, 2016, https://time.com/4277510/porn-and-the-threat-to-virility.

22. Julian, "Why Are Young People?"

23. Julian, "Why Are Young People?"

24. "General Happiness," Trends: Gender & Marriage, GSS Data Explorer, https://gssdataexplorer.norc.org/trends/Gender%20&%20Marriage?measure=happy.

25. Wilcox and Stone, "The Happiness Recession."

26. Lyman Stone, "Sex Ratios in the Pews: Is There Really a Deficit of Men in American Churches?," Institute for Family Studies, August 12, 2019, https://ifstudies.org/blog/sex-ratios-in-the-pews-is-there-really-a-deficit-of-men-in-american-churches.

27. Charles Fain Lehman, "'Sex Recession'? Blame Marriage Stagnation," Institute for Family Studies, November 19, 2018, https://ifstudies.org/blog/sex-recession-blame-marriage-stagnation.

28. Wilcox and Stone, "The Happiness Recession."

29. Lois M. Collins, "BYU and Baylor Study: Religious Couples Report Greater Sexual Satisfaction," *Deseret News*, April 23, 2019, www.deseret.com/2019/4/24/20671562/byu-and-baylor-study-religious-couples-report-greater-sexual-satisfaction.

30. Sam Allberry, *Why Does God Care Who I Sleep With?* (Charlotte, NC: Good Book, 2020), 23.

31. Becket Cook, "From Gay to Gospel: The Fascinating Story of Becket Cook," interview with Brett McCracken, The Gospel Coalition, August 23, 2019, www.thegospelcoalition.org/article/gay-gospel-becket-cook.

32. Cook, "From Gay to Gospel."

33. Cook, "From Gay to Gospel."

34. Sam Allberry, "How Celibacy Can Fulfill Your Sexuality," The Gospel Coalition, August 26, 2016, www.thegospelcoalition.org/article/how-celibacy-can-fulfill-your-sexuality.

35. Cook, "From Gay to Gospel."

36. Cook, "From Gay to Gospel."

37. Justin Lonas, "Why It's Better to Trade than to Give," The Gospel Coalition, January 22, 2020, www.thegospelcoalition.org/article/better-trade-give.

38. Lonas, "Why It's Better."

39. Lauren Tara LaCapra, "Top Lobbying Banks Got Biggest Bailouts: Study," Reuters, May 26, 2011, www.reuters.com/article/us-lobbying -imfreport/top-lobbying-banks-got-biggest-bailouts-study-idUSTRE 74P7AF20110526.

40. Bernie Madoff, quoted in Steve Fishman, "The Madoff Tapes," *New York*, February 25, 2011, https://nymag.com/news/features/berniemadoff -2011-3.

41. Kevin McCoy, "Court Filing Reveals Madoff's Net Worth at Least $823 Million," ABC News, March 13, 2009, https://abcnews.go.com/Business/ story?id=7080697&page=1.

42. "Our Take on the 10 Biggest Frauds in Recent U.S. History," *Forbes*, www.forbes.com/pictures/efik45ekdjl/our-take-on-the-10-biggest-frauds -in-recent-u-s-history-2/#1c5cf12f775a.

43. Madoff, quoted in Fishman, "The Madoff Tapes."

44. Madoff, quoted in Fishman, "The Madoff Tapes."

45. "Purpose and Values," Eventide, www.eventidefunds.com/purpose-and -values.

46. "The Eventide Gilead Fund Ranks Top 1 Percent Within All Mid-Cap Growth Funds for 1 Year, 3 Years, and 5 Years," Eventide, July 19, 2013, www.eventidefunds.com/news/the-eventide-gilead-fund-ranks-top-1 -percent-within-all-mid-cap-growth-funds-for-1-year-3-years-and-5 -years.

47. "Eventide Gilead Fund Ranked Best Performing Mutual Fund by the New York Times for the Five-Year Period Ending September 30, 2013 Based on Total Returns," Yahoo! Finance, October 21, 2013, https:// finance.yahoo.com/news/eventide-gilead-fund-ranked-best-124500306 .html.

48. "The Eventide Gilead Fund Ranks Top 1 Percent."

49. "The Eventide Gilead Fund Ranks Top 1 Percent."

Chapter 4:
Gospelbound Christians
Suffer with Joy

SOME MATERIAL FROM this chapter has been adapted and updated from the following previously published articles: Sarah Eekhoff Zylstra, "The Final Call of John Perkins," The Gospel Coalition, April 2, 2018, www.thegospelcoalition .org/article/final-charge-john-m-perkins; Sarah Eekhoff Zylstra, "How Chinese Pastors Developed Their Theology for Suffering," The Gospel Coalition, April 22, 2020, www.thegospelcoalition.org/article/how-chinese-pastors-developed -their-theology-for-suffering; Luke Goodrich, "How to Prepare for the Most Intense Opposition We've Faced," interview by Collin Hansen, *Gospelbound* podcast, The Gospel Coalition, June 17, 2020, www.thegospelcoalition.org/ podcasts/gospelbound/how-to-prepare-for-the-most-intense-opposition-weve

-faced. Quotations from the interviews that occurred for these articles are not cited separately here.

1. I gathered this story as she spoke to groups over several days (January 30–31, 2020), then confirmed with her later.
2. Personal interview by Sarah Eekhoff Zylstra, January 29, 2020.
3. Personal interview by Sarah Eekhoff Zylstra, January 30, 2020.
4. Tim Keller, "Truth Without Love, Love Without Truth" (sermon, Gospel and Culture Conference, Kuala Lumpur, Malaysia, January 2020), www.youtube.com/watch?v=Mg7Ir0uXplE.
5. Luke Goodrich, *Free to Believe: The Battle over Religious Liberty in America* (Colorado Springs, CO: Multnomah, 2019).
6. Costi Hinn, "Benny Hinn Is My Uncle, but Prosperity Preaching Isn't for Me," *Christianity Today*, September 20, 2017, www.christianitytoday.com/ct/2017/october/benny-hinn-costi-uncle-prosperity-preaching-testimony.html.
7. Joel Osteen, "The Power of 'I Am' " (sermon, Lakewood Church, Houston, TX, October 28, 2012), www.youtube.com/watch?v=_kjSK-PcU9o. Further quotes from this sermon are given in the text.
8. Tim Challies, "The Joel Osteen Sermon That Changed Oprah's Life," Challies, July 26, 2018, www.challies.com/vlog/the-joel-osteen-sermon-that-changed-oprahs-life.
9. Russell S. Woodbridge, "Prosperity Gospel Born in the USA," The Gospel Coalition, June 4, 2015, www.thegospelcoalition.org/article/prosperity-gospel-born-in-the-usa.
10. John M. Perkins, *One Blood: Parting Words to the Church on Race* (Chicago: Moody, 2018), 37.
11. John M. Perkins, "Let Justice Roll Down: John M. Perkins in Conversation with Charles Marsh," interview by Charles Marsh, Spring Institute for Lived Theology, Charlottesville, VA, 2009, www.livedtheology.org/resources/let-justice-roll-down.
12. Debbie Elliott, "Integrating Ole Miss: A Transformative, Deadly Riot," NPR, October 1, 2012, www.npr.org/2012/10/01/161573289/integrating-ole-miss-a-transformative-deadly-riot.
13. Trip Burns, "Real Violence: 50 Years Ago at Woolworth," *Jackson Free Press*, May 23, 2013, www.jacksonfreepress.com/news/2013/may/23/real-violence-50-years-ago-woolworth.
14. Jerry Mitchell, "Klansman Who Orchestrated Mississippi Burning Killings Dies in Prison," *Mississippi Clarion-Ledger*, January 12, 2018, www.clarionledger.com/story/news/local/journeytojustice/2018/01/12/klansman-who-orchestrated-mississippi-burning-killings-dies-prison/1028454001.
15. John M. Perkins, "Oral History Interview with John Perkins, 19 June 1987," interview by Paul Erickson, Wheaton College, Billy Graham

Center Archives, collection 367, audio tape T1, https://archives.wheaton
.edu/repositories/4/archival_objects/240378.

16. John M. Perkins, *Let Justice Roll Down* (Grand Rapids, MI: Baker Books, 1976), 192.

17. Perkins, *One Blood*, 81–82.

18. Jemar Tisby, "John Perkins Wants to Keep the Dream Alive Through Love," The Gospel Coalition, April 17, 2017, www.thegospelcoalition .org/reviews/dream-with-me-john-perkins.

19. Timothy C. Morgan with reports from Associated Baptist Press, "Racist No More? Black Leaders Ask," *Christianity Today*, August 1, 1995, www .christianitytoday.com/ct/1995/august1/5t9053.html.

20. Sarah Eekhoff Zylstra, "Southern Baptists Repudiate the Confederate Flag," *Christianity Today*, June 14, 2016, www.christianitytoday.com/news/ 2016/june/southern-baptists-racial-reconciliation-sbc-civilitas-pca.html.

21. Kate Shellnutt, "Southern Baptists Approve Alternate Resolution Against the Alt-Right," *Christianity Today*, June 14, 2017, www.christianity today.com/news/2017/june/southern-baptists-vote-resolution-against -alt-right-sbc17.html.

22. Sarah Eekhoff Zylstra, "Presbyterian Church in America Apologizes for Old and New Racism," *Christianity Today*, June 24, 2016, www.christianity today.com/news/2016/june/pca-apologizes-for-new-and-old-racism .html.

23. Perkins, *One Blood*, 33.

24. See "Time with a Living Legacy of the Chinese Church—Cultural Revolution Experiences," China Partnership, September 8, 2016, www.china partnership.org/blog/2016/8/time-with-a-living-legacy-of-the-chinese -church-cultural-revolution-experiences.

25. "Chinese Pastor Roundtable: A Big Crisis Will Be the Next Generation," China Partnership, October 18, 2017, www.chinapartnership.org/ blog/2017/10/chinese-pastor-roundtable-a-big-crisis-will-be-the-next -generation?rq=roundtable.

26. Richard B. Gaffin Jr., "The Usefulness of the Cross," *Westminster Theological Journal* 41, no. 2 (Spring 1979): 228–46.

27. Gaffin, "Usefulness of the Cross."

28. Sarah Eekhoff Zylstra, "Red Tape: China Wants to Constrict Christian Activities with 26 New Rules," *Christianity Today*, October 3, 2016, www .christianitytoday.com/news/2016/october/red-tape-china-constricts -christian-activities-sara.html.

29. Wang Jianguo, "116 Chinese Pastors Sign Joint Statement on the New Religious Regulations," China Partnership, September 2, 2018, www .chinapartnership.org/blog/2018/9/116-chinese-pastors-sign-joint -statement-on-the-new-religious-regulations.

30. Wang Yi, quoted in Joe Carter, "Persecuted Chinese Pastor Issues a 'Declaration of Faithful Disobedience,'" The Gospel Coalition, Decem-

ber 17, 2018, www.thegospelcoalition.org/article/persecuted-chinese
-pastor-issues-declaration-faithful-disobedience.

31. "Outspoken Chinese Pastor Wang Yi Sentenced to 9 Years in Prison,"
Christianity Today, December 30, 2019, www.christianitytoday.com/
news/2019/december/chinese-pastor-wang-yi-early-rain-house-church
-sentence-pri.html.

32. Wang, quoted in Carter, "Persecuted Chinese Pastor."

33. Closed session (for privacy) at the Gospel and Culture Conference,
Kuala Lumpur, Malaysia, January 29–31, 2020.

34. Personal interview by Sarah Eekhoff Zylstra, January 30, 2020.

35. Tim Keller, "In the World, Not of the World" (sermon, Gospel and
Culture Conference, Kuala Lumpur, Malaysia, January 29, 2020), www
.youtube.com/watch?v=Q85QOlQAWsY.

36. Keller, "Truth Without Love."

37. Keller, "In the World."

38. Keller, "In the World."

39. Keller, "In the World."

Chapter 5:
Gospelbound Christians
Care for the Weak

SOME MATERIAL FROM this chapter has been adapted and updated from the following previously published articles: Sarah Eekhoff Zylstra, "While Celebrating Progress, IJM Digs into New Problem," The Gospel Coalition, August 13,
2018, www.thegospelcoalition.org/article/ijm-won-fight-sexual-abuse-worse;
Sarah Eekhoff Zylstra, "Riots in John Piper's Neighborhood," The Gospel Coalition, August 24, 2020, www.thegospelcoalition.org/article/riots-john-pipers
-neighborhood; Tom Holland, "The Revolution the West Wishes It Could
Forget," interview by Collin Hansen, *Gospelbound* podcast, The Gospel Coalition, March 10, 2020, www.thegospelcoalition.org/podcasts/gospelbound/the
-revolution-the-west-wishes-it-could-forget; Sarah Eekhoff Zylstra, "Sharing
Dinner and Jesus with Strippers," The Gospel Coalition, May 4, 2017, www
.thegospelcoalition.org/article/sharing-dinner-and-jesus-with-strippers; Sarah
Eekhoff Zylstra, " 'Worth Laying Down Your Life': The Missionary Adventures
of Rick Sacra," The Gospel Coalition, January 28, 2019, www.thegospelcoalition
.org/article/worth-laying-life-missionary-adventures-rick-sacra; Sarah Eekhoff
Zylstra, "Why There Are Way More Pro-Life Protesters Than You Think," The
Gospel Coalition, January 15, 2020, www.thegospelcoalition.org/article/way-pro
-life-protesters-think. Quotations from the interviews that occurred for these articles are not cited separately here.

1. Robin Haarr, *Evaluation of the Program to Combat Sex Trafficking of Children in the Philippines: 2003–2015* (International Justice Mission, August

2017), 166, www.ijm.org/documents/studies/philippines-csec-program
-evaluation.pdf.

2. *Cybersex Trafficking*, IJM Casework Series (International Justice Mission, September 2016), www.ijm.org/sites/default/files/IJM_2016_Casework _FactSheets_CybersexTrafficking.pdf.

3. Personal interview by Sarah Eekhoff Zylstra, July 16, 2020.

4. "The Compassion of Early Christians," Bible Mesh, February 7, 2020, https://biblemesh.com/blog/the-compassion-of-early-christians.

5. Julian, "To Arsacius, High-Priest of Galatia," in *The Works of the Emperor Julian*, trans. Wilmer Cave Wright (London: William Heineman, 1923), 3:71.

6. Beatriz Carrillo, Johanna Hood, and Paul Kadetz, introduction to *Handbook of Welfare in China*, ed. Beatriz Carrillo, Johanna Hood, and Paul Kadetz (Cheltenham, UK: Edward Elgar, 2017), 3, www.researchgate .net/publication/318125448_Handbook_of_Welfare_in_China.

7. Michael S. Rosenwald, "Hitler Hated Judaism. But He Loathed Christianity, Too," *Washington Post*, April 20, 2019, www.washingtonpost .com/history/2019/04/20/hitler-hated-judaism-he-loathed-christianity -too.

8. Friedrich Nietzsche, *Beyond Good and Evil: Prelude to a Philosophy of the Future*, ed. Rolf-Peter Horstmann and Judith Norman, trans. Judith Norman (Cambridge: Cambridge University Press, 2002), 56–57.

9. Margaret Sanger, "The Eugenic Value of Birth Control Propaganda," *Birth Control Review* 5, no. 10 (October 1921): 5, https://babel.hathitrust .org/cgi/pt?id=coo.31924007352325&view=1up&seq=193.

10. Margaret Sanger, "My Way to Peace" (speech, New History Society, January 17, 1932), www.nyu.edu/projects/sanger/webedition/app/ documents/show.php?sangerDoc=129037.xml.

11. Samantha Schmidt, "Planned Parenthood to Remove Margaret Sanger's Name from N.Y. Clinic over Views on Eugenics," *Washington Post*, July 21, 2020, www.washingtonpost.com/history/2020/07/21/margaret -sanger-planned-parenthood-eugenics.

12. "Our History," Planned Parenthood, www.plannedparenthood.org/ about-us/who-we-are/our-history.

13. Tom Holland, *Dominion: How the Christian Revolution Remade the World* (New York: Basic Books, 2019).

14. Conrad Hackett and David McClendon, "Christians Remain World's Largest Religious Group, but They Are Declining in Europe," Pew Research Center, April 5, 2017, www.pewresearch.org/fact-tank/2017/04/ 05/christians-remain-worlds-largest-religious-group-but-they-are -declining-in-europe.

15. "The Universal Declaration of Human Rights," United Nations, December 10, 1948, www.un.org/en/universal-declaration-human -rights.

16. Brittney Wacek, "Factors Which Put Social Workers at a Greater Risk

for Burnout," St. Catherine University School of Social Work, May 2017, https://sophia.stkate.edu/cgi/viewcontent.cgi?article=1806& context=msw_papers.

17. David Daniels, "Scarlet Hope: Loving Strippers Where They Are," *Good News Today*, April 2015, http://thegoodnewstoday.org/scarlet-hope -loving-strippers-where-they-are.

18. Kevin Sieff, "Liberia Already Had Only a Few Dozen of Its Own Doctors. Then Came Ebola," *Washington Post*, October 11, 2014, www .washingtonpost.com/world/africa/liberia-already-had-only-a-few-dozen -of-its-own-doctors-then-came-ebola/2014/10/11/dcf87c5c-50ac-11e4 -aa5e-7153e466a02d_story.html.

19. Chelsea Rice, "Dr. Rick Sacra, Now Ebola-Free, Returning to Liberia to Help Rebuild," Boston.com, January 12, 2015, comments section, www .boston.com/culture/health/2015/01/12/dr-rick-sacra-now-ebola-free -returning-to-liberia-to-help-rebuild#comments.

20. Kenneth Berding, "How Did Early Christians Respond to Plagues? Historical Reflections as the Coronavirus Spreads," *Good Book Blog*, Biola University, March 16, 2020, www.biola.edu/blogs/good-book-blog/ 2020/how-did-early-christians-respond-to-plagues.

21. Sarah Willey, "Ebola Survivor Richard Sacra Honored for Selfless Work in Liberia," UMass Med News, February 1, 2019, www.umassmed.edu/ news/news-archives/2019/02/ebola-survivor-richard-sacra-honored-for -selfless-work-in-liberia.

22. Alexandra Zavis, "American Ebola Survivor Dr. Rick Sacra Returns to Liberia This Week," *Los Angeles Times*, January 12, 2015, www.latimes .com/world/africa/la-fg-ebola-rick-sacra-20150112-story.html; Meredith Engel, "Ebola Survivor Rick Sacra Talks About His Decision to Return to Liberia," *New York Daily News*, January 12, 2015, www.nydaily news.com/life-style/health/ebola-survivor-rick-sacra-talks-returning -liberia-article-1.2074783.

23. David von Drehle, "The Ebola Fighters," *Time*, December 10, 2014, https://time.com/time-person-of-the-year-ebola-fighters.

24. Randy Alcorn, "A Letter from Jail," Eternal Perspective Ministries, December 22, 2010, www.epm.org/resources/2010/Dec/22/letter-jail.

25. Tamar Lewin, "With Thin Staff and Thick Debt, Anti-Abortion Group Faces Struggle," *New York Times*, June 11, 1990, www.nytimes.com/ 1990/06/11/us/with-thin-staff-and-thick-debt-anti-abortion-group-faces -struggle.html.

26. "1,000 Arrested in Blockades of Abortion Clinics," *Los Angeles Times*, October 30, 1988, www.latimes.com/archives/la-xpm-1988-10-30-mn -962-story.html.

27. *2018 Violence and Disruption Statistics* (National Abortion Federation, 2018), 7, https://prochoice.org/wp-content/uploads/2018-Anti-Abortion -Violence-and-Disruption.pdf.

28. Jerry Schwartz, "400 Are Arrested in Atlanta Abortion Protests," *New*

York Times, October 5, 1988, www.nytimes.com/1988/10/05/us/400-are
-arrested-in-atlanta-abortion-protests.html.

29. Lynne Duke and Michael Abramowitz, "Anti-Abortion Protesters
    Blockade Clinic in Va.," *Washington Post*, October 30, 1988, www
    .washingtonpost.com/archive/local/1988/10/30/anti-abortion-protesters
    -blockade-clinic-in-va/bc324721-4785-4bc7-9deb-8b3cbd269373.
30. Scott Harris and Nancy Wride, "Huge Protest at Abortion Clinic Turns
    Violent," *Los Angeles Times*, April 15, 1990, www.latimes.com/archives/la
    -xpm-1990-04-15-mn-1974-story.html.
31. Harris and Wride, "Huge Protest at Abortion Clinic."
32. Richard L. Hughes, "'The Civil Rights Movement of the 1990s?': The
    Anti-Abortion Movement and the Struggle for Racial Justice," *Oral His-
    tory Review* 33, no. 2 (Summer–Autumn 2006): 1–24, https://pubmed
    .ncbi.nlm.nih.gov/17115517.
33. "Selma, Alabama: The Role of News Media in the Civil Rights Move-
    ment | The African Americans," PBS, www.pbslearningmedia.org/
    resource/mr13.socst.us.selma/selma-alabama-the-role-of-news-media-in
    -the-civil-rights-movement; William G. Thomas III, "Television News
    and the Civil Rights Struggle: The Views in Virginia and Mississippi,"
    Southern Spaces, November 3, 2004, https://southernspaces.org/2004/
    television-news-and-civil-rights-struggle-views-virginia-and-mississippi.
34. David Shaw, "Abortion Bias Seeps into News," *Los Angeles Times*, July 1,
    1990, www.latimes.com/food/la-me-shaw01jul01-story.html.
35. Liam Stack, "A Brief History of Deadly Attacks on Abortion Providers,"
    New York Times, November 29, 2015, www.nytimes.com/interactive/
    2015/11/29/us/30abortion-clinic-violence.html.
36. *2018 Violence and Disruption Statistics*, 7.
37. David H. Weaver and G. Cleveland Wilhoit, *The American Journalist in
    the 1990s: U.S. News People at the End of an Era* (Mahwah, NJ: Lawrence
    Erlbaum, 1996), 17.
38. "Press Sees Coverage as Having Hurt Bush Election Chances," Pew
    Research Center, December 20, 1992, www.pewresearch.org/politics/
    1992/12/20/press-sees-coverage-as-having-hurt-bush-election-chances.
39. Crisis Pregnancy Center Map, https://crisispregnancycentermap.com;
    "Data Center," Guttmacher Institute, https://data.guttmacher.org/
    states/table?state=US&topics=57+71&dataset=data.
40. "An Overview of Abortion Laws," Guttmacher Institute, October 1,
    2020, www.guttmacher.org/state-policy/explore/overview-abortion-laws.
41. *2018 Violence and Disruption Statistics*, 2.
42. Sarah Tuttle-Singer, Twitter, May 15, 2019, https://twitter.com/Tuttle
    Singer/status/1128739808178843649.
43. Joshua Ryan Butler, Twitter, May 17, 2019, https://twitter.com/butler
    josh/status/1129495969274318848.
44. Trevin Wax, Twitter, May 15, 2019, https://twitter.com/TrevinWax/
    status/1128823307917242368.

45. Trillia Newbell, Twitter, May 16, 2019, https://twitter.com/trillia newbell/status/1128985844390551552.

46. "Who Gives Most to Charity?," Philanthropy Roundtable, www .philanthropyroundtable.org/almanac/statistics/who-gives; "Religion in Everyday Life," Pew Research Center, April 12, 2016, www.pewforum .org/2016/04/12/highly-religious-people-not-distinctive-in-all-aspects -of-everyday-life.

Chapter 6:
Gospelbound Christians
Set Another Seat at the Table

SOME MATERIAL FROM this chapter has been adapted and updated from the following previously published articles: Sarah Eekhoff Zylstra, "The Exponential Growth of Classical Christian Education," The Gospel Coalition, January 9, 2017, www.thegospelcoalition.org/article/the-exponential-growth-of-classical -christian-education; Sarah Eekhoff Zylstra, "Riots in John Piper's Neighborhood," The Gospel Coalition, August 24, 2020, www.thegospelcoalition.org/ article/riots-john-pipers-neighborhood; Sarah Eekhoff Zylstra, "Black and White Together: An Unusual Church Merger in Iowa," The Gospel Coalition, August 2, 2019, www.thegospelcoalition.org/article/black-and-white-together-an -unusual-church-merger-in-iowa. Quotations from the interviews that occurred for these articles are not cited separately here.

1. Rosaria Butterfield, "The Gospel Comes with a House Key" (breakout, The Gospel Coalition women's conference, Indianapolis, IN, June 15, 2018), www.youtube.com/watch?v=9aaWG6V5phI.

2. *Loneliness and the Workplace: 2020 U.S. Report* (Cigna, January 2020), 3–4, www.cigna.com/static/www-cigna-com/docs/about-us/newsroom/studies -and-reports/combatting-loneliness/cigna-2020-loneliness-report.pdf.

3. Tamara Lush, "Poll: Americans Are the Unhappiest They've Been in 50 Years," AP News, June 16, 2020, https://apnews.com/article/ 0f6b9be04fa0d3194401821a72665a50.

4. W. Bradford Wilcox, "Marriage with Family at Its Center," *Wall Street Journal*, March 28, 2020, www.wsj.com/articles/marriage-with-family-at -its-center-11585368060.

5. Mollie Moric, "US Divorce Rates Soar During COVID-19 Crisis," Legal Templates, July 29, 2020, https://legaltemplates.net/resources/ personal-family/divorce-rates-covid-19.

6. W. Bradford Wilcox and Lyman Stone, "Divorce Is Down, Despite Covid-19," *Washington Post*, October 21, 2020, www.washingtonpost .com/opinions/2020/10/21/divorce-is-down-despite-covid-19.

7. Cary Funk and Alec Tyson, "Partisan Differences over the Pandemic Response Are Growing," Pew Research Center, June 3, 2020, www

.pewresearch.org/science/2020/06/03/partisan-differences-over-the
-pandemic-response-are-growing.

8. Brett McCracken, "Church, Don't Let Coronavirus Divide You," The Gospel Coalition, May 15, 2020, www.thegospelcoalition.org/article/church-dont-let-coronavirus-divide.

9. Richard Fry, "The Number of People in the Average U.S. Household Is Going Up for the First Time in over 160 Years," Pew Research Center, October 1, 2019, www.pewresearch.org/fact-tank/2019/10/01/the-number-of-people-in-the-average-u-s-household-is-going-up-for-the-first-time-in-over-160-years.

10. Joe Carter, "When Did the Decline of Marriage Begin in America?," The Gospel Coalition, August 28, 2015, www.thegospelcoalition.org/article/when-did-the-decline-of-marriage-begin-in-america.

11. Kim Parker and Renee Stepler, "As U.S. Marriage Rate Hovers at 50%, Education Gap in Marital Status Widens," Pew Research Center, September 14, 2017, www.pewresearch.org/fact-tank/2017/09/14/as-u-s-marriage-rate-hovers-at-50-education-gap-in-marital-status-widens.

12. A. W. Geiger and Gretchen Livingston, "8 Facts About Love and Marriage in America," Pew Research Center, February 13, 2019, www.pewresearch.org/fact-tank/2019/02/13/8-facts-about-love-and-marriage.

13. Fry, "Number of People"; "Total Fertility Rate in the United States in 2018, by Ethnicity of Mother," Statista, www.statista.com/statistics/226292/us-fertility-rates-by-race-and-ethnicity.

14. Fry, "Number of People."

15. Lyman Stone, *Promise and Peril: The History of American Religiosity and Its Recent Decline* (American Enterprise Institute, April 2020), 45–48, www.aei.org/wp-content/uploads/2020/04/Promise-and-Peril.pdf.

16. "Marital Status," Pew Research Center Religious Landscape Study, 2014, www.pewforum.org/religious-landscape-study/marital-status.

17. Stone, *Promise and Peril*, 46–48.

18. Rebecca McLaughlin, "5 Reasons Why I Don't Always Sit with My Husband in Church," RebeccaMcLaughlin.org, February 18, 2018, www.rebeccamclaughlin.org/post/2018/02/18/5-reasons-why-i-don-t-always-sit-with-my-husband-in-church.

19. Personal interview by Sarah Eekhoff Zylstra, May 4, 2020.

20. McLaughlin, "5 Reasons."

21. Personal interview by Sarah Eekhoff Zylstra, May 4, 2020.

22. Personal interview by Sarah Eekhoff Zylstra, May 4, 2020.

23. Stone, *Promise and Peril*, 42–45.

24. Robert Littlejohn and Charles T. Evans, *Wisdom and Eloquence: A Christian Paradigm for Classical Learning* (Wheaton, IL: Crossway Books, 2006), 19.

25. *The New England Primer* (ca. 1688; repr., Worcester, MA: S. A. Howland, n.d.), 10–11.

26. Stone, *Promise and Peril*, 31.

27. John Dewey, "The Influence of Darwinism on Philosophy," in *The Influence of Darwin on Philosophy and Other Essays in Contemporary Thought* (New York: Henry Holt, 1910), 1–19.

28. Stone, *Promise and Peril*, 44.

29. Stone, *Promise and Peril*, 45.

30. Stone, *Promise and Peril*, 44.

31. Stone, *Promise and Peril*, 44–45.

32. "Phillips Neighborhood in Minneapolis, Minnesota," City-Data.com, www.city-data.com/neighborhood/Phillips-Minneapolis-MN.html; Libor Jany, "Minneapolis Police Beef Up Patrols After South Minneapolis Violence," *Star Tribune*, April 7, 2015, www.startribune.com/minneapolis -police-beef-up-patrols-after-south-minneapolis-violence/298980661.

33. Christopher Magan, "Here's Where Minnesota Schools Get Their Money and How It Is Spent," *Pioneer Press*, October 27, 2019, www .twincities.com/2019/10/27/heres-where-minnesota-schools-get-their -money-and-how-it-is-spent.

34. Rebecca McLaughlin, "The Most Diverse Movement in History," *Christianity Today*, October 14, 2019, www.christianitytoday.com/women/2019/ october/most-diverse-movement-history-mclaughlin-confronting.html.

35. McLaughlin, "Most Diverse Movement in History."

36. "The Global Religious Landscape," Pew Research Center, December 18, 2012, www.pewforum.org/2012/12/18/global-religious-landscape-exec.

37. Martin Luther King Jr., "Paul's Letter to American Christians," November 4, 1956, Martin Luther King, Jr. Research and Education Institute, https://kinginstitute.stanford.edu/king-papers/publications/knock -midnight-inspiration-great-sermons-reverend-martin-luther-king-jr-1.

38. "Multiracial Congregations Have Nearly Doubled, but They Still Lag Behind the Makeup of Neighborhoods," Baylor University, June 20, 2018, www.baylor.edu/mediacommunications/news.php?action=story& story=199850.

39. "Cedar Rapids City, Iowa," United States Census Bureau, www.census .gov/quickfacts/cedarrapidscityiowa.

40. "Cedar Rapids, Iowa," City-Data.com, www.city-data.com/city/Cedar -Rapids-Iowa.html.

41. Molly Duffy, "At Cedar Rapids Church, a Journey to Togetherness," *Gazette*, April 20, 2019, www.thegazette.com/subject/news/education/at -cedar-rapids-church-a-journey-to-togetherness-20190420; Stephanie Johnson, "Two Churches Come Together for One Message," CBS2Iowa .com, November 6, 2017, https://cbs2iowa.com/news/local/two -churches-one-message.

42. "Multiracial Congregations Have Nearly Doubled."

43. Adelle M. Banks, "More Multiracial Churches Led by Black, Hispanic Pastors," *Christianity Today*, January 17, 2020, www.christianitytoday .com/news/2020/january/more-multiracial-churches-black-hispanic -pastors-mosaix.html.

Chapter 7:
Gospelbound Christians
Love Their Enemies

SOME MATERIAL FROM this chapter has been adapted and updated from the following previously published articles: Sarah Eekhoff Zylstra, "'An Unlikely Ally': What a Secular Atheist Is Teaching Christian Leaders," The Gospel Coalition, February 28, 2018, www.thegospelcoalition.org/article/what-a-secular-atheist -is-teaching-christian-leaders; Sarah Eekhoff Zylstra, "Breaking Racial Barriers in Post-Apartheid South Africa," The Gospel Coalition, October 20, 2017, www.thegospelcoalition.org/article/breaking-racial-barriers-church-in-post -apartheid-south-africa; Sarah Eekhoff Zylstra, "Riots in John Piper's Neighborhood," The Gospel Coalition, August 24, 2020, www.thegospelcoalition.org/ article/riots-john-pipers-neighborhood. Quotations from the interviews that occurred for these articles are not cited separately here.

1. Anna Brown, "Most Democrats Who Are Looking for a Relationship Would Not Consider Dating a Trump Voter," Pew Research Center, April 24, 2020, www.pewresearch.org/fact-tank/2020/04/24/most -democrats-who-are-looking-for-a-relationship-would-not-consider -dating-a-trump-voter.
2. "The Partisan Divide on Political Values Grows Even Wider," Pew Research Center, October 5, 2017, www.people-press.org/2017/10/05/ the-partisan-divide-on-political-values-grows-even-wider.
3. Carroll Doherty and Jocelyn Kiley, "Key Facts About Partisanship and Political Animosity in America," Pew Research Center, June 22, 2016, www.pewresearch.org/fact-tank/2016/06/22/key-facts-partisanship.
4. Doherty and Kiley, "Key Facts"; "Partisan Antipathy: More Intense, More Personal," Pew Research Center, October 10, 2019, www.pew research.org/politics/2019/10/10/partisan-antipathy-more-intense -more-personal; "The Partisan Landscape and Views of the Parties," Pew Research Center, October 10, 2019, www.pewresearch.org/politics/ 2019/10/10/the-partisan-landscape-and-views-of-the-parties.
5. Greg Martin and Steven Webster, "The Real Culprit Behind Geographic Polarization," Atlantic, November 26, 2018, www.theatlantic .com/ideas/archive/2018/11/why-are-americans-so-geographically -polarized/575881.
6. Lee de-Wit, Sander van der Linden, and Cameron Brick, "What Are the Solutions to Political Polarization?," Greater Good Magazine, July 2, 2019, https://greatergood.berkeley.edu/article/item/what_are_the _solutions_to_political_polarization.
7. Pietro S. Nivola, "Thinking About Political Polarization," Brookings, January 1, 2005, www.brookings.edu/research/thinking-about-political -polarization.
8. Russell Berman, "What's the Answer to Political Polarization in the

U.S.?," *Atlantic*, March 8, 2016, www.theatlantic.com/politics/archive/2016/03/whats-the-answer-to-political-polarization/470163.

9. Rhitu Chatterjee, "Stressed Out by Politics? Here's How to Keep Caring Without Losing Your Cool," NPR, September 25, 2019, www.npr.org/sections/health-shots/2019/09/25/764216567/is-politics-stressing-you-out-heres-how-to-keep-caring-without-losing-your-cool.

10. Nicole Spector, " 'Election Stress Disorder': How to Cope with the Anxiety as Political Tensions Intensify," NBC News, March 3, 2020, www.nbcnews.com/better/lifestyle/election-stress-disorder-how-cope-anxiety-political-tensions-intensify-ncna1146951.

11. Ruben Banerjee, "Staines' Killing: Murder of Australian Missionary and His Two Sons in Orissa Shocks India," *India Today*, February 8, 1999, www.indiatoday.in/magazine/cover-story/story/19990208-staines-killing-murder-of-australian-missionary-and-his-two-sons-in-orissa-shocks-india-780092-1999-02-08.

12. "Bible Translated in Oriya Dialect," *Hindustan Times*, November 25, 2006, www.hindustantimes.com/india/bible-translated-in-oriya-dialect/story-Kk7xAxiP8nCw9eVXw79cJO.html.

13. "What Happened to Gladys Staines Following Her Husband's Murder?," CBN India, April 3, 2019, www.youtube.com/watch?v=r_m0OiZu7e8&list=PLgl7ryoHplachu7wuAac0PkMLEpCye8Hv&index=15&t=0s&app.

14. "Report of the Justice D. P. Wadhwa Commission of Inquiry: Judicial Commission or Injudicious Cover Up?," South Asia Human Rights Documentation Centre, August 25, 1999, www.oocities.org/indianfascism/fascism/wadhwa_commission.htm.

15. Gladys Staines, "Gladys Staines Interview for The Least of These Movie," interview by Rod Hopping, Heritage Films, May 20, 2019, www.youtube.com/watch?v=7UUqtT_NAec.

16. Staines, "Gladys Staines Interview."

17. "India: Funeral of Slain Australian Missionary," Associated Press, January 26, 1999, www.youtube.com/watch?v=Lun16mrcSgA.

18. Barry Bearak, "Baripada Journal; Forgiving Her Family's Killers, but Not Their Sins," *New York Times*, September 3, 1999, www.nytimes.com/1999/09/03/world/baripada-journal-forgiving-her-family-s-killers-but-not-their-sins.html.

19. Ruben Banerjee, "Inability of Orissa Govt to Capture Dara Singh Points to a Criminal-Politician Nexus," *India Today*, September 13, 1999, www.indiatoday.in/magazine/crime/story/19990913-inability-of-orissa-govt-to-capture-dara-singh-points-to-a-criminal-politician-nexus-824227-1999-09-13; "Staines Murder Cause: A Chronology," *Outlook*, January 21, 2011, www.outlookindia.com/newswire/story/staines-murder-case-a-chronology/709203.

20. "Graham Staines Murder Case: Accused on the Run for Two Decades Arrested," *Hindustan Times*, September 21, 2019, www.hindustantimes

.com/india-news/graham-staines-murder-case-accused-on-the-run-for
-two-decades-arrested/story-KWQCp1u4rvaUnlJ4ftUf3L.html;
"Supreme Court Upholds Life Sentence for Killer of Two Missionaries,"
AsiaNews, October 10, 2007, www.asianews.it/news-en/Supreme
-Court-upholds-life-sentence-for-killer-of-two-missionaries-10519
.html.

21. Krishnadas Rajagopal, "SC Spares Dara Death, Says His Triple Murder
Was to Teach a Lesson," *Indian Express*, January 22, 2011, http://indian
express.com/article/news-archive/web/sc-spares-dara-death-says-his
-triple-murder-was-to-teach-a-lesson.

22. Morgan Lee, "Forgiver of Missionary Martyrdoms Wins India's Mother
Teresa Award," *Christianity Today*, December 15, 2015, www.christianity
today.com/news/2015/december/forgiver-india-mother-teresa-award
-gladys-staines-martyrdom.html.

23. Staines, "Gladys Staines Interview."

24. Staines, "Gladys Staines Interview."

25. Joseph Shapiro, "Amish Forgive School Shooter, Struggle with Grief,"
NPR, October 2, 2007, www.npr.org/templates/story/story.php?storyId
=14900930.

26. Staines, "Gladys Staines Interview."

27. Robert D. Putnam and David E. Campbell, *American Grace: How Religion Divides and Unites Us* (New York: Simon & Schuster, 2010), 461.

28. Russell Moore, Twitter, December 18, 2014, https://twitter.com/
drmoore/status/545690015834312704.

29. Jonathan Haidt, *The Righteous Mind: Why Good People Are Divided by Politics and Religion* (New York: Vintage Books, 2012), 119.

30. Sarah Posner, *Unholy: Why White Evangelicals Worship at the Altar of Donald Trump* (New York: Random House, 2020); Terry Gross and Linda
Kay Klein, "Memoirist: Evangelical Purity Movement Sees Women's
Bodies as a 'Threat,'" NPR, September 18, 2018, www.npr.org/2018/
09/18/648737143/memoirist-evangelical-purity-movement-sees
-womens-bodies-as-a-threat.

31. Haidt, *Righteous Mind*, xix–xx.

32. Trevin Wax, "The 6 Moral Foundations of Politics," The Gospel Coalition, January 13, 2015, www.thegospelcoalition.org/blogs/trevin-wax/
the-6-moral-foundations-of-politics.

33. Haidt, *Righteous Mind*, 179.

34. Haidt, *Righteous Mind*, 281.

35. Evan Low and Barry H. Corey, "We First Battled over LGBT and Religious Rights. Here's How We Became Unlikely Friends," *Washington Post*, March 3, 2017, www.washingtonpost.com/news/acts-of-faith/wp/
2017/03/03/we-first-battled-over-lgbt-and-religious-rights-heres-how
-we-became-unlikely-friends/?utm_term=.e1b71176c61d.

36. Sam Nkomo, "Gospel and Race Part 2 Interview with Emily Rahube
and Sam Nkomo," Christ Church Midrand, https://soundcloud.com/

christ-church-midrand/gospel-and-race-part-2-interview-with-emily
-and-sam.

37. "Apartheid and Reactions to It," South African History Online, August 27, 2019, www.sahistory.org.za/article/apartheid-and-reactions-it.

38. Marissa Evans, "Apartheid (1948–1994)," Black Past, February 21, 2009, www.blackpast.org/gah/apartheid-1948-1994; "Early Apartheid: 1948–1970," Facing History and Ourselves, www.facinghistory.org/confronting-apartheid/chapter-2/introduction.

39. "The United Nations—Partner in the Struggle Against Apartheid," United Nations, www.un.org/en/events/mandeladay/un_against_apartheid.shtml.

40. "Nelson Mandela's Prison Numbers," Nelson Mandela Foundation, www.nelsonmandela.org/content/page/prison-timeline.

41. "Apartheid," History.com, March 3, 2020, www.history.com/topics/africa/apartheid.

42. Steven Mufson, "It Had Been 26 Years Since I'd Seen South Africa. How It Changed—and How It Hadn't," *Washington Post*, January 2, 2014, www.washingtonpost.com/opinions/it-had-been-26-years-since-id-seen-south-africa-how-it-changed--and-how-it-hadnt/2014/01/02/204269aa-6f2b-11e3-b405-7e360f7e9fd2_story.html.

43. Ed Stoddard, "South Africa to Limit Farm Sizes to Speed Land Redistribution," Reuters, May 21, 2016, www.reuters.com/article/us-safrica-landrights-reform/south-africa-to-limit-farm-sizes-to-speed-land-redistribution-idUSKCN0YC0GJ.

44. Frank Chung, "'Bury Them Alive!': White South Africans Fear for Their Future as Horrific Farm Attacks Escalate," News.com.au, March 25, 2017, www.news.com.au/finance/economy/world-economy/bury-them-alive-white-south-africans-fear-for-their-future-as-horrific-farm-attacks-escalate/news-story/3a63389a1b0066b6b0b77522c06d6476.

45. Thomas Harding, "Black South African Politician Andile Mngxitama Calls for Mugabe-Style 'Land Grab,'" Independent, August 27, 2016, www.independent.co.uk/news/world/africa/andile-mngxitama-black-south-african-politician-calls-for-mugabe-style-land-grab-a7212856.html.

46. Robyn Dixon, "A Night of Violence That Shattered a South African's View of Her White Privilege," *Los Angeles Times*, December 11, 2015, www.latimes.com/world/great-reads/la-fg-c1-south-africa-white-privilege-20151211-story.html.

47. "Lilly Million and Blaque Nubon @ Christ Church Midrand," video, 3:51, July 28, 2013, www.youtube.com/watch?v=s-Qrp0kF1lI.

48. Erin Conway-Smith, "South Africa Starts 2016 with Racism Outcry," *USA Today*, January 7, 2016, www.usatoday.com/story/news/world/2016/01/07/south-africa-racism-fight/78404322.

49. Verashni Pillay, "Mandela and the Confessions of a Closet Christian," *Mail & Guardian*, December 12, 2013, https://mg.co.za/article/2013-12-12-mandela-and-the-confessions-of-a-closet-christian.

Chapter 8:
Gospelbound Christians
Give Away Their Freedom

SOME MATERIAL FROM this chapter has been adapted and updated from the following previously published articles: Sarah Eekhoff Zylstra, "How John Piper's Seashells Swept Over a Generation," The Gospel Coalition, March 20, 2017, www.thegospelcoalition.org/article/how-john-pipers-seashells-swept-over-a-generation; Sarah Eekhoff Zylstra, "America's Epidemic: How Opioid Addicts Find Help in the Church," The Gospel Coalition, August 31, 2017, www.thegospelcoalition.org/article/americas-epidemic-how-opioid-addicts-find-help-in-the-church; Sarah Eekhoff Zylstra, "The Friendship That Battled the Prosperity Gospel to Treat Africa's HIV Crisis," The Gospel Coalition, May 21, 2018, www.thegospelcoalition.org/article/friendship-battled-prosperity-gospel-treat-africa-hiv-aids-crisis; Sarah Eekhoff Zylstra, "Why Indianapolis Megachurch Members Are Joining God in the 'Swamp,'" The Gospel Coalition, July 30, 2018, www.thegospelcoalition.org/article/why-indianapolis-megachurch-members-joining-god-swamp; Sarah Eekhoff Zylstra, "Alex and Brett Harris Are Doing Hard Things," The Gospel Coalition, November 5, 2014, www.thegospelcoalition.org/article/alex-and-brett-harris-are-doing-hard-things. Quotations from the interviews that occurred for these articles are not cited separately here.

1. John Piper, "Boasting Only in the Cross" (sermon, Passion OneDay 2000, Memphis, TN, May 20, 2000), www.desiringgod.org/messages/boasting-only-in-the-cross.

2. John Piper, *Don't Waste Your Life* (Wheaton, IL: Crossway, 2003); John Piper, *Don't Waste Your Life Study Guide* (Wheaton, IL: Crossway, 2007); John Piper, *Don't Waste Your Life Tracts* (Wheaton, IL: Crossway, 2010); Lecrae, "Don't Waste Your Life," featuring Dwayne Tryumf, *Rebel*, Reach Records, 2008.

3. Matt Carter, Twitter, August 23, 2016, https://twitter.com/_Matt_Carter/status/768290293724491776.

4. Richard Fry, "It's Becoming More Common for Young Adults to Live at Home—and for Longer Stretches," Pew Research Center, May 5, 2017, www.pewresearch.org/fact-tank/2017/05/05/its-becoming-more-common-for-young-adults-to-live-at-home-and-for-longer-stretches.

5. Juliana Menasce Horowitz, Nikki Graf, and Gretchen Livingston, "Marriage and Cohabitation in the U.S.," Pew Research Center, November 6, 2019, www.pewsocialtrends.org/2019/11/06/marriage-and-cohabitation-in-the-u-s.

6. Gretchen Livingston, "Is U.S. Fertility at an All-Time Low? Two of Three Measures Point to Yes," Pew Research Center, May 22, 2019, www.pewresearch.org/fact-tank/2019/05/22/u-s-fertility-rate-explained.

7. Marisa Crane, "6 of the Hardest Drugs to Quit," American Addiction

Centers, November 25, 2019, https://americanaddictioncenters.org/adult-addiction-treatment-programs/hardest-quit.

8. Lindsay Kramer, "Why Is Opiate Addiction So Hard to Treat?," Recovery.org, February 25, 2015, www.recovery.org/pro/articles/why-are-opiate-addicts-so-hard-to-treat.

9. Holly Hedegaard, Arialdi M. Miniño, and Margaret Warner, *Drug Overdose Deaths in the United States, 1999–2018*, NCHS Data Brief, January 2020, 1, 3, www.cdc.gov/nchs/data/databriefs/db356-h.pdf.

10. Josh Katz, "Drug Deaths in America Are Rising Faster than Ever," *New York Times*, June 5, 2017, www.nytimes.com/interactive/2017/06/05/upshot/opioid-epidemic-drug-overdose-deaths-are-rising-faster-than-ever.html?_r=0.

11. Paul Hemez, "Nonmarital Sex by Age 25: Generational Differences Between Baby Boomers & Millennials," National Center for Family & Marriage Research at Bowling Green State University, 2017, www.bgsu.edu/ncfmr/resources/data/family-profiles/hemez-nonmarital-sex-by-age-25-boomers-millennials-fp-17-11.html.

12. *Porn Statistics* (Owosso, MI: Covenant Eyes, 2020), 9, 15–16, www.covenanteyes.com/pornstats.

13. Brian Krans, "Can Porn Induce Erectile Dysfunction?," October 10, 2019, Healthline, www.healthline.com/health/erectile-dysfunction/porn-induced-ed#sexual-appetite.

14. Dennis Thompson, "Study Links Preference for Pornography with Real-World Sexual Dysfunction," UPI, May 12, 2017, www.upi.com/Health_News/2017/05/12/Study-links-preference-for-pornography-with-real-world-sexual-dysfunction/5641494620190.

15. Philip Zimbardo, "Is Porn Good for Us or Bad for Us?," *Psychology Today*, March 1, 2016, www.psychologytoday.com/us/blog/hero/201603/is-porn-good-us-or-bad-us.

16. Melissa Batchelor Warnke, "Opinion: Millennials Are Having Less Sex than Any Generation in 60 Years. Here's Why It Matters," *Los Angeles Times*, August 3, 2016, www.latimes.com/opinion/opinion-la/la-ol-millennials-less-sex-20160802-snap-story.html.

17. David Sheff, "The Rolling Stone Survey: On Sex, Drugs and Rock & Roll," *Rolling Stone*, May 5, 1988, www.rollingstone.com/culture/culture-news/the-rolling-stone-survey-on-sex-drugs-and-rock-roll-81616.

18. "Drug and Alcohol Abuse Across Generations," DrugAbuse.com, https://drugabuse.com/featured/drug-and-alcohol-abuse-across-generations.

19. Sheff, "Rolling Stone Survey."

20. Derek Rishmawy, "False Freedom and the Slavery of Autonomy," The Gospel Coalition, September 2, 2013, www.thegospelcoalition.org/article/false-freedom-and-the-slavery-of-autonomy.

21. Rishmawy, "False Freedom."

22. Scott Sonenshein, "How Constraints Force Your Brain to Be More Cre-

ative," *Fast Company*, February 7, 2017, www.fastcompany.com/3067925/
how-constraints-force-your-brain-to-be-more-creative.

23. Horowitz, Graf, and Livingston, "Marriage and Cohabitation in the
U.S."; Linda Bloom and Charlie Bloom, "Want More and Better Sex?
Get Married and Stay Married," *Huffington Post*, July 13, 2017, www
.huffpost.com/entry/want-more-and-better-sex-get-married-and-stay
-married_b_5967b618e4b022bb9372aff2.

24. Many of the students who successfully make the transfer from a community college to a four-year university *do* graduate. But most community
college students don't transfer, even though 80 percent started their college education aiming for a bachelor's degree. See D. Jenkins and J. Fink,
What We Know About Transfer, Community College Research Center,
January 2015, https://ccrc.tc.columbia.edu/media/k2/attachments/what
-we-know-about-transfer.pdf.

25. *Global HIV & AIDS Statistics—2020 Fact Sheet* (UNAIDS, 2020), 5, www
.unaids.org/sites/default/files/media_asset/UNAIDS_FactSheet_en.pdf.

26. "Sub-Saharan Africa," in *2006 AIDS Epidemic Update* (World Health
Organization, 2006), 10, www.who.int/hiv/mediacentre/04-Sub_Saharan
_Africa_2006_EpiUpdate_eng.pdf.

27. Fyodor Dostoyevsky, *The Brothers Karamazov*, trans. Richard Pevear and
Larissa Volokhonsky (New York: Farrar, Straus and Giroux, 2002), 58.

28. John F. Haines, *History of Hamilton County, Indiana: Her People, Industries
and Institutions* (Indianapolis: B. F. Bowen, 1915), 241.

29. "Best Places to Live," CNN Money, September 2012, https://money
.cnn.com/magazines/moneymag/best-places/2012/top100.

30. Sam Dangremond, "The Best Place to Live in America Is a City You've
Never Heard Of," *Town & Country*, March 6, 2018, www.townand
countrymag.com/leisure/a9280984/best-place-to-live-in-
america.

31. "Carmel City, Indiana," United States Census Bureau, www.census.gov/
quickfacts/fact/table/carmelcityindiana/PST045219.

32. "Carmel Police ID Victim, Suspect Killed in Monday Shooting,"
WishTV.com, July 28, 2020, www.wishtv.com/news/crime-watch-8/
carmel-police-id-victim-suspect-killed-in-monday-shooting; Summer
Ballentine, Allison Prang, and Steph Solis, "Carmel Murder-Suicide
Hits O'Malia Family, Friends," *Indianapolis Star*, July 27, 2014, www
.indystar.com/story/news/local/hamilton-county/2014/07/27/carmel
-couple-die-apparent-murder-suicide/13255503.

33. *2019 Annual Report* (Indianapolis: College Park Church, 2019), https://
256469dc8dd9b78e41a9-ba52a0b241f891ac68e37b761b226571.ssl.cf2
.rackcdn.com/uploaded/2/0e10420772_1589983305_2019-annual
-report.pdf.

34. "Indianapolis, IN (Brookside Parkway South Dr/N Sherman Dr),"
Neighborhood Scout, www.neighborhoodscout.com/in/indianapolis/
brookside-parkway-south-dr#overview.

35. "Near Eastside Neighborhood Area," Indy Vitals, https://indyvitals.org/NearEastside#; *LISC Sustainable Communities Initiative Neighborhood Quality Monitoring Report: Near Eastside Neighborhood, Indianapolis, IN* (SAVI, June 4, 2014), www.savi.org/savi/documents/LISC_FINAL/NEAST_Report2.pdf.

36. Jordan Fischer, "As Near Eastside Poised to Be Deadliest Neighborhood Again, Residents Offer Muted Hope for Renewal," WRTV, Novemer 4, 2016, www.wrtv.com/longform/as-near-eastside-poised-to-be-deadliest-neighborhood-again-residents-offer-muted-hope-about-renewal.

37. Fanchon Stinger, "East Side Neighborhood Attributes Positive Transformation to 5 Community Pillars," Fox59, October 27, 2016, http://fox59.com/2016/10/27/east-side-neighborhood-attributes-positive-transformation-to-5-community-pillars.

38. Jordan Fischer, "Bodies of Three Dogs Dumped in Near Eastside Alley," WRTV Indianapolis, June 21, 2018, www.theindychannel.com/news/local-news/crime/bodies-of-three-dogs-dumped-in-near-eastside-alley.

39. "Shooting on Near East Side Leaves 1 Dead, 1 Injured," Fox59, July 28, 2020, https://fox59.com/news/shooting-on-near-east-side-leaves-1-dead-1-injured.

40. Jordan Fischer, "PC: Plot to Rob Alleged Drug Dealer Ended with Brookside Man's Murder," WRTV Indianapolis, June 26, 2017, www.wrtv.com/news/crime/pc-plot-to-rob-alleged-drug-dealer-ended-with-brookside-mans-murder.

41. Sierra Hignite, "Child Shot on Near East Side, One of Many Similar Cases in the Area," WishTV.com, June 29, 2020, www.wishtv.com/news/local-news/child-shot-on-near-east-side.

42. Alex Harris and Brett Harris, *Do Hard Things: A Teenage Rebellion Against Low Expectations* (Colorado Springs, CO: Multnomah, 2008).

43. Alex Harris and Brett Harris, *Start Here: Doing Hard Things Right Where You Are* (Colorado Springs, CO: Multnomah, 2010).

Conclusion:
No Apology Needed

1. Carl F. H. Henry, *The Uneasy Conscience of Modern Fundamentalism* (Grand Rapids, MI: Eerdmans, 2003), 88–89.

2. Larry W. Hurtado, introduction to *Destroyer of the Gods: Early Christian Distinctiveness in the Roman World* (Waco, TX: Baylor University Press, 2016).

3. Alan Kreider, *The Patient Ferment of the Early Church: The Improbable Rise of Christianity in the Roman Empire* (Grand Rapids, MI: Baker Academic, 2016), 51.

4. Vermon Pierre, "Forgiveness Is a Marathon," The Gospel Coalition,

August 12, 2015, www.thegospelcoalition.org/article/forgiveness-is-a
-marathon.

5. Timothy Keller, *How to Reach the West Again: Six Essential Elements of a
Missionary Encounter* (New York: Redeemer City to City, 2020), 12.

6. Carl R. Trueman, *The Rise and Triumph of the Modern Self: Cultural
Amnesia, Expressive Individualism, and the Road to Sexual Revolution*
(Wheaton, IL: Crossway, 2020), 407.

ABOUT THE AUTHORS

Collin Hansen serves as the vice president of content and editor in chief of The Gospel Coalition (TGC), where for the last decade he's overseen all content, including books, conferences, articles, podcasts, newsletters, social media, and more. He is the author of several books, including *Young, Restless, Reformed: A Journalist's Journey with the New Calvinists* (his debut), *Blind Spots: Becoming a Courageous, Compassionate, and Commissioned Church*, and *A God-Sized Vision: Revival Stories That Stretch and Stir* (with John Woodbridge). He hosts the *Gospelbound* podcast for TGC and cohosts the *Life and Books and Everything* podcast with his friends Kevin DeYoung and Justin Taylor. His edited works include *Our Secular Age: Ten Years of Reading and Applying Charles Taylor* and *The New City Catechism Devotional*.

Collin grew up on a farm in South Dakota, where his parents still live. He earned a bachelor's degree in journalism and history from Northwestern University, went on to work as news editor for *Christianity Today*, and then earned an MDiv at Trinity Evangelical Divinity School. He serves as an elder for Redeemer Community Church in Birmingham, Alabama, and he and his wife have two young children. He serves on the advisory board of Beeson Divinity School and regularly lectures and leads tours about civil rights history.

Sarah Eekhoff Zylstra is a senior writer for TGC, where she also oversees faith and work coverage. Her features on trends in religion and church leadership are regularly rated among TGC's most popular and valuable content. Previously, she reported news for

Christianity Today for more than a decade, freelanced regularly for a local daily paper, taught at Trinity Christian College, and home-schooled her children. This is her first book.

Sarah grew up in a small farming community in Iowa. She earned a bachelor's degree in English and communication from Dordt University, followed by a master's degree from Medill School of Journalism at Northwestern University. She and her husband have settled down in the suburbs of Chicago with their two sons. They are active members at Orland Park Christian Reformed Church.

ABOUT THE TYPE

The text of this book was set in Janson, a typeface designed about 1690 by Nicholas Kis (1650–1702), a Hungarian living in Amsterdam, and for many years mistakenly attributed to the Dutch printer Anton Janson. In 1919, the matrices became the property of the Stempel Foundry in Frankfurt. It is an old-style book face of excellent clarity and sharpness. Janson serifs are concave and splayed; the contrast between thick and thin strokes is marked.